The University of Notre Dame

A Portrait of Its History and Campus

Thomas J. Schlereth

The University of Notre Dame

University of Notre Dame Press   Notre Dame / London

A Portrait of Its History and Campus

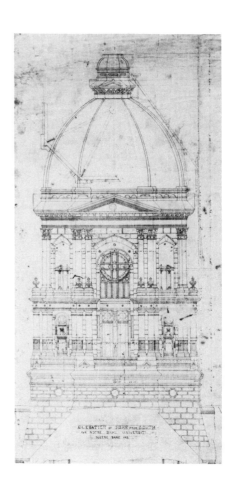

Copyright © 1976 by University of Notre Dame Press
Notre Dame, Indiana 46556

Library of Congress Cataloging in Publication Data

Schlereth, Thomas J
  The University of Notre Dame.
  Bibliography: p.
  Includes index.
  1. Notre Dame, Ind. University—History.
I. Title.
LD4113.S34   378.772′89   75–43747
ISBN 0–268–01905–3
ISBN 0–268–01906–1 pbk.

Manufactured in the United States of America

For FATHER JEROME J. WILSON, C.S.C.
who first made it possible for me to know Notre Dame

Table of Contents

Acknowledgments

My intellectual and methodological obligations to other scholars and authors are recorded in the introductory essay and selected bibliography. I would like to acknowledge here the numerous individuals who, in various ways, have encouraged and assisted me in researching and writing this book.

Many alumni and friends of Notre Dame have shared their knowledge and, in several instances, their photographs with me. I would like to thank Donald C. Grant, William D. Farmer, Paul R. Byrne, Grover F. Miller, Robert P. Best, Kenneth W. McCandless, and Robert J. Schultz.

Two University staff members, Shirley Schneck of the faculty stenographic pool and Karen Kolber, secretary to the Program in American Studies, patiently typed and retyped my manuscript drafts with consistent carefulness, patience, and good spirits.

It is one of the delightful rewards of scholarship that it is social as well as solitary. My fellow members of the American studies faculty—Edward A. Fischer, Sister Madonna Kolbenschlag, Thomas J. Stritch, and Ronald Weber—perceptively read and greatly improved my early manuscript or contributed ideas toward its design. Other Notre Dame colleagues—Jay P. Dolan of the history department, Father John C. Gerber, local superior of the Congregation of Holy Cross, Donald P. Costello of the English department, and Steven W. Hurtt of the architecture department—gave my drafts their professional scrutiny. I am particularly grateful to Steven Hurtt for encouraging my forays into the field of architectural history.

I would like to express my appreciation to the staffs of several archival facilities where I have worked during the past three years. I am particularly indebted to the University of Notre Dame Archives, its archivist, Father Thomas E. Blantz, C.S.C., and the archival staff—Mercedes Muenz, Carmine T. Buonaiuto, Wendy Clauson Schlereth, and Lawrence J. Bradley—who have been industrious, persevering, and knowledgeable fellow-researchers in my project. Father Thomas F. Elliott, C.S.C., archivist of the Indiana Province of the Congregation of Holy Cross, has also been an energetic supporter of my work. For assisting me in my search in both verbal and visual evidence, I would also like to thank Jay J. Kane, assistant director of the University's information services; Anton C. Masin, director of special collections, Memorial Library; Brother James Morony, C.S.C., archivist of the Indiana Province of the Brothers of Holy Cross (South Bend, Indiana); Sister Kathryn Marie, C.S.C., archivist, and her assistant, Sister M. Alma Louise, C.S.C., of the Provincial Archives of the Sisters of the Holy Cross (Notre Dame, Indiana); Sister Bernadette Marie, C.S.C., archivist, St. Mary's College (Notre Dame, Indiana); and James Sullivan, director, Northern Indiana Historical Society (South Bend, Indiana).

Writing this history has been one task; designing it, in some respects, proved to be an even more formidable undertaking. In the latter endeavor, I have had the good fortune to work with genuine professionals. James R. Langford, a fellow historian and director of the University of Notre Dame Press, has taken a personal interest in every aspect of the book's evolution, from my original idea of it through to the final page proofs. His vision of the University Press as an integral part of the University's intellectual life augurs well for Notre Dame's future academic history. The staff of the University Press has also given me extensive practical assistance in the final crafting of the book. I thank John E. Ehmann for his conscientious attention to numerous production details and Betty Scates for her patient and careful proofreading. A special accolade is due my copy editor, Bruce M. Fingerhut, whose sympathetic grasp of the total concept of my work combined with a relentless attention to minute detail never impaired my original style.

Two individuals are particularly responsible for the visual delight of the book: Donald J. Nelson, of the University's Office of Printing and Publications, whose design of its pages so fully and yet unobtrusively realized my original intent of the volume; and Joseph A. St. Jean, a senior student in the University's School of Architecture, whose deft draftsmanship and fine architectural sensibilities have made our collaboration a rewarding learning experience for me and, I anticipate, my readers. Mr. St. Jean drew the master map, the walker's guide, and the six individual walk maps, plus the historical reconstructions and other modern cartography I have used in the volume.

Several people have helped me in extraordinary ways. Francis P. Clark, head of the University's microfilm department, has given generously of his time and of his personal photographic and documentary holdings concerning Notre Dame's history. Mr. Clark's collection of Catholic Americana, a worthy successor to the one assembled by James F. Edwards in the nineteenth century, has been a constant and abundant source of rare monographs, newspapers, and photographs for my research. Richard W. Conklin, director of the University's information services, in addition to reading my manuscript, also provided me with much photographic and documentary data on twentieth-century Notre Dame. Mr. Conklin also authorized an expenditure from his department's budget that enabled the University photographer's office to assist me in the conservation and reproduction of many original nineteenth-century photographs. James F. Newkirk, a former member of the University photographer's staff, was largely responsible for most of this salvage work. Mr. Newkirk, a young man of genuine historical sensitivity, photographic skill, and indefatigable energy, painstakingly helped preserve and expand the visual record of Notre Dame's history. I, as well as the University, am beholden to him in many ways.

In one sense this book probably would never have been written were it not for the man to whom it is dedicated. Father Jerome J. Wilson, C.S.C., found a way for a young man to come to Notre Dame in 1959; because of his concern, I am in his debt in ways that can never be fully acknowledged. Those who know this compassionate priest and friend will understand why he so rightly deserves my dedication.

Finally, the greatest debt in the actual researching and writing of this book is owed to my wife, Wendy Clauson Schlereth. As a historian and archivist, she has an aversion to the kind of effusive acknowledgment that ascribes all the inspiration, all the merit, to the writer's wife. I appreciate this sentiment and indeed share it, but as a historian myself, I am obliged to record the simple truth: while I could have written this book without my wife, I could not have written it so soon, so well, or with so much pleasure; she has carefully read and perceptively criticized every part of it, from the title to the bibliography, often several times, and made invaluable suggestions. I am especially indebted to her consummate editorial and literary skill; she has transformed my often ponderous prose into articulate exposition. Her standards are strenuous, and she is not to blame if I have not always met them.

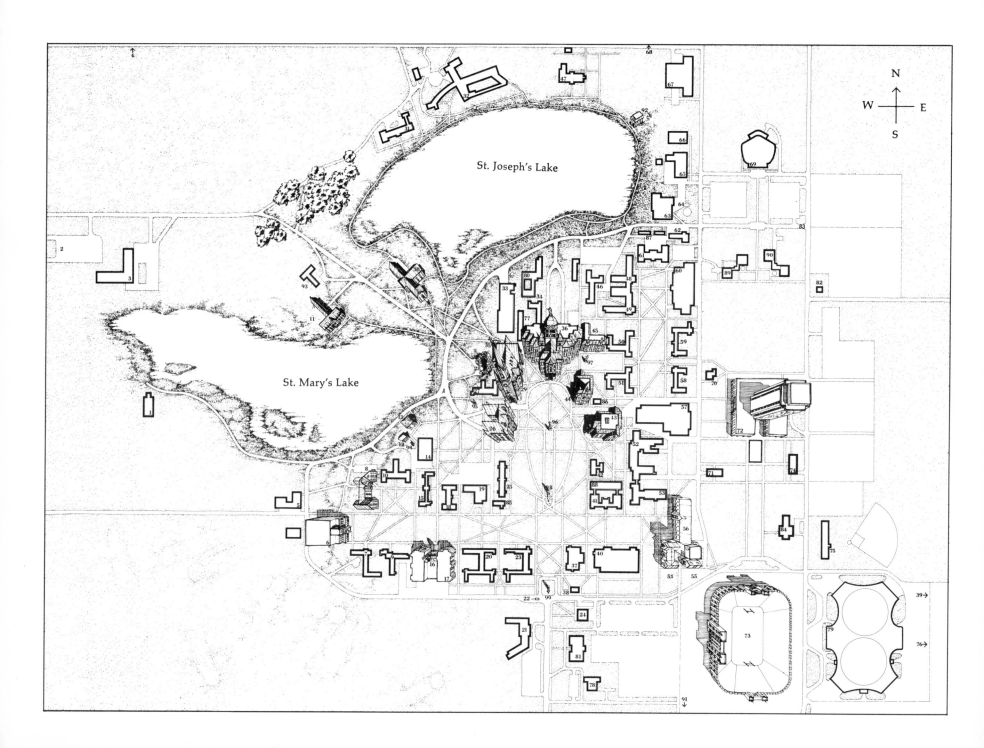

St. Joseph's Lake

St. Mary's Lake

N
W E
S

Map Legend

1 Carroll Hall
2 Fatima Shrine
3 Fatima Retreat House
4 University Village
5 ROTC Building
6 Rockne Memorial
7 Pangborn Hall
8 Lyons Hall
9 Fisher Hall
10 Morrissey Hall
11 Holy Cross Hall
12 Log Chapel
13 Old College
14 Architecture Building
15 Howard Hall
16 Cafeteria (The Oak Room)
17 South Dining Hall
18 Badin Hall
19 Hammes Notre Dame Bookstore
20 Dillon Hall
21 Morris Inn
22 Main Gate
23 Alumni Hall
24 Post Office
25 Walsh Hall
26 Sorin Hall

27 Corby Hall
28 Grotto of Our Lady of Lourdes
29 Sacred Heart Church
30 Columba Hall
31 St. Joseph Hall
32 Moreau Seminary
33 Laundry
34 Freshman Year Building and Brownson Hall
35 Presbytery
36 Administration Building
37 Law School
38 Lewis Bus Shelter
39 Tennis Courts
40 Cushing Hall of Engineering
41 Hurley College of Business Administration
42 Hoynes Hall
43 LaFortune Student Center
44 Washington Hall
45 St. Edward's Hall
46 Student Infirmary
47 Holy Cross House
48 Stanford Hall
49 Keenan Hall
50 Zahm Hall

51 Cavanaugh Hall
52 Nieuwland Science Hall
53 Chemical Engineering Hall
54 Art Gallery (O'Shaughnessy Hall)
55 Sculpture Studio
56 O'Shaughnessy Hall of Liberal and Fine Arts
57 The Old Fieldhouse
58 Breen-Phillips Hall
59 Farley Hall
60 North Dining Hall
61 Haggar Hall
62 Fire Station
63 Power Plant and Utilities
64 Water Tower
65 Ave Maria Press
66 Mechanical Engineering Lab
67 Maintenance Center
68 Reyniers Germfree Life Building
69 Stepan Center
70 WNDU, Radio and Television
71 Radiation Research Building
72 Notre Dame Memorial Library
73 Stadium
74 Computing Center and Mathematics Building

75 Aerospace Engineering Lab
76 Cartier Field
77 Earth Sciences Building
78 University Club
79 Athletic and Convocation Center
80 Lewis Hall
81 Center for Continuing Education
82 Bulla Shed (Campus Ministry)
83 East Gate
84 Paul V. Galvin Life Science Center
85 Knights of Columbus Council Home
86 Band Building
87 Medical Science Building
88 Hayes-Healy Center
89 Flanner Tower
90 Grace Tower
91 Alumni-Senior Club
92 Boat House
93 Holy Cross Annex
94 Founders' Monument
95 William J. Corby Statue
96 Sacred Heart Statue
97 St. Edward's Statue
98 Edward Sorin Statue
99 Our Lady of the University Statue

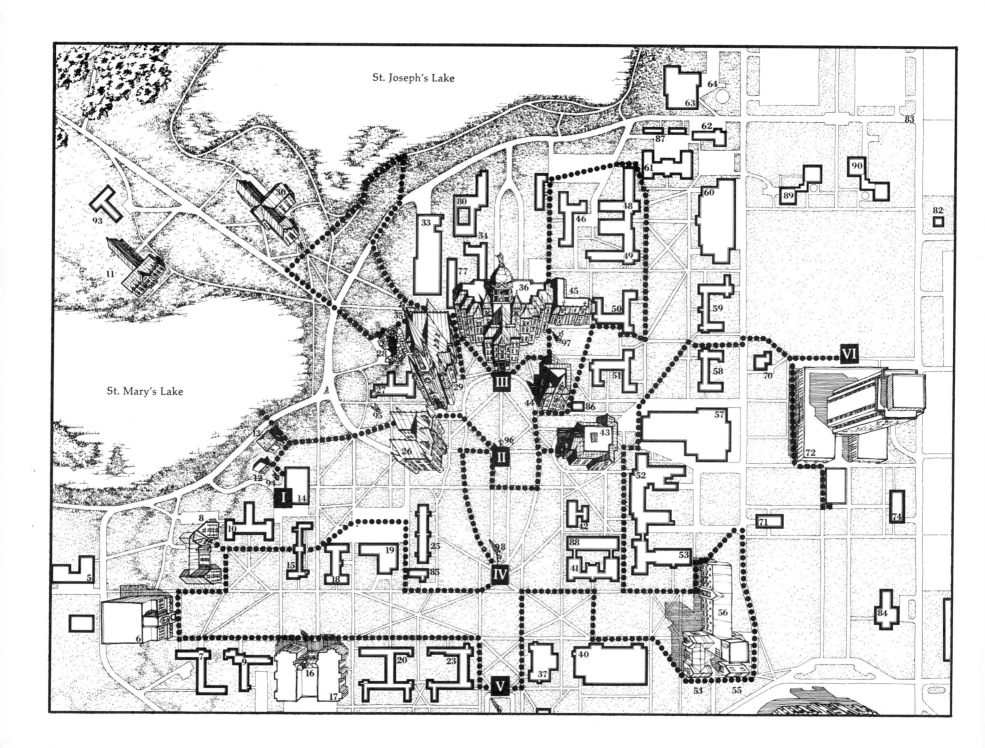

St. Joseph's Lake

St. Mary's Lake

A Note to the Reader

THIS BOOK is designed to serve several purposes: it is a narrative history of the University of Notre Dame from 1842 to 1976; it is also a detailed walking guide to the University's campus development and architecture, an extensive collection of graphic evidence, and, finally, a brief reference work containing appropriate statistical data and bibliographical material about Notre Dame. While a multipurpose book, I hope it will intrigue a single clientele of readers, namely, readers who are willing to page back and forth in the book, test the comparisons I suggest, watch for the visual clues I point out, and, when possible, energetically tramp over the campus itself, visualizing how it must have been to live, work, study, and teach here as early as 1844 or as recently as 1942. My aspiration is that such readers will discover the delight of doing history themselves: in print, photography, and in person, they will experience the history of Notre Dame in a uniquely personal way.

To elicit and narrate this personal understanding of the University's past, I have chosen the metaphor of a walk. I invite readers to take several walks with me, a historian, through the past that has been Notre Dame. A reader can journey through this past vicariously by reading the following narrative and carefully examining its accompanying sequence of images and maps. If the reader is on the campus, he can explore it, book in hand, reading the narrative, studying the graphic materials, and observing the various extant artifacts of the campus that the book also uses as historical evidence.

For the reader who chooses to use the book as a historical Baedeker, a few words of general orientation are necessary. Notre Dame grew in a series of definable geographical directions that have a surprising historical continuity. A master map of the University (turn back one page to view this map) and a walker's guide (left) designate this growth; six walks, corresponding to the six chapters in the book, are plotted on the guide. Both map and guide are drawn on axonometric projections with the Sorin statue in the center of the campus as its base point, and both are keyed (see master map legend) to extant structures (arabic numerals) on the modern University campus. Thus the first walk begins at the Founders' Monument (94), and the last walk concludes at the front of Memorial Library (72)

In each chapter a more detailed map precedes the narrative text. The walk maps are correlated with the master map and contain the precise route that the reader should follow if he wishes to "walk through" the history that is explored in the various chapters. Appropriate directions (italicized), keyed to the walk maps by boldface capital letters when the directions call for moving from area to area, are to be found in the narrative text. Within the narrative text the reader will also find references to graphic materials reproduced in the book. Such references have two parts: a roman numeral to designate the chapter and an arabic numeral to denote the position of the illustration in that chapter. For example, I–7 is the seventh illustration in Chapter I.

Each chapter contains certain information that the reader is encouraged to use to interpolate much of the University's history for himself. Comparisons can be made, for instance, between the large overviews that commence and conclude each chapter for a sense of Notre Dame's chronological and physical development. A reader can also trace certain demographic patterns in the statistical data provided at the beginning of each chapter; the changing composition of students and faculty can be extrapolated by juxtaposing the various photographs found at the conclusion of each chapter. Within chapters there are numerous cross-references whereby the reader can engage in his personal historical analysis and speculation.

In the textual narrative all religious personnel can be assumed to be members of the Congregation of Holy Cross (C.S.C.) unless otherwise noted. The dimensions of buildings are cited in the standard sequence of length, width, and height. A selected bibliography is included for those who wish to pursue various topics discussed in the text. Likewise, the appendices attempt to satisfy special interests of readers who wish to examine campus art, architecture, and sculpture in greater detail. An index to persons and buildings has been prepared to assist the individual using the work as a reference tool.

While the book is a history of the University of Notre Dame, it is not intended to be an official history in either comprehensiveness or interpretation. It is merely one historian's personal journey through the past that has been Notre Dame.

Discovering the Past in Print, Person, and Photography

NO SINGLE medium can adequately express the total history of Notre Dame. However, by utilizing several types of evidence (documentary records, architecture, topography, and photography) and the insights of several disciplines (cultural history, architectural history, historical geography, and material culture studies), it has been possible to formulate a multifaceted appraisal of the University's past. The chapters that follow attempt to unify different data and methods in a historical interpretation that enables the reader to re-create and to understand Notre Dame as it appeared to the successive generations of people who have lived, studied, taught, and worked here. I am hopeful that this approach will encourage similar scholarship by other historians working in the fields of social and cultural history. I cherish the belief that my approach will be suggestive to individual readers of the ways that they can discover the past, not only in history books, but also in the buildings that they inhabit or the photographic albums that they save. In these introductory remarks I would, therefore, like to identify and explain briefly the types of evidence and methods I have employed in this attempt to create a historical portrait of Notre Dame.

No historian researching a university history would neglect the documentary sources of that institution's archives. In addition to the University of Notre Dame Archives, I have also found it important to research the respective archival holdings of the Priests of Holy Cross, the Brothers of Holy Cross, and the Sisters of the Holy Cross. My debt to the published record of Notre Dame's history as narrated in official histories, monographs, dissertations and other published and unpublished studies is recorded in the selected bibliography.

Unfortunately this documentary material, while abundant in quantitative terms, has at least one serious deficiency. Both the official archival records and most printed sources (even the student press) are all too brief in their treatment of routine student and faculty life in all periods except that of the most recent past. In order to overcome this inadequacy in the documentary evidence, I have employed the techniques of oral history, interviewing faculty and staff members as well as alumni of the University in an effort to ascertain what it was actually like to be a student or a faculty member at Notre Dame at various periods in the institution's twentieth-century history. The insights of these "living histories" have been invaluable in expanding and informing my own interpretation of Notre Dame's development, and I have frequently regretted not having similar oral evidence regarding the college's intellectual and social history in the nineteenth century. I have been greatly assisted in gathering this oral evidence by being invited to participate in the Oral History Project of the University Archives first begun in 1969 by Father Thomas Blantz, C.S.C.

In addition to oral history I have turned to architecture and geography as sources for documenting and widening my understanding of Notre Dame's history. The extant physical plant of the University is assuredly a tangible, organic expression of its past. As Professor Richard Sullivan has suggested, "walking over the campus you can trace your way back in time from now to the 1840's, simply by looking carefully at what you pass" (*Notre Dame: Reminiscences of an Era* [Notre Dame, Ind., 1951]). In several ways, the surviving part of the institution's built environment can be "read" as something of a palimpsest, a material document latent with much historical data embedded in its physical forms.

I argue, for example, that one can deduce a great deal about the cultural temper and aspirations of a community by tracing the evolution of its building styles. The development of Notre Dame's architecture —the utilitarian log and clapboard structures of the 1840s, the mansarded, Second Empire brick buildings of the 1870s, the eclectic "modern Gothic" of the 1880s, the few neoclassical structures of the 1910s, the collegiate Gothic revivals of the 1920s, the strictly functional buildings of the 1950s, and finally, the high-rise towers of the late 1960s—can be as important a chronicle to the historian as the documentary sources with which he usually interprets the past. In reconstructing the architectural history of Notre Dame, I have profited from Francis Kervick's *Architecture at Notre Dame* (Notre Dame, Ind., 1938), and Marcus Whifflin's more general survey, *American Architecture since 1780: A Guide to the Styles* (Cambridge, Mass., 1969).

The metamorphoses of facade and function that vintage structures often undergo over time can also serve as historical evidence to the alert interpreter. Visible architectural modifications and renovations of buildings (altered rooflines, changed fenestration, additions or removals) such as the Old College (I–25–28) or Hoynes Hall (III–54–57) have prompted me to undertake the type of historical speculation and inquiry that scholars like Kevin Lynch (*What Time Is This Place?* [Cambridge, Mass., 1972]) and Grady Clay (*Close-Up: How to Read the American City* [New York, 1973]) encourage in their investigations of the built environment. Actual historical change is vividly present in a collage of old and new architectural features frozen in time in much of the University's architecture that has been readapted for different uses over the past decades. One of my objectives in this book is to stimulate readers to discover and decipher these facades as visual clues to the past.

Architecture, by definition, is much more than exterior facades. It is a structural art that combines external form and interior space. Several interior spaces exist on the University's campus that are suggestive of the academic achievement, ambition, or ambivalence of Notre Dame at different junctures of its history. I encourage the reader to experience first hand spaces such as Willoughby Edbrooke's Administration Building of 1879 or Ralph Adams Cram's South Dining Hall of 1927. The comparative analysis of other interiors, usually done via architectural drawings or historical photography, is another technique of the architectural historian that is quite useful to the historian of an institution. For instance, a chronological sequence of photographs of the interior of Sacred Heart Church (II–7–9) accentuates the significant changes in liturgical theory and practice that have occurred in campus worship during the building's seventy-five-year history. The changing social mores and cultural interests of students can be similarly plotted by juxtaposing a nineteenth-century interior of Sorin Hall (III–65) with one recreated in the same structure (VI–45) by contemporary undergraduates.

A final way in which I have employed architecture as historical evidence is much indebted to that branch of American studies scholarship that has been interested in the symbolic dimensions of material culture. John Kouwenhoven's *The Arts in Modern American Civilization* (New York, 1948) and Alan Trachtenberg's *The Brooklyn Bridge, Fact & Symbol* (New York, 1965) are typical models for the type of cultural analysis I perform on selected campus architectural artifacts. The 1879 Administration Building, for example, has been examined as a physical embodiment of much of the cultural style and intellectual ambience of nineteenth-century Notre Dame. The building's central location on the campus, its status as a focal point, its multiple uses over practically a century, and its deliberately planned dome of gold have provided me with a rich symbol around which to recognize much of Chapter II. There are other physical objects—the grotto, the Sorin statue, the Lyons arch, the stadium, the Memorial Library—which are also latent with symbolic meaning in the history of the University.

The land itself—its geological, topographical, and geographical pasts—has also served as evidence in the study that follows. The physical terrain on which Notre Dame's history has taken place is significant in several ways. The marl and limestone deposits provided brick and plaster necessary to erect most of the nineteenth-century buildings; the land's original timber cover was a constant source of lumber; agricultural products from the sand-loam soil and fish from the spring-fed lakes provided sustenance for the community.

In his article, "Time, Space and the Geographic Past: A Prospectus for Historical Geography" (*American Historical Review*, October 1971), John T. Jakle rightly points out that historians have often neglected natural topographic features, natural resources, landscape design, public planning, and changing land use as potential historical data. A significant exception is the scholarship of Richard Wade and Harold Mayer who, in their classic study, *Chicago: Growth of a Metropolis* (Chicago, 1969), demonstrate how writing the "history of a place" requires the tools of both the historian and the geographer—the former with his emphasis on the texture of life and the latter with his concern for spatial relations. The Mayer and Wade synthesis has been a prototype for my own investigation into the field of historical geography.

Notre Dame has always had an overwhelming "sense of place." Presidents from Sorin to Hesburgh have seen the campus—really a self-contained village with its twin lakes, formal tree-lined quadrangles, informal wooded areas, and isolation from the city of South Bend—as a unique learning environment. Recently in a study of environmental design ("The Endangered Domain: A Review and Analysis of Campus Planning and Design at the University of Notre Dame"), Kenneth W. McCandless has sought to identify "those physical features, natural or introduced, and design concepts, planning and architectural, which collectively have established the particular character which is the Domain of Notre Dame." Following McCandless's lead, I have tried to interpret the meaning of the "domain" in historical sequence. In so doing I have paid considerable attention to how and why the campus was originally designed as it was and how, in what ways, and for what reasons it expanded as it did. Naturally, I have been interested in the spatial relations between individual buildings and their siting on the land; I have likewise been concerned to join the land and its

buildings with successive generations of campus inhabitants and their activities.

To conduct such an inquiry I have relied on lithographic and engraved overviews of the campus, contour maps, nineteenth-century manuscript cartography, plus various types of aerial photography. A careful examination of the actual physical terrain of the campus and its environs was, of course, vital to my research. I invite readers to continue such an investigation as they tramp over the campus or as they compare the opening and closing perspectives that are included in each chapter. A sense of Notre Dame's geographical growth can also be extracted from the cartographic data that I have reconstructed and/or reproduced.

It should be pointed out that architectural and geographic evidence, like documentary data, also has its limitations for historical inquiry. Occasionally nineteenth-century lithographers or engravers took artistic liberties with the subjects that they were assigned to replicate. Lakes sometimes appear as rivers (I–53), plains may be exaggerated into rolling hills (IV–1), and a simple facade may become elaborated

into an ornate style. Such evidence, therefore, must be confirmed with other data in order to insure accuracy. Yet some discovered distortions are potential evidence for the cultural historian; the fanciful projections of campus lithography are often indicators of the University's aspirations at various points in its history. The historian who uses architectural evidence labors under a final burden: often the buildings in which he is interested simply no longer exist, or the architect's sketches, measured drawings, and blueprints do not survive.

In an attempt to fill gaps in the evidential record of Notre Dame's history, I have turned to historical photography. The University's history fortuitously coincides with photography's history. Louis Jacques Mandé Daguerre announced the discovery of the photographic process which bears his name only three years before his fellow countryman, Edward Sorin, founded Notre Dame du Lac. A daguerreotypist studio existed in the University's Main Building II erected in 1865, and photography classes, usually taught in the science department, were popular throughout the nineteenth century. As will be evident, the photographic

material that has survived is a varied but impressive lot: tintypes, glass-plate negatives, yearbook photos, rotogravures, student snapshot albums, stereographs, and newspaper half-tones.

I should point out an important methodological premise that underlies my use of historical photography. This book differs from other "pictorial histories" because it attempts to employ photography as evidence instead of mere illustration. Usually historians have added pictures to their narratives in order to illustrate the text or to make an event or a personality more exciting and compelling to their readers. Such "illustrated histories" are often beautifully and effectively executed. This study, however, purports to consider the photographic image as a significant historical document in its own right.

The surviving photography of the University—of buildings, lands, people, activities—has first been helpful to me in the most elemental work of the historian, the task of establishing an accurate and comprehensive chronology of events. Photography, as Beaumont Newhall has thoroughly shown (*The History of Photography*, [New York, 1964]), has its own technical history: daguerreotypes preceded ambrotypes; the *carte-de-viste* came before the ferrotype; the Kodak print (1888) predated the autochrome color process (1903). Photographers also have a history. In South Bend for instance, Albert McDonald was practicing his trade before James Bonney set up his studio. Both took numerous photographs of the University and the chronological limits of their careers assists the historian in dating their photographs. In turn, once a photograph can be identified as to its chemical composition or photographer, then its subject matter can be located in time.

Frequently the photograph confirms the chronology of events already available from the documentary record, but occasionally it fills in a gap that previously existed in the record or even challenges the traditional sequence of that record. The accurately dated photograph itself becomes a reference point for comparative research with other photographs. It also can be used to widen our knowledge of a single point in time. For instance, figure III–21 below documents that in 1888 the University crew practiced on St. Joseph's Lake. Upon careful exam-

ination this photograph also reveals that the University had built on the southwest shore a large ice house—a fact that the documentary record neglects entirely. The photograph gives the researcher not only the exact geographic location of the structure but also provides him with an accurate architectural rendering. Photographs, likewise, have been invaluable in the historical reconstructions that I have done of certain parts of the nineteenth-century campus. The cartographic re-creations of the University's farms (see below, I–34) or its service facilities (III–10) are greatly indebted to photographic evidence.

Glen Holt has argued persuasively ("Chicago through a Camera Lens: An Essay on Photography as History," *Chicago History*, 1971) that photographic documentation is especially useful in researching and describing the physical growth and internal spatial patterns of any urban environment. I have adopted his technique of doing urban history to my study of campus history. By using the various panoramas that photographers have taken from atop vantage points such as the farmyard windmill, the Sacred Heart Church steeple, the Administration Building

dome, or the Cartier Field tower, I have been able to document successive stages of campus development. Such photographic views coupled later with aerial photography depict quite clearly the transformation of the Indiana landscape from forest to open farmland to a highly developed built environment. In a novel way the camera records for the historian a visual census of an area, providing him with information he cannot get easily or at all in other ways. For instance, the changing mixtures of agricultural, recreational, academic, industrial, and residential land usage are clearly displayed; the relation of the campus to the lakes, to neighboring St. Mary's College, to the surrounding countryside, and to the city of South Bend is demonstrated. The changing pattern of campus planning (or the lack thereof) is depicted by a series of aerial views; the shifting texture and importance of certain locales or focal points are likewise captured by views of the same place taken over several decades. In each case a photograph handles the problem of scale—the size of things in the environment—in a method that quantitative data or even narrative prose could never quite achieve.

Sociologists such as Howard Becker ("Photography and Sociology," *Studies in the Anthropology of Visual Communications*, 1974) and anthropologists like John Collier (*Visual Anthropology: Photography as a Research Method*, [New York, 1967]) have recognized the value of photography for social history. My use of photography for this purpose is much in debt to their pioneering scholarship. I have found that photographs have been useful in attempting to reconstruct how former University students, faculty, and staff lived. Photographs, in addition to preserving the vanished faces of who we have been, have the marvelous ability to dramatize the normal. They help satisfy our overwhelming curiosity about how students dressed and dined, how they studied and worked on the campus, or how they amused themselves. Photographs speak to these simple but profoundly human questions with an emotive power that prompts us to realize both the sameness and strangeness of the past.

In order to capture the total social context of an era, I have usually depended upon a collage of images to "tell" the history of Notre Dame. Occasionally, however, a photograph completely capsulized my understanding of a certain personality, social atmosphere, representative situation, or significant event in one single compelling image. The photographer Henri Cartier-Bresson coined the phrase "the decisive moment" to refer to this special instant when things fall into place in the viewfinder in such a way as to render accurately a larger perception. Such breakthroughs have been rare in my patient research through numerous photographic archives. Yet the brooding portrait of Father John Zahm (III–46), the simple interior of St. Edward's dormitory (III–12), and the intense student-faculty confrontation of figure VI–20 connote meaning beyond the confines of the photograph's frame.

Like other types of evidence, historical photography has its limitations. Every photographer is well aware that he, no less than any other observer, exerts considerable control over the information and message that a photograph contains. The historian who uses photography as evidence must totally abandon the folk notion that the camera records objectively what is there for it to record. One must be aware of the cultural biases of the photographer who pushes the shutter button. Technical as well as personal biases likewise must be acknowledged when using photography as a historical source. The choice of film, of development and printing processes, of lens and camera, of exposure and framing, all influence the final photograph. Most cameras—especially in the hands of the amateurs who took the majority of the photographs I have used—worked best in strong light. Thus the photographic record that survives contains few views of activities which took place inside the University's buildings, or of its campus at night or on inclement days. The experience of the excessively overcast, unusually rainy northern Indiana winter is therefore missing from the photographic evidence and, consequently, from the historical experience that was (and is) Notre Dame.

Any one photographer will, of course, only capture but a fraction of an institution's diverse communal life; even taken as a group, photographers of Notre Dame have missed many aspects of the institution's past. The numerous fires that the University has suffered and nationally prominent athletic events were usually witnessed by many cameras. The routine daily life of the dormitories and the campus passed largely unnoticed. Activities of the University's classrooms, libraries, study halls, laboratories, and lecture halls are unfortunately largely unrecorded by both nineteenth- and twentieth-century photographers.

A final qualifying factor regarding the veracity of photographic documentation is what one critic has called "the fecklessness of historic preservation," whereby one photograph is salvaged while another is lost. Nowhere is this better demonstrated than in the one attempt by the University to prepare a visual census of the entire campus for an exhibit at the Chicago Columbian Exposition in 1893. Of the 125 oversized (14" × 20") photographs taken by Alexander Kirsch's photography class, only 67 appear to have survived. One can only speculate on the extent of other losses. Much of the blame for such carelessness must be assumed by historians. In our past scholarship we have used photography only marginally, causing libraries and archives to neglect collecting such data in any systematic fashion.

As a historian I have become convinced that the various artifacts of a past time and place—documents, architecture, cartography, photography—are vital in helping each of us to understand the past more fully as well as to comprehend more knowledgeably the increased velocity of change in our own lifetimes. I am therefore hopeful that this book, in addition to stimulating and expanding an interest in Notre Dame's history, will give readers a heightened sense of the history that pervades their environment—be it town, neighborhood, or campus. As will be evident from the chapters that follow, history can be read in stone and steel, wood and brick, map and photograph, as well as in libraries and archives; the past is visual as well as verbal. I wish that readers might acquire from this book a "visual historical literacy," whereby they might better interpret the abundant and diverse evidence that looms so important for our understanding of the modern past.

Thomas J. Schlereth
26 November 1975

I. The University in 1844

I–1. Notre Dame, ca. 1848. Earliest extant overview of the campus from a copperplate engraving drawn by John Manz of Chicago shows (l. to r.) the Old College, the bakery, the brothers' novitiate, the first main church, the first Main Building. In addition to the entrance gates and porter's lodge, playing fields in the foreground, the two-storey Manual Labor Training School, and its apprentice shops front the campus.

Beginning at the Founders' Monument (94) behind the northwest corner of the Architecture Building (14), Walk I explores the historical background of the University's founding and its growth up to the Civil War. A walk of 250 yards, it moves from the earliest locale of the University's life—Log Chapel (12) and Old College (13)—to the southeast bank of St. Mary's Lake to explain the buildings and activities around this natural feature of the campus. Then, following the expansion of Notre Dame eastward in the 1840s and 1850s, the walk covers the terrain of the first University farm, proceeds by the William Corby Monument (95) and Corby Hall (27), and ends at the site of Main Building I, constructed in 1844, the same year the University was incorporated by the State of Indiana.

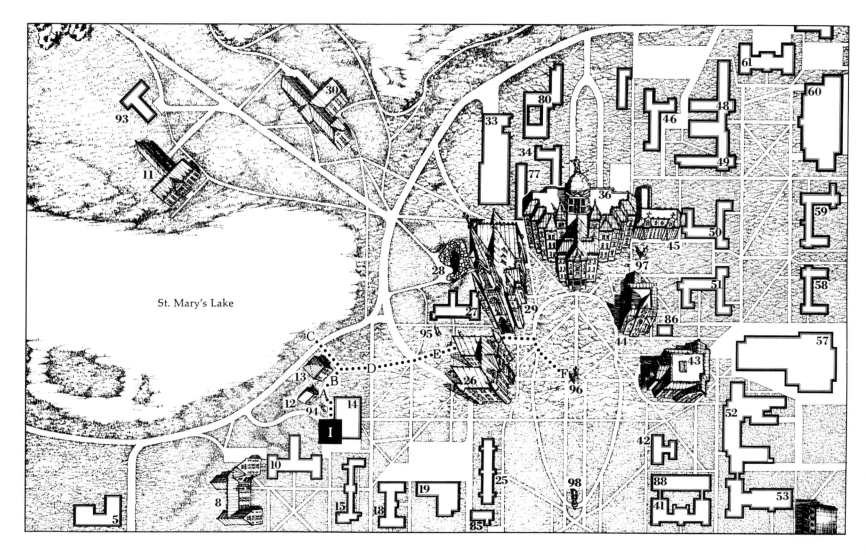

Origins, Founding, Early Growth

THE HISTORY of a place does not really begin in any one place. Nonetheless, men mark their land in order to remember its past and to recollect where their story as a people, an institution, or a community could be said to have begun. Early in this century, Notre Dame recalled its nineteenth-century origins by erecting a monument to its French founders (I–2, 94), a priest and six brothers, all of the religious community eventually known as the *Congregatio a Sancta Cruce*, or the Congregation of Holy Cross (C.S.C.). From this site in the late afternoon on November 26, 1842, Father Edward Sorin and his fellow religious first viewed the land on which they were to build, in less than two years, a Catholic men's college, a preparatory high school, an apprentices' vocational school, and a religious novitiate. In an early letter back to his community in France, the twenty-eight-year-old

Notre Dame in 1844

Acreage: 524   Buildings: 5
Faculty: 8   Tuition: $100
Students: 25   Room/board: $65

Sorin recorded the moment's elation: "Everything was frozen and yet the landscape appeared so beautiful. The lake, with its mantle of resplendent white snow, was to us a symbol of the purity of Our Lady, whose name it bears and also of the purity of soul which should characterize the new inhabitants of these lovely shores." Because of the heavy snow-cover, Sorin initially had no way of knowing that there were actually two lakes on his land grant. He therefore named his new home, in honor of his special spiritual patroness, *Notre Dame du Lac*, or Our Lady of the Lake.

Others had also come to this lake vista before Sorin, left their traces, and were a part of its history. Potawatomi, Miami, and Chippewa Indians had roamed these shores for centuries. Père Jacques Marquette, S.J., may have been the first European to explore the area as early as 1675, but if not he, then assuredly his countryman, Robert Sieur de La Salle, canoed upriver from St. Joseph, Michigan (where he established Fort Miami in 1679), to the southern bend of the St. Joseph River, roughly one-half mile west

of the present Notre Dame campus (I–3). La Salle and his fourteen-man party followed the Indian portage across the marsh to the Kankakee River, on to the Illinois, and then down the Mississippi, claiming all the territory they traversed for God and country.

In their exploration and colonization of the Mississippi Valley, the French allied sacred and secular concerns, the *père* accompanied the *coureur de bois*. Shortly after La Salle's visit, a French Jesuit, Claude Allouez, established St. Joseph's Mission (1680) at Niles, Michigan, where the French eventually also constructed Fort St. Joseph (I–3). In 1686 Allouez founded another mission at the same lakeshore site where Sorin would arrive 150 years later. Allouez, more knowledgeable of the area's topography than Sorin, named the mission Ste-Marie-des-Lacs (I–3). During both the French and English colonial occupation of this part of northern Indiana, a log chapel-cabin and a few small sheds in a little clearing served as a missionary base for itinerant French clerics attempting to Christianize the native Indians and minister to

I–2. Founders' Monument (94)
This historical marker was originally surmounted by an eight-foot statue of St. Joseph, patron of the Brothers of St. Joseph. Sorin also considered Joseph a special protector of Notre Dame, located as it was in St. Joseph County, close to the St. Joseph River and St. Joseph, Michigan. On the western face of the monument is an erroneous claim that credits Sorin and six brothers standing on this spot November 26, 1842. Actually only Sorin and Brothers Francis Xavier (I–19), Gatien, and probably Patrick and Basil were there that historic winter afternoon. Brothers Lawrence (I–36), Vincent (I–17), and Joachim arrived the following spring, and Anselm in 1844.

I–3. St. Joseph Valley Settlement, 1679–1835
A modern map reconstructed from documentary sources of the period showing the principal settlements in northern Indiana and southern Michigan.

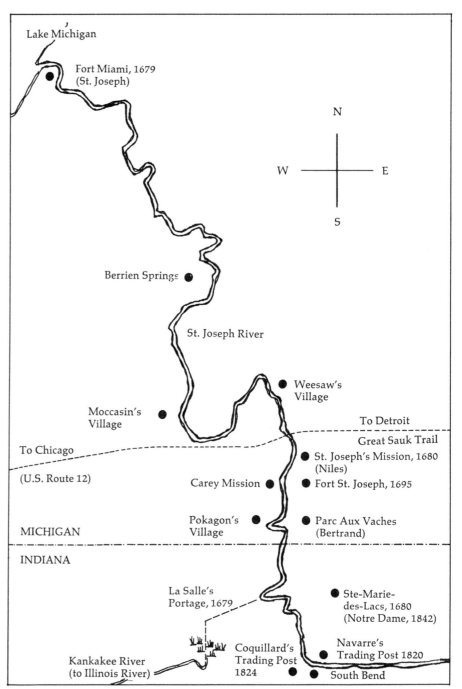

I–3

the few European Catholics in the region. Even after the ecclesiastical jurisdiction of the area passed in 1790 to the first American bishop, John Carroll (II–62), the Indiana Territory still remained, in terms of Catholic missionary effort, the particular province and responsibility of the French. The consequences of this distinctive European heritage, wrote one local historian, was that early Notre Dame was "French in conception, nomenclature, personnel, methods, ideas and aims."

Secular missionary priests Stephen Badin (I–8), who came to the northern Indiana frontier in 1830, Louis De Seille (I–13), who would die in Badin's cabin-chapel, and Benjamin Petit, who accompanied his Indian converts when they were forcibly removed farther west to the Indian territory in 1839, each continued the work begun by Allouez at Ste-Marie-des-Lacs. They also served as exemplars to Sorin, who later had them buried at Notre Dame. Other Frenchmen also had a part in the early history of the University. Simon Gabriel Bruté, an emigré from the French Revolution, a priest in the Society of Saint

Sulpice, and first bishop of Vincennes, had traveled to Europe in 1836 to raise money and clergy for his newly created (1834) American diocese (I–4).

Among those who heard Bruté's pleas at the major seminary at Le Mans in western France was Edward Sorin, a restless, twenty-two-year-old curate who felt his ambition and energy stifled by minimal pastoral duties in the neighboring village of Parcé. While at Le Mans, Sorin had become acquainted with one of the seminary's professors, Abbé Basil Anthony Moreau (I–7), who was in the process of gathering a group of French clerics into a religious community then known as the Auxiliary Priests of Le Mans. Moreau had previously inherited the responsibility of governing a group of religious brothers, the Josephites, or Brothers of Saint Joseph, which had been founded by James Francis Dujarie in 1820. He eventually combined the priests and brothers, along with a group of religious women (Sisters of the Holy Cross), into a thriving religious community that was recognized by the papal authorities in 1857 and

I–4. Catholic Development in the Midwest, 1835
Bishop Simon Bruté's hand-drawn map of the extent of his Vincennes diocese as of February 11, 1835, indicates South Bend's location as well as the various modes of water transport—lake, river, canal—vital to the development of the Midwest.

I–4

called the Congregation of Holy Cross (C.S.C.).

As a newly ordained diocesan priest, Edward Sorin was attracted to the work of the Le Mans Auxiliaries who made it their special province to minister in poor, understaffed parishes and schools. In 1840 he joined Moreau's religious community. Sorin, like so many men who would figure prominently in the nineteenth-century history of Notre Dame, was a Breton. So was a former lawyer of Rennes, Celestine de la Hailandière (I–6), who had become a missionary priest to America and who was named Bruté's successor as bishop of Vincennes in 1839. De la Hailandière and Sorin shared other traits in addition to their regional origin: a high sense of vocation, practicality, individuality, and audacity. It was no wonder southern Indiana proved too small for the two of them.

De la Hailandière, as Bruté's vicar-general, had been in France when his superior died, attempting to persuade Father Moreau to send a colony of his brothers to work and teach in the far-flung Vincennes diocese (I–4). Moreau responded

I–5–8. Benefactors of Early Notre Dame
Four clerics whose vision and energy figured in the inspiration, founding, and support of the University are: Simon Bruté (1779–1839) (I–5), first bishop of Vincennes, whose preaching in France in 1836 inspired young Sorin to a missionary career; Celestine de la Hailandière (1798–1882) (I–6), who persuaded Basil Anthony Moreau (1799–1873) (I–7), founder and first superior-general of Holy Cross, to send Sorin and his brothers to St. Peter's, Indiana. When Sorin requested another site on which to build a novitiate and a college, Hailandière gave him the 524 acres in northern Indiana donated earlier to the Vincennes diocese by Stephen Badin (1768–1853) (I–8), first priest ordained in the U.S. and veteran missionary for sixty years in the Ohio and Mississippi valleys.

by sending to America in 1841 six brothers, with Edward Sorin as their religious superior and advisor. De la Hailandière settled them on a 160-acre farm and mission station called St. Peter's, twenty-seven miles east of Vincennes in southern Indiana. Despite their inability to speak even the most rudimentary English, the new missionaries quickly set up a primary school and their first religious house; they gained twelve new recruits for the brotherhood and began to consider themselves rather permanently established in the United States.

Sorin soon decided he wanted to build a college. In the spring of 1842, without consulting Moreau or de la Hailandière, he and the brothers began gathering building materials, borrowed money from the Bank of Vincennes, and proceeded to construct a small building. Much to Sorin's chagrin, de la Hailandière strenuously objected to the unauthorized project principally because a Catholic college, St. Gabriel's, conducted by the Eudist Fathers, existed only thirty miles away. De la Hailandière, however, aware of Sorin's determination and aspira-

tions, told the young priest he might build a college elsewhere in the diocese. Sorin welcomed his offer of an alternative site in spite of, or perhaps because of, the fact that de la Hailandière suggested a location at the furthermost limits of the diocese in sparsely settled northern Indiana.

Father Stephen Badin (I–8), who had purchased the site in several parcels from the U.S. Government and early settlers in 1830–32, had sold it for a nominal fee to the Vincennes diocese in 1835 with the express hope that a school and an orphanage be established there. In 1840 the property was offered to Father Ferdinand D. Bach of the Fathers of Mercy in the hope that he would establish an educational institution at Ste-Marie-des-Lacs. As a result of his appointment to another post, Bach was forced to abandon the contemplated establishment at the lakes, and the land reverted to the bishop of Vincennes. De la Hailandière now promised to give Sorin and the Holy Cross community title to the property if Sorin, within two years time, could reopen the mission sta-

I–5

I–6

I–7

I–8

I–9. South Bend, 1831
This historical reconstruction looking southwest from the Niles Road (now Niles Avenue) across St. Joseph River was drawn by O. E. Stelzer in 1931. Despite some visual distortions, the map illustrates residences and businesses of several South Bend supporters of Notre Dame. The campus would be located two miles to the north along the Niles Road.

O.E.STELZER, DES.

1. *Lathrop M. Taylor's first Trading Post, established in 1827*
2. *Alexis Coquillard's Trading Store, Meeting Place of County Commissioners*
3. *The "Fairplay", N. B. Griffith's Ferry*
4. *Frederick Bainter's Brick House*
5. *A. Coquillard's new Frame House*
6. *Strayer Gun Shop*
7. *Alexis Coquillard's First Trading Post, "Big St. Joseph Station", built in 1823*

VIEW
of
SOUTH BEND
in
1831

8. *L. M. Taylor's second Trading Post, Residence and Post Office, first called "Southold"*
9. *Peter Johnson's Michigan Hotel*
10. *Benjamin Coquillard's Tavern*
11. *Calvin Lilly's Tavern*
12. *Wm. Stanfield's Residence*
13. *Stockade started in 1831 before the Black Hawk War*
14. *Jefferson School House*

I–10–11. Local Founding Fathers
Alexis Coquillard (1795–1855) (I–10), French Catholic, agent of the American Fur Company, cofounder of South Bend, extended the University credit and materials during its early years; his nephew and namesake, Alexis T. Coquillard (1825–90), was Notre Dame's first day student. Chief Leopold Pokagon (1775–1841) (I–11), renowned civil chief of the Potawatomis, in 1830 requested the bishop of Detroit to send a priest (Badin, as it turned out) to reopen the local Indian missions. Pokagon's son Simon (1830–99) (I–56), like a number of Potawatomi and Miami young men, attended Notre Dame.

I–12. Bertrand Mission, Michigan, 1912
In 1814 Joseph Bertrand, French trader who had taken a Potawatomi wife, set up his fur press at Parc Aux Vaches on the north side of the Chicago Road (Great Sauk Trail) and named the settlement after himself. Bertrand, a lifelong friend of Sorin, helped him establish St. Mary's Academy not far from this site in 1844. When the Academy (later, St. Mary's College) moved to its present Indiana

tion, establish a brothers' novitiate, and build his projected college.

In addition to the approximately two hundred local Indian Catholics led by Leopold Pokagon (I–11), and later his son Simon (I–57), Sorin would also have the responsibility for the spiritual welfare of thirty (mostly French Canadian) Catholic families settled in the village (approximately 1,000 population) of South Bend (I–9), as well as those located in neighboring northern Indiana and southern Michigan settlements (I–12). De la Hailandière instructed Sorin to seek assistance and credit in South Bend from Alexis Coquillard (I–10), trader-agent of the American Fur Company and town father, who, along with Lathrop Taylor, had platted the village in 1831. On November 16, 1842, Sorin with seven brothers, a small bill of credit, and slightly over $300, set out from St. Peter's to make contact with Coquillard and to take possession of the land he had been tentatively given. After an arduous 250-mile overland journey, Sorin and at least four of his companions arrived (I–15–16) in the late afternoon of November 26,

I–10

I–11

I–12

site ten years later, Sorin and the sisters of Holy Cross acknowledged their debt to the trader by naming the first St. Mary's building Bertrand Hall (II–29).

I–13. Last Eucharist of Louis DeSeille, 1837
A painting completed by Notre Dame faculty member John Worden after an unfinished sketch by Professor Paul Wood, the original oil canvas now hangs on the west interior wall of the Log Chapel (12). According to differing traditions, the white man assisting the dying DeSeille is either Joseph Bertrand or Benjamin Coquillard, father of the first Notre Dame day student.

I–13

I–14. Badin Memorial, 1906
Affixed to the east wall of the replica of Badin's 1831 Log Chapel (12), this historical marker denotes the priest's contributions to the early history of the University. Badin, for whom Badin Hall (18) is named, was also a part-time faculty member who taught "Evidences of Christianity."

1842, in the vicinity of the present Founders' Monument (94). Three other brothers followed at a slower pace with oxen, wagons, supplies, and equipment.

A *Walk west, down the path to the front of the Log Chapel (12).*

Shortly after reaching Ste-Marie-des-Lacs, Sorin, in addition to re-naming it Notre Dame du Lac (which became the University's corporate title in 1844), began to expand his primitive settlement. Buildings already there included a one-and-one-half-storey log cabin-chapel erected by Badin (I–14) in 1831; a two-storey clapboard house inhabited by Charron, an Indian interpreter, and his family; and a small log shed. The present Log Chapel (12) is a historical reconstruction of Badin's original structure (I–20, 22) in which Sorin and his brothers first resided. The ground floor served as their living quarters and the attic as their chapel. The colony immediately began felling trees and preparing lumber for another larger, but similar, log house which Sorin located just east of the Badin chapel. Scattered

I–15

I–15–16. The Founding, November 26, 1842
The beginnings of the University were depicted by two Notre Dame artists-in-residence: in 1883 Luigi Gregori (II–12) created a full-length wall mural (presently in the trunk room of St. Edward's Hall) for the Sorin Association (I–16). It illustrates an encounter that occurred shortly after the arrival of Sorin. Fourteen Indians had requested baptism. Sorin invited them to stay overnight in Badin's log cabin–chapel. After Sorin performed the baptisms the next morning, an Indian woman, as a token of gratitude, gave Sorin seven rings. Francis X. Ackerman, professor of mechanical drawing, did

the above line drawing (I–15) of Sorin's arrival but took a number of liberties with the historical event. The colony did not all arrive at once, nor did they come by stagecoach, and there is no evidence that Charron, the Indian interpreter who lived in the area, was there to welcome them.

Born in the village of La Roche (Ahuille) near Laval in the province of La Mayenne, son of a respected middle-class farming family, Sorin was the product of the local schools, private tutoring, the Colleges of Laval and Precigne. He was ordained in 1838 and soon joined the newly organized (1840) Auxiliary Priests of Abbé Moreau. Despite his youth (twenty-eight years), his lack of experience, and his brevity as a religious, Sorin was the logical choice to lead the new community's first missionary effort to the United States; he was a leader with indefatigable energy, stubborn ambition, and undaunted optimism. Nineteenth-century Notre Dame was, without a doubt, the lengthened shadow of this brash, dynamic, visionary man.

Catholic families, white and Indian alike, assisted the Holy Cross community in raising the walls of this building before work had to cease due to a typically bitter northern Indiana winter in 1842. When a second contingent of eleven brothers led by Brother Vincent Pieau (I–17) arrived from Vincennes in February 1843, construction was resumed so that by March 19th, the Feast of St. Joseph, Sorin could dedicate the first of the thirty-four buildings he would erect in the creation of the Notre Dame campus.

B *Walk to the southeast side of the Old College (13) and face the marble historical marker on its southeast wall.*

With the completion of Sorin's log building, Badin's cabin-chapel assumed two new functions: Brother Francis Patois (I–19) established a carpentry shop on the first floor, and the second storey became a crowded dormitory for the brothers who now numbered eighteen men. Under Patois's direction, the brothers began to prepare more lumber and to secure building materials for a major college structure. Sorin had

I–17. Brother Vincent (1797–1890)
Born Jean Pieau at Courbeville, France, the son of a weaver but orphaned at an early age, he was the first to join Father Dujarie's new community of brothers formed at Ruille in 1821. A veteran teacher and administrator, in 1842 he was the oldest (forty-five years) of the Holy Cross colony sent to Indiana with Sorin. The latter's father, heartbroken over his son's departure for America, employed Vincent to be Fr. Sorin's surrogate-father. Vincent also served Sorin as confidant, novice master, University trustee, faculty member, and administrative officer for over fifty years.

I–18

I–19. Brother Francis Xavier (1820–96)
Born René Patois at Clermont, La Sarthe, he was a carpenter and mason before entering the religious life, shortly after his twentieth birthday. Among the youngest (twenty-one years) members of the missionary colony, Brother Xavier brought his manual skills to the founding of Notre Dame. A self-taught architect, he, along with Brother Charles Harding, designed many of the University's nineteenth-century buildings. He was also the University mortician, coffinmaker, and steward of both the Community (I–29) and Cedar Grove Cemeteries.

I–20

I–20. Badin Chapel Marker, 1895
Although Badin's original chapel burnt in 1858, its site remained a hallowed spot in Notre Dame's collective memory. The location of the first home of Sorin and his band was mounded, maintained, and marked by a twelve-foot iron cross.

I–22. Log Chapel, ca. 1955
A reconstruction of Badin's Log Chapel (12) was built in 1906 from the manuscript (I–21) by William Arnett, an ex-slave from Kentucky. A storey-and-a-half cedar cabin (40' × 24'), hand-hewn by broadaxe, the chapel is still used for religious services.

I–22

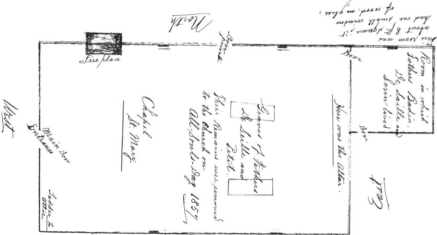

Old French Brother Francis Xavier stated the chapel to have been 20 ft. wide by 35 feet long. He weatherboarded it, and his statement ought to be correct. On each side North and South were 2 small windows. It was a Log-chapel, covered outside with weatherboards; it burned down in the winter 1856–57 —

I–21

I–21. Badin Chapel Floor Plan, ca. 1900
An interior plan as drawn by Brother Boniface from the reminiscences of men (particularly Brother Francis Xavier) who had lived in the structure before it burnt.

I–23. Log Chapel Interior, 1975
Now used principally for vesper services,
student retreats, and marriage liturgies,
the chapel interior has undergone various
renovations since 1906.

**I–24. Early Advertisement of the
University, South Bend Free Press, 1843.**

left southern Indiana with a set of
architectural plans and the understanding that Mr. Marsile, a
Vincennes constructor who had
prepared the drawings, would come
to Notre Dame the following spring
and erect a four-and-one-half-storey
Main Building. When Marsile failed
to arrive as promised, the always
impatient Sorin determined to put
up a small brick building which
would dramatize, if only in a token
fashion, the college's establishment
and credibility.

With bricks donated by Benjamin
Coquillard (Alexis's brother and
a South Bend general merchant),
Sorin and Brother Francis designed
a squat, two-storey structure (later
expanded to four storeys) to house
classrooms, a student dormitory, a
dining hall, a dormitory for the faculty (brothers), a clothes room, and
a kitchen. This multipurpose building, originally only intended as an
expedient until a major Main Building could be constructed, survives
on the present campus as the only
extant original landmark of the
University in its first decade. As its
historical marker indicates, the "Old
College" has served as a convent

I–23

UNIVERSITY OF NOTRE-DAME-DU-LAC,

SOUTH BEND, ST. JOSEPH COUNTY, INDIANA.

Under the direction of the Priests of the Holy Cross, associated with the Brothers of St. Joseph.

THIS Institution is now opened for the reception of Youth, under the auspices of the Rt. Rev'd Bishop of Vincennes, who presented to the Brothers, the beautiful and elegant site upon which the buildings are erected.

Notre-Dame-du-Lac, is at a distance of one mile from South Bend, the County seat; 80 miles from Chicago, Illinois; 180 from Detroit, Mich. and 80 from Fort Wayne, Ia.

The erection of a Seminary here, was contemplated many years ago; the location being so eminently adapted for the purpose, but it was only within the last year that the Bishop was enabled to accomplish this design. All the advantages of convenience, attractive scenery, pure and invigorating air, and excellent springs, combine here to form not only a healthful abode, but also, an agreeable solitude, which facilitates so effectually the intellectual improvement of youth.

The edifice is of brick, four and a half stories high and not inferior in point of style or structure, to any of the Colleges of the United States, and is situated upon a commanding eminence on the verge of two picturesque and commodious Lakes, which with the river St. Joseph and the surrounding country, present a most magnificent prospect. The rooms are spacious, well ventilated and furnished with everything conducive to regularity and comfort.

A Gymnasium will be erected near the Seminary on a large and improved plan, and will be under the direction of a careful and experienced master.

THE INFIRMARY is intrusted to Sisters, similar in their Institute to the Sisters of Charity; Their well known kindness and skill are a sufficient guarantee, that the invalids will be attended to with all the diligence and care, which devotion and affection can suggest. One of the Brothers is a Physician, but for greater security, the services of the most experienced of the faculty will be procured in cases of serious diseases.

The disciplinary government will be mild, yet sufficiently energetic, to preserve that good order, so essential to the well being of the Institution. The morals and general deportment of the pupils will be watched over with the greatest assiduity and solicitude; and no pains will be spared to prepare them for fulfilling their respective duties in society. In their daily recreations, they will be always accompanied by a member of the Institution; all books in their possession will be subject to the inspection of the Prefect of Studies; and none will be allowed circulation without his consent. Corporal punishment will never be inflicted, but more conciliatory and effective means of correction will be judiciously used; should a pupil prove refractory, and incorrigible, he will be dismissed.

The faculty will be formed from the Priests of the Holy Cross, and the most competent Brothers, one of whom has just returned from Europe, having completed arrangements for any additional aid which may be hereafter found requisite.

In the reception of pupils, no distinction of creed will be made, and the parents of those, not professing the Catholic Faith, may rest assured that there will be no interference with their religious tenets; they will be required only to attend to the religious exercises with decorum, this being in conformity with the rules of all Catholic Colleges in the United States.

TERMS.

Board, washing, mending and medical attendance, with the English Course, embracing all the branches of a practical education; Orthography, Reading, Writing, Arithmetic, Grammar and Composition, to which particular attention will be paid; Geography, Ancient and Modern History; the most approved method of Book-keeping, Surveying, Mensuration, Mathematics, Astronomy, the use of the Globes, Rhetoric, Vocal

Music, &c.	$100 per ann.
Half Boarders	40 " "
Day scholars in the above course	20 " "
The same in the preparatory School	16 " "
The classical course with the higher branches of education, an additional sum of	20 " "
The French, German, Spanish and Italian languages are taught at an extra charge of	8 " " each
Instrumental Music and Drawing	20 " " each

Class Books, Stationery, and Medicines furnished at the usual rates.

The payments must be made semi annually, in advance; from this rule there can be no deviation whatever, as the charges are based upon the lowest estimate, the object of the Institution being to increase the facilities of instruction, without any view to pecuniary reward.

The vacation will begin on the 1st of August and end on the 1st of September. it is desirable that pupils attend punctually on this day, being the commencement of the academic year.

No boarder will be received for a shorter term than half a year, and no deduction made for absence, except in case of sickness or dismission.

Examinations will take place at the end of each Quarter, and reports forwarded semi annually to parents, informing them of the progress, health, &c. of their children. Public examinations, and distribution of premiums, will take place in the last week of July in every year.

DIRECTIONS FOR PARENTS.

Each pupil must be provided with bed and bedding, (if furnished by the Institution, they form an extra charge,) six shirts, six pair of stockings, six pocket handkerchiefs, six towels, (all of which must be marked) a knife and fork, a table and tea spoon, a hat and cap, two suits of clothes, an over coat, a pair of shoes and a pair of boots for winter; three suits and two pairs of shoes for summer. No advances will be made by the Institution for clothing or other expenses.

The pupils will not be allowed to have money in their possession; their pocket money must be deposited in the Treasurer's hands, in order to guard against abuses, and to enable the Institution to apply the money as an incentive to virtue and industry. When parents wish to have their children sent home, they must give timely notice, settle all accounts, and supply means to defray their travelling expenses.

Visitors cannot be permitted to interrupt the pupils during the hours of study; the mid-day recreation commences at half past twelve and ends at half past one o'clock. This is the most appropriate time for the visits of parents and friends.

All letters to pupils or members of the Institution must be post paid.

E. SORIN, Superior
of the Brothers of St. Joseph,
South Bend, St. Joseph County, Indiana.

☞ This Institution was Incorporated by the Indiana Legislature at its last session, 1843.

[W. & J. Millikan Pr's South Bend, Ia.

I–25–28. Old College Multiple Uses
I–25, farmhouse, ca. 1870; I–26, bakery and farmhouse, ca. 1892; I–27, house of studies for brothers, ca. 1906; I–28, Holy Cross Mission Band headquarters, 1936.

I–25

I–26

(as early as the summer of 1843 Sorin recruited four sisters of the Holy Cross to assume the domestic tasks of his institution), a bakery, farmhouse, house of studies for teaching brothers, headquarters for the Holy Cross Mission Band, student dormitory, and retreat house (I–25–28). Despite all the alterations wrought to its interior arrangement, exterior facades, and surrounding landscape, it remains a simple, candid expression of the inauspicious beginnings of Notre Dame.

C *Walk to the front door of the Old College (13), descend the stairs and path to the right, and walk across the road to the shore of St. Mary's Lake.*

In addition to the Old College, other structures were soon erected around St. Mary's Lake, a seventeen-acre, twenty-two-foot deep, spring-fed body whose perimeters in the 1840s were larger, more irregular and marsh-bordered than the present shoreline. This lake, in the University's first few years, became the focal point of communal existence. It was an industrial site,

I–27

I–28

I–29. University Lakes, 1878
Lithograph map by Charles Shober of
Chicago shows the lime kilns (92, 93,
97), brick kilns, and brick yard (101, 102),
St. Aloysius (priests') Novitiate (78), Holy
Sepulchre (87), Community Cemetery
(86), St. Joseph's (brothers') Novitiate
(68), and the Chapel of the Holy Angels
(64). The Rush dam was located (108)
along St. Mary's Creek. (Numbers
correspond to this map's legend.)

I–29

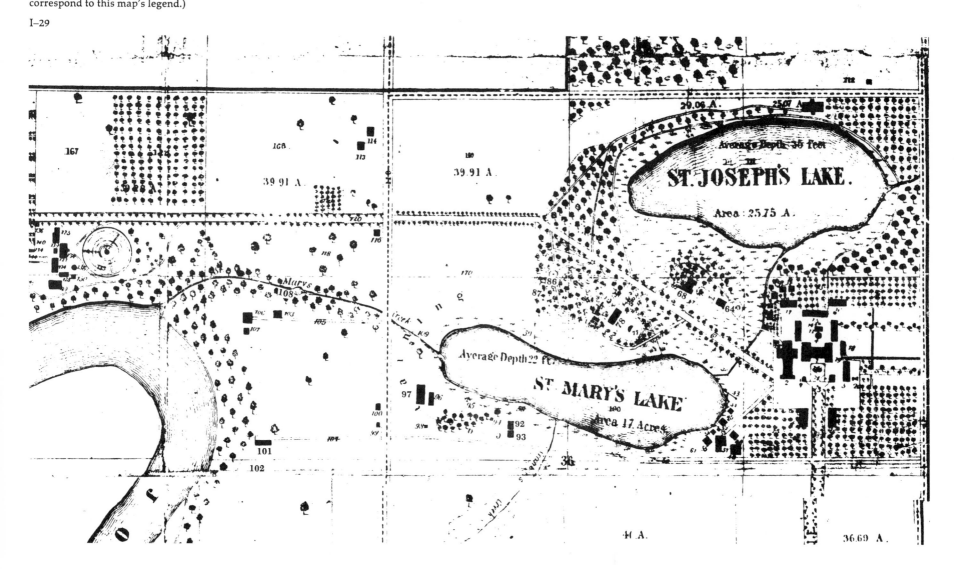

I–30. St. Mary's Lake, 1906
Pond to the right of Carroll Hall (1), formerly Dujarie Institute, is a vestige of where marl was dug in the nineteenth century. St. Mary's Creek flows out of the lake at its extreme western shore and eventually passes to the left of St. Mary's College in the distance. Holy Cross Seminary (building with bell cupola and now Holy Cross Hall [11]) occupied the site of the former priests' novitiate (I–31). The foundation site of the University bakery (I–40) can be seen at the bottom of the photograph.

I–30

an economic resource, a spiritual inspiration, and a source of life and death.

To the left of the present (1) Carroll Hall (formerly Dujarie Institute, built in 1906 as a residence for Holy Cross brothers and named for their founder) were the University's first industries (I–29). Rich marl deposits yielded raw materials for brick production which began as early as 1843. A year later lime kilns were also in operation. By 1847, small residences, built to house hired men who assisted the brothers in the manufacturing processes, lined the road that now winds toward Carroll Hall. Until the early 1880s the University kilns produced the lime (vital for plaster and mortar) and the distinctive yellow-buff "Notre Dame brick" (by 1858 one-half million were produced annually for sale) used in all Notre Dame's buildings erected during that period. With certain exceptions, the University has maintained a visual continuity with this aspect of its past by using Belden brick, of similar hue and texture, in most of its new construction.

To the right and west of Carroll Hall lies the St. Mary's Lake outlet which once drained, by means of St. Mary's Creek, into the St. Joseph River, one-half mile to the west (I–29). As early as 1847, the University's Council of Administration attempted to buy the farm property along this stream. Initially they desired access to the river for its transport and commercial possibilities and also hoped to incorporate the mill, farm buildings, and competing lime kiln that a Mr. Rush had already built on the land adjacent to their own holdings. Rush repeatedly refused to sell despite the University's annual offers. Notre Dame officials were also anxious to control the creek and the dam on it so that they could lower the level of their lakes thereby draining the surrounding marsh and exposing more valuable marl.

Father Sorin, nineteenth-century entrepreneur that he was, saw these commercial prospects, but also coveted the Rush property for another reason. He had become convinced that the high water level and the stagnant marsh between the two lakes caused the malarial fever and cholera that had continually afflicted

I–31. Holy Cross Community Buildings
Located on the nineteenth-century "Island," the buildings are (l. to r.): the Holy Sepulchre shrine (13), the Community Cemetery (large cross), the St. Aloysius (priests') Novitiate (12), the St. Joseph's (brothers') Novitiate (11), and the Chapel of the Holy Angels and shrine (10). (Numbers correspond to the lithograph's legend.)

I–31

his faculty and student body since 1847. By 1855, twenty-three priests, brothers, sisters, and students had died, and Sorin felt the sickness had reached epidemic proportions. Faced with a decimated community, a desperate Sorin approached Rush again and, to his surprise, Rush now appeared willing to sell. The initial legal papers were drawn up, but Rush suddenly left town without signing them. Sorin, not a man accustomed to be kept waiting, felt a decision had been agreed upon in the spirit if not the letter of the law. Without hesitation he dispatched six burly workmen to destroy Rush's dam while he went off to celebrate the Holy Thursday Eucharist in memory of those who had died during the epidemic. Rush, upon his return, accepted the *fait accompli* and closed the sale for $8,000 as originally arranged. The University was expanded by 185 acres, the lake level sank, the marsh dried, and the cholera vanished.

The shores of St. Mary's Lake also became the forested preserve of several religious houses of formation for the expanding Holy Cross community. On the site of the pres-

ent (11) Holy Cross Hall (I–32), almost directly across the lake from the Old College, was St. Aloysius Novitiate (also known as Our Lady of Holy Cross), erected in 1852–53 for the training of C.S.C. priests (I–31). Behind this novitiate were replicas of important artifacts of Christian history designed to inspire spiritual meditation: the tomb of the Virgin Mary and a *via dolorosa* that led to a Holy Sepulchre modeled after the original shrine at

Jerusalem. Behind this house of formation was, and still is, the Holy Cross Community Cemetery (I–31). Here, marked by uniformly unpretentious white crosses in graves democratically arranged in chronological order of death, lie buried many men who have been significant in Notre Dame's history.

To the right of Holy Cross Hall is the present Columba Hall (30), located on a protuberance referred to in the 1840s as "the Island."

Here St. Joseph's Novitiate for the brothers and a chapel (Our Lady of the Angels) were built in 1844 (I–33). Before the marsh was drained, the lowland between the lakes frequently flooded, thereby creating an "Island" (really a peninsula) which Sorin saw as a natural cloister for religious contemplation. Accessible first only by boat, then bridge, and finally plank road, the isolated spot remained a favorite place for spiritual exercises

I–32. Holy Cross Seminary
Built in 1886 on the site of the first priests' novitiate (I–29, 31), a new front facade was added to the structure in 1926. Formerly a house for men studying for the Holy Cross priesthood, it was converted to a student residence hall in 1967.

I–33. Holy Cross Community House, ca. 1900
Also known as Mount St. Vincent, this building complex was erected on the site of the brothers' first (St. Joseph's) novitiate (I–29, 31). Renamed Columba Hall in 1954 in honor of Brother Columba, it now serves as a residence for the brothers' community on the University campus.

throughout the nineteenth century. In a formal garden of serpentine walks, a chapel and shrine of Our Lady of Angels were built (II–24). The chapel became a venerated shrine for pilgrimages by American Catholics.

D *Turn around and walk back up the steps beside the Old College (13); then proceed left (east) along its entrance walk to the first intersecting path. Turn around and face the Old College.*

Notre Dame's principal endowment throughout much of its history has been its land. Brother Lawrence Menage (I–36), one of Sorin's original companions and a farmer from La Sarthe, found approximately ten acres cleared when the first colony arrived in 1842. Two years later he had over 120 acres of wheat, potatoes, and corn under cultivation. Menage also had Brother Xavier (I–19), the first University architect, construct a series of farm buildings (I–34) along the lake shore. Figure I–38 depicts the extent of the farm complex by the 1860s, and figure I–39 delineates its growth by 1893.

Standing on the present walk from the Old College, one could have seen, in 1893, by facing that structure (which periodically served as a farmhouse) and turning slowly (counterclockwise) toward the intersecting path, a panorama of over twenty farm buildings erected throughout the nineteenth century. Behind the Old College was an ice house, farther up the hill a slaughter house and a huge pigsty (I–35). A large cow barn, several animal sheds, and a three-storey (80' × 40') hay barn occupied the present site of Howard (15) and Morrissey (10) Halls. Parallel to the Old College and just beyond the Founders' Monument were a sugar house, horse shed, and implement barn. Where the Architecture Building (14) now stands would have been a large wagon shed, tool house, another stable, and a windmill (I–39), and beyond that the wheat granary and corncribs shown in figure I–41. East of the corncribs was the Manual Labor and Industrial School complex (see chapter IV, figures IV–10–14). Turning toward the lake (again counterclockwise), one would have seen the University bakery

I–32

I–33

I–34. Notre Dame Farm, ca. 1895
The first University farm buildings at their greatest extent included: a) icehouse, b) slaughterhouse, c) hog shed, d) horse barn, e) sugarhouse, f) horse shed, g) cattle barn, h) wagon shed, i) dairy barn, j) toolhouse, k) windmill, l) corn-cribs, m) wheat granary, n) apprentice's recreation hall, o) coal shed, p) Manual Labor School, q) bakery, r) flour storage sheds, s) baker's residence, t) privy,

u) farmhouse, and v) privy. Those structures that were in place in 1895 and survive on the present campus are: Old College (13), Sorin Hall (26), and Corby Hall (27). Those structures erected later on the site include the Log Chapel (12) and the Architecture Building (14). The capital letter **D** denotes the position of the walker as described in the text.

I–35. Back of the Farms, 1888
The hog yard is seen with its lakeside watering hole; in the foreground is the ice house. Visible beyond the Old College is the roof of the bakery (I–40) and, to the right of Old College among the tree cover, the windmill that was in the center of the farmyard.

I–36. Brother Lawrence (1815–73)
Born John Menage at Rece, France, son of peasant farmers, Lawrence was one of Sorin's original companions in 1842. An unlettered, simple man who possessed a shrewd business acumen, he was the University steward and was in charge of all its farms.

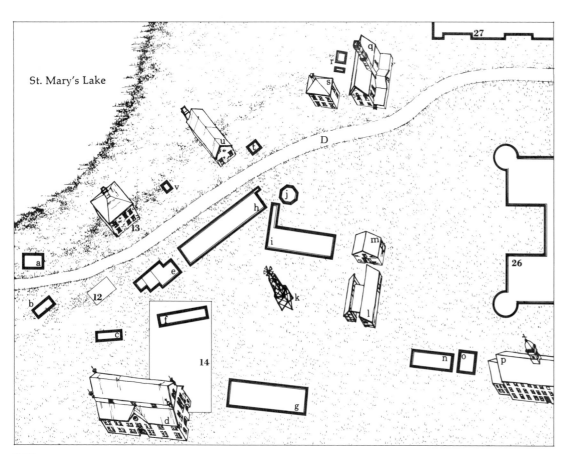

I–34

I–35

I–36

I–37. University Barn, 1893
Built at a cost of approximately $750 and the largest of several barns in the area (see I–34), this structure housed the college livery. In use until 1896, the University occasionally held its summer closing exercises here.

I–38–39. University Farms, 1865–88
Two views of the farm: I–38, a pastoral engraving from a southwest perspective, ca. 1865, showing six buildings surrounding the Old College and appropriate livestock grazing in split-railed pastures. A photograph (I–39), taken from the northwestern shore of St. Mary's Lake, summer of 1888, noting (l. to r.) Sacred Heart Church, implement shed, bakery and grain-storage shed,

Vagnier family residence, brothers' farmhouse, roofline of wagonshed, sail of windmill, Old College, and a barn roof in the trees behind Old College.

I–37

I–38

I–39

I–40. Bakery and Vagnier Residence, ca. 1900

Built in 1850s and removed in 1902, the bakery had its major ovens flued by the visible chimney with adjoining wood-, coal-, and grain-storage buildings to its rear. The two-storey farmhouse built by the Vagnier and Howard families in 1866, was the residence of both the bakery staff and farm workers. Beyond this house (extreme left) can be seen the Old College.

I–41–42. University Farms, 1885, 1890

I–41, photographed from atop the farmyard windmill, here is shown (l. to r.) wheat granary, two corncribs and the back of the Manual Labor School (IV–10–11) recreation hall; I–42, photographed from farm road (now walk from Old College) showing to the left of the road, the Vagnier house, the bakery, and an implement shed. Beyond the shed were the botanical gardens laid out by Father Joseph Carrier in the spring of 1867. The fenced pasture in both views was planted with fruit trees.

(I–40) located at the corner where the main road turns up the hill toward Corby Hall, then the baker's residence and adjoining flour storage sheds, another large farmhouse (known as Mr. Vagnier's house), and several privies.

E *Turn around and walk northeast to the main road and proceed to the William J. Corby Monument (I–44) in front of Corby Hall.*

In addition to its physical expansion to the north and east, during its first two decades, the University also extended its horizons beyond its campus confines. The Brothers of St. Joseph went from "the Island" novitiate to establish primary and secondary schools in nine states by the end of the nineteenth century. These schools recruited students for the University's secondary and vocational programs as well as the college. Father Sorin also sent three brothers along with four laymen on a prospecting expedition to the California gold fields in 1850. The expedition, legally organized as the St. Joseph's Company of Notre Dame du Lac, despite its patronage (spiritual and financial), found no

I–40

I–42

I–41

I–43. Father Corby Blessing the Troops, 1863
A panorama done in oil by Paul Wood in 1871 to commemorate Chaplain Corby's giving general absolution to the Irish Brigade about to enter battle at Gettysburg, July 2, 1863.

I–44. William Corby Monument
A bronze statue depicts Corby at the Gettysburg National Battlefield in Pennsylvania; the similar campus monument was erected by student subscriptions and unveiled in 1911.

gold and cost the Notre Dame community several of its members by death and desertion.

Shortly after the Civil War broke out in 1861, Indiana's governor asked Sorin to supply Catholic chaplains for the Union Army. Eight Holy Cross priests (I–45) responded, the most colorful being William J. Corby (I–44), who served with the Army of the Potomac, wrote an autobiography of his experiences (*Memoirs of a Chaplain's Life*), and later served two terms (1866–72 and 1877–81) as University president. Corby, for whom Corby Hall is named, gave general absolution to General George Meade's Irish Brigade before the crucial battle of Gettysburg in 1863 (I–43). That act, as well as his long service to the Union cause, is memorialized at the Gettysburg battlefield by a statue (I–44), which is replicated on the campus.

F *Walk in front of Sacred Heart Church to the Sacred Heart Statue (96) in the center of the Main Quadrangle and stand facing south toward Notre Dame Avenue.*

In addition to its involvement in certain national events, Notre Dame also expanded into the surrounding local community. In 1855 the Council of Administration, largely at Sorin's urging, decided to develop some of its real estate located approximately one mile south of its campus along the present Notre Dame Avenue (I–47). Several farm fields were platted into individual lots, and a school was erected and staffed by University personnel. Catholic laborers (especially the Irish who had come to work on the canals and railroads) were encouraged to settle in a subdivision that not unexpectedly came to be called "Sorinsville" (I–46). Lots in the planned town could be purchased for a down payment of $25, with the rest being paid in labor, trade, or long-term credit installments. The University, on a few occasions, also built faculty houses in the area (I–48). Throughout the nineteenth century the neighborhood provided the college with a dedicated labor force, students, apprentices, and religious vocations.

Turn around to face the Administration Building (36).

I–43

I–44

I–46. Sorinsville, ca. 1873
Also known as the "village catholique"
and "little Dublin," Sorin's 120-acre real
estate development can still be identified
by various streets named for personalities
or patrons important in the early history
of Notre Dame: Abbé Moreau, Brothers
Vincent, Francis, and Basil, Saints
Aloysius and Joseph, Pope Pius IX, and

Napoleon III. Sorin also planned and
platted another nineteenth-century town
in Nebraska which he named St. Edward's
after his own patron.

I–47. Notre Dame Avenue, 1888
A tree-lined "grand avenue" envisioned
by Sorin as early as 1849, this street
remains the principal entrance to the
University. Just over a mile from Sorin
Street to the Main Building, this vertical
axis connected the outskirts of the towns
of Lowell and South Bend with the
University.

I–45. Notre Dame Civil War Chaplains
(sitting) Capt. J. J. McCormick, James
Dillon, C.S.C., William Corby, C.S.C.;
(standing) Patrick Dillon, C.S.C., Dr.
K. O'Hanlon. Eighty-nine Holy Cross
sisters from Notre Dame and St. Mary's
ministered to the sick in military and
naval hospitals during the war.

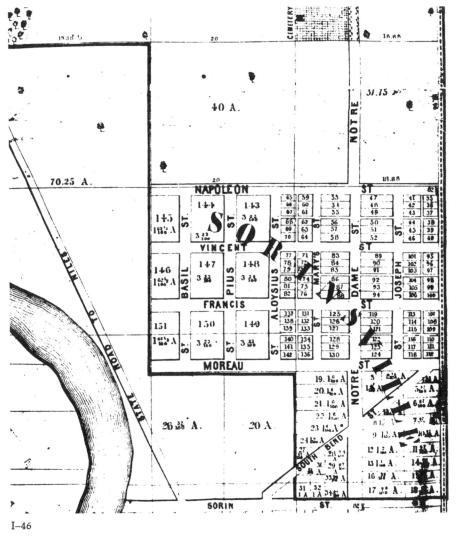

I–46

I–47

In 1844 two important events occurred that affected the future development of Notre Dame. John D. Defrees, who was a Methodist, South Bend attorney, and state senator, secured for Sorin's unseasoned institution an extremely comprehensive charter of incorporation as a full-fledged, degree-granting University from the Indiana legislature. Secondly, the University's Council of Administration decided to locate its main campus on a north-south axis with its first Main Building erected roughly on the site of the present Administration Building. Although no master plan existed in the 1840s, it is obvious that the nineteenth-century French academic interpretation of classical planning was the Cartesian model for the future growth of what came to be known as the Main Quadrangle.

Work had been proceeding on the Old College building in August 1843, when Marsile, the Vincennes architect originally commissioned to construct a Main Building, belatedly arrived at Notre Dame. Sorin quickly persuaded a local merchant to grant him more credit ($500) and

a fellow C.S.C. priest to donate his family patrimony ($1,200) to the University's first building fund. At the laying of the cornerstone, Sorin passed a collection plate among those whom he had invited, raising another $250. Construction of Main Building I continued into December when the brick building was finally under roof. By June 1844 the structure was ready for occupancy and in August the first closing exercises took place within its walls.

Although no daguerreotype or other early photographic reproduction of the actual building seems to survive, several engraved sketches (I–49–52) generally correspond to the written accounts of the structure. In 1853, due to bequest of $10,000, two 40' × 60' wings were added and the building took the form of an H or "double hammer." The structure was a multifunctional dwelling modeled on Sorin's conception of a typical French boarding lycée. The first, or ground, floor housed a refectory, kitchens, recreation hall, and washrooms, while study halls, classrooms, an art gallery, and the president's rooms and office were on the second floor.

I–48. Maurice Francis Egan Home, 1136 North Notre Dame Avenue
Built in 1889 by the University President Thomas Walsh for the noted Catholic poet, novelist, and editor of the New York *Freeman's Journal* who assumed the "Chair of Literature" at the University, it was christened "the Lilacs" by Egan and still serves as a faculty residence.

I–49–52. Main Building I Views, 1844–65
I–49, earliest extant view; I–50, a perspective from the west in the Greek revival mode with a front portico and an iron cross; I–51, an 1853 treatment from the east with the portico replaced by a staircase porch and a different belfry to house a new bell sent by Moreau; I–52, view from the south, ca. 1865, showing development of the college yard and a bronzed statue of the Virgin atop a small tower.

I–48

I–49

I–50

I–51

I–52

I–53. **Campus View, ca. 1856**
Moving counterclockwise from Main Building I are located the first main church, the brothers' novitiate, the priests' novitiate, St. Mary's Lake, Old College and two adjacent farm buildings, the Manual Labor School, porter's lodge, post office, and to the right of Main Building I, the University infirmary.

Nine private rooms for priests and lay faculty, as well as several student dormitories, comprised the third floor, with the next storey being divided into other dormitories, the museum, and an armory. The garret served as sleeping quarters for hired men and working boarders. Thus, practically every segment of the University—faculty, administration, students, staff—lived together under one roof. Heated by woodburning stoves until 1853, when steam heat was introduced, lacking indoor plumbing (chamber pots are numerous on an 1856 inventory), this first Main Building served the University until 1865, when it was replaced by an expanded second structure (see chapter II, II–2–4).

Three levels of academic instruction were offered in Main Building I. The Minim Department schooled the youngest boys (I–55) in elementary arithmetic, reading, grammar, and history. The Junior Department, administering a college preparatory program, provided its students with coursework in Latin, Greek, English, history, and composition. The Senior Department, the only real collegiate

I–53

dimension of the University, was a version of the *ratio studiorum* used by the Jesuits at St. Louis University in Missouri. This classical collegiate curriculum, which never attracted more than a dozen students yearly in the first decades, included four years of humanities, poetry, rhetoric, and philosophy. In addition, French, German, Spanish, and Italian were taught as well as various forms of music and drawing. By 1855 a student could take a two-year course designed to give him "a fund of general information indispensable to young merchants." In 1861 this program was formalized as a Commercial Department, No theology courses were included in the formal curriculum (nor would they be until 1920), although religious ex-

I–54. Preparatory Students as Continental Cadets

I–55. Hans Schremmer

ercises were held daily on the campus.

No young man or boy was turned away who wished to attend Notre Dame and who could, by one means or another (cash, labor, barter), pay some sort of tuition for his support. There were no entrance requirements, and students (I–56–59) were simply placed wherever they seemed to fit into the curriculum. Students arrived and departed at odd times during the year, as did their professors. Most students, lacking extensive common-school education and being of diverse backgrounds and abilities, required preparatory training or extensive remedial work before going on to the collegiate level. All students followed the same daily schedule, six days a week rising at 5:30 A.M. (5:00 A.M. from May to August). An academic day consisted of study periods, classes, meals, and recreation periods from 7:30 A.M. until supper at 6:00 P.M. It was a regimen typical of the French educational practice, designed to keep a student so active he had neither time nor energy to get into mischief. All students remained on the grounds at all times

I–54

I–55

I–56. Simon Pokagon, Potawatomi Indian Student

I–57. Neil H. Gillespie, First A.B. Degree Student

I–58. Alexis T. Coquillard

except on Wednesday and Sunday afternoon walks. One of the few breaks from the daily routine was on Saturday afternoon when history and geography courses gave way to the traditional end-of-week bath.

The major portion of the University's activities occurred within the multipurpose Main Building (I–49–52) which loomed as the tallest building in the surrounding countryside. Sorin deliberately located it on a "grand avenue" (now Notre Dame Avenue) to be continued, in his words, "as straight as possible as far as our land extends" (I–47). In addition to its monumentality, the four-storey brick structure had a disarming charm with its large stone steps, classical portico, conspicuous public clock in its central pediment, and oak shingle roof which, as a contemporary account records, "turned up and warped beautifully in the sun and thus ventilated the attic." In its early history (I–50) the building was surmounted by a bell tower upon which first stood an iron cross eighteen feet high, and later (I–52) a statue of Our Lady protected by a belvedere.

As shown in an early engraving of the building (I–53), Main Building I was soon surrounded by a series of ancilliary structures. An early student left a diary account of how this area looked in 1845–46: "The yard in front of the college contained about half an acre, with here and there a fine oak, while thence on to South Bend was a dense forest. . . . The front yard fence was flanked by two small one-storey cottages, one occupied by Mr. Stever as a little finishing store; the other by the good old porter, Brother Cyprian, who was the shoemaker of the community. At the rear of the college, to the east, stood the Manual Labor establishment, having a tailor shop under the care of Brother Augustus and a printing office under Brother Joseph. . . . Still a little further back stood the carpenter shop, a log building under Brother William. To the east of it stood the blacksmith shop and the gardener's house."

By 1844 the outline of nineteenth-century Notre Dame was established; at the end of Sorin's presidency in 1865, that vision was becoming a reality. A college, pre-

I–56

I–57

I–58

I–59. Dennis Foley and Sorin's Velocipede

I–60. Father Alexis Granger, Vice-President and Prefect of Religion

I–61. Lucius G. Tong, Professor of Law and Bookkeeping

I–62. Arthur J. Stace, Professor of Civil Engineering

I–63. Brother Peter Fitzpatrick, Professor of Astronomy

paratory and grade schools, religious novitiates, and a Manual Labor School were all going concerns under Sorin's imperial direction. In the history of nineteenth-century American higher education, however, a high rate of failure accompanied the college-building boom years prior to the Civil War. Only nine other Catholic colleges existed when Notre Dame was founded but that number had grown to fifty-one by 1861. Presently only seven of these antebellum institutions still exist. One historian estimates a mortality rate of approximately 80 percent among Notre Dame's contemporary secular institutions. Yet Notre Dame survived. Why? From Europe came men, money, and Catholic immigrants with sons requiring education; likewise from America came philanthropy in land and cash grants and in the dedicated lives of faculty and staff (I–60–63). The college's position in time and place was also fortuitous: Notre Dame was founded just as the Midwest was opened by canals and railroads; for most of the 1840s Notre Dame was the only Catholic college of conse-

quence with access to such cities as Toledo, Cleveland, Detroit, Milwaukee, and particularly, the rapid-growing city of Chicago. The college's geographic proximity to South Bend, a community soon to be a center of agriculture and industry, aided its growth. And, of course, there was the indomitable Edward Sorin—master entrepreneur, gambler, diplomat, legerdemain, adventurer, man of faith—who, more than any other single man, created and molded Notre Dame out of his willful, optimistic, aggressive personality. John Wack, a historian of the University's foundation, succinctly summarized its stature at the end of its first decades: "a properly chartered, substantially constructed, modestly successful seat of learning—inadequately endowed in faculty, students, and funds, but at least minimally endowed in all of these, not bankrupt, not intellectually destitute, not unattended, not without hope."

I–60

I–61

I–62

I–63

**I–64. Notre Dame University, St. Joseph
County, Indiana**

II. The University in 1879

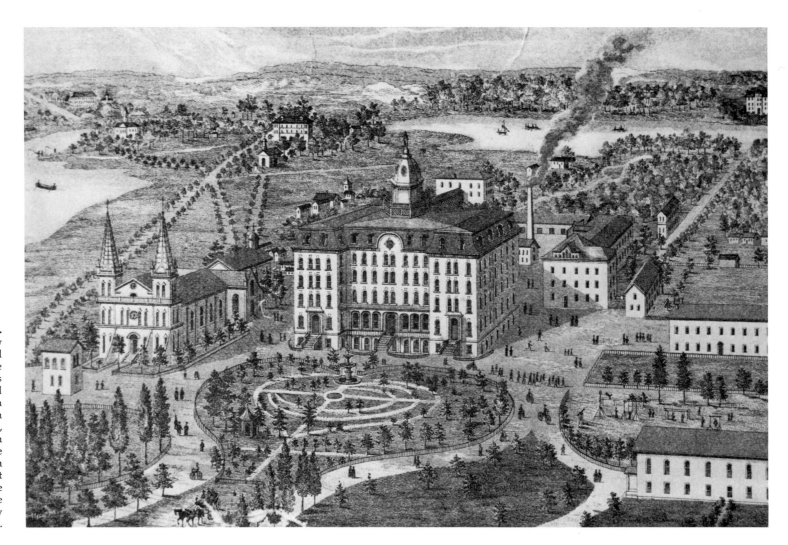

II–1. Notre Dame, ca. 1866. A supposed bird's-eye-view illustrates how the second Main Building, even more than its predecessor, was designed as an architectural focal point around which clustered (l. to r.) the main church, service buildings, infirmary, and exhibition and recreation halls. The design of the formal garden was in the shape of a heart to remind its visitors of the Divine Heart of Jesus, one of the emblems of the Holy Cross community.

Beginning at the Sacred Heart statue (96) in the center of the Main Quadrangle, Walk II explores the expansion of the University from the late 1840s to the early 1880s. A walk of 350 yards, it begins at the site of the early Main Buildings and churches and continues through the Sacred Heart Church (29) to an area developed in the 1850s and known as the French Quarter—presbytery (35), earth sciences (77), and Brownson Hall (34). Then, the tour proceeds west to the buildings around St. Joseph's Lake and illustrates Notre Dame's historic relationship with St. Mary's College. Returning to the Main Quadrangle via the Lourdes grotto (28), the walk ends with a description of the Great Fire of 1879 and a tour through the present Administration Building (36).

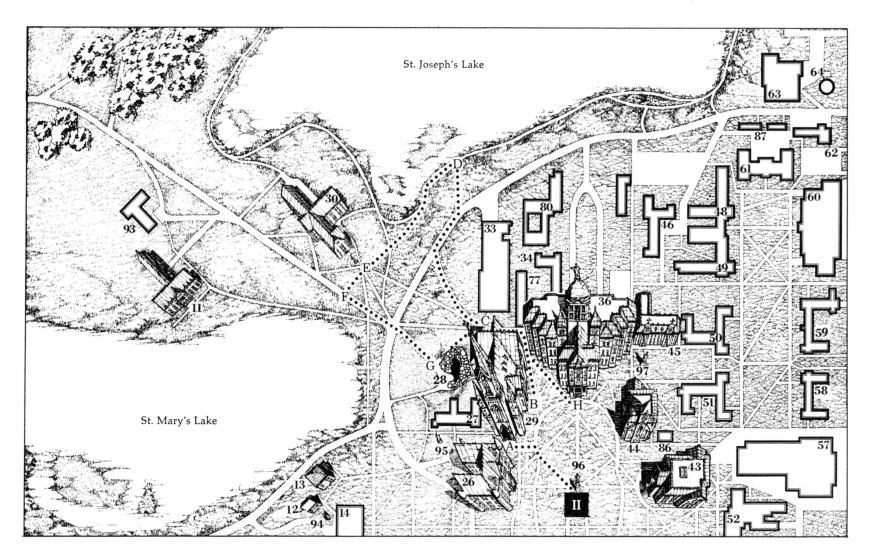

Expansion, Calamity, Recovery

BY 1879 NOTRE DAME had begun to assume some of the basic characteristics of a respectable midwestern college. Departments in commerce (1861), science (1865), law (1869), and engineering (1873) expanded the classical, liberal arts curriculum. The University had established an academic press that published scholarly and literary works, a weekly religious periodical (*The Ave Maria*), and a collegiate magazine (*The Scholastic*). In 1865 the fledgling institution had celebrated the silver jubilee of its founding with a week-long "Parisian fete" and the publication of its first official history. An alumni association was formed in 1868. That same year, Father Sorin, who had delegated the University presidency to Father Patrick Dillon in 1865, was elected superior-general of the Congregation of Holy Cross. Sorin, charged with the responsibility of governing his religious community's

---

Notre Dame in 1879

Acreage: 925   Buildings: 18
Faculty: 34   Tuition: $125
Students: 395   Room/board: $125

---

spiritual and educational activities in Europe, Asia, and the Americas, transferred the C.S.C. international headquarters from Le Mans, France, to Notre Dame, thereby increasing the American institution's power and influence in the congregation's affairs. As superior-general, Sorin would superintend the succession of presidents of Notre Dame and govern and channel their efforts.

In 1863, despite the financial strains imposed by the disruptive Civil War, Sorin decided to expand Notre Dame by commissioning the erection of Main Building II. Dillon, who had been in charge of the early construction of St. Mary's College (II–29), had William Thomas, a Chicago architect, draw up plans for a structure that would utilize a major part of Main Building I (I–49–52) and be built on the same site. Construction began after the spring semester of 1865, and by September the six-storey brick structure (II–2–4) was occupied by the returning student body. A white dome with a statue of Our Lady was set in place the following year.

A *Walk left and west to the front of Sacred Heart Church (29).*

Religious belief and practice permeate Notre Dame's history. Since 1848 this spirituality has had its most public manifestation in the two main collegiate churches dedicated to the Sacred Heart. University officials purposefully located these churches in obvious proximity to successive Main Buildings in order to dramatize the institution's mutual dedication to the mind and the spirit. The first edifice (II–5), a double-spired, carpenter-Gothic structure, was begun in 1848 and completed in 1852, with the steeple being constructed by a local carpenter in payment for his son's college education. A twenty-three-bell carillon that Sorin had purchased in France was too heavy to hang in its tower, so a "temporary ground belfry" (II–2) was erected in 1856 to house the prized instrument.

In the spring of 1869, Superior-General Sorin, now also chairman of the University Board of Trustees and absolute policymaker at Notre Dame, decided to build a bigger church to accommodate an anticipated increase in the student body. Patrick C. Keeley, the most re-

nowned American Catholic church architect and recipient of Notre Dame's Laetare Medal in 1884, was commissioned to begin preliminary drawings. Keeley modeled his design on that of the baroque church of the Gesú in Rome: a cruciform, 200 feet in length, with three naves, and a transept large enough to seat 2,000 people. A large dome (perhaps to parallel the Main Building's) was to be placed over the intersection of the transept at the central nave, and there were to be two large bell towers. The architect estimated the ambitious project would cost over one hundred thousand dollars.

Even the expansionist Sorin thought the plans too grandiose for the University's limited budget. He decided instead to have Father Alexis Granger (I–60), longtime pastor of Sacred Heart parish, and Brother Charles Harding, a talented amateur architect and builder, collaborate with him in a more modest design. Figure II–6 is reputed to be one of Harding's first renderings of their collective effort, a treatment remarkably similar to the main church in Sorin's hometown of

II–3. The University, ca. 1868
Assembled are student body and faculty in front of completed Main Building II with a French summer house (left) and the first University observatory (right). Another observatory was later located above the roof under the tin dome. A circular walk surrounded the dome, and atop it was a statue of Our Lady. In the building itself there were two large refectories, with washroom facilities in its basement; three study halls were located on the first floor—two for preparatory students and one for the collegians. The third floor, reached by a double flight of stairs, housed thirteen classrooms and five sleeping rooms for faculty. The fourth, fifth, and sixth floors were all dormitories. In the front of the sixth floor (note circular stained-glass window) was a chapel.

II–2. Main Building II, ca. 1866
A photograph taken from the west atop the Manual Labor School (IV–12) indicates the new Main Building's relation to the first main church (with its temporary two-storey bell tower in front of it) and to the surrounding area that eventually became the Main Quad. Documentary and visual sources suggest that the gabled roof of Main Building I was removed, its porch and middle facade altered, and several extra floors added, along with a mansard roof, to create this structure. Its dimensions were 160 feet long (exactly the size of Main Building I), 80 feet wide, and 90 feet, or six storeys, high.

11–3

II–5. The Church of the Sacred Heart, 1865
Built in 1848–52, this wooden structure (90′ × 38′ × 25′) served the University community until 1870. Its interior furnishings were highly prized: statuary donated by King Louis Phillipe, stained-glass windows (including a western rose window) by the Carmelites at Le Mans, and a chancel organ (1,527 pipes) in front of the congregation.

II–4. Main Building II, ca. 1866
A view from the east shows (l. to r.) the first main church and, directly behind it, William Phelan Hall, Main Building II, and the student infirmary. The Main Building also housed a lecture hall, a museum, and for a while, an armory of fifty-two stands of medieval arms.

II–5

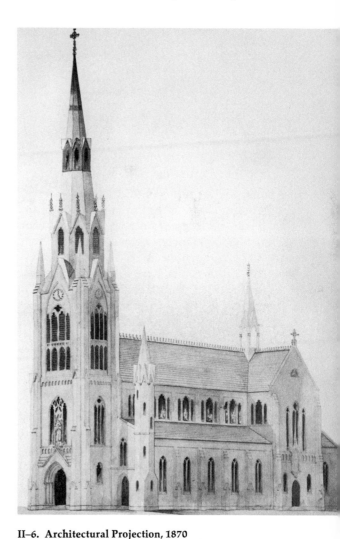

II–6. Architectural Projection, 1870
Brother Charles Harding, working in the French Gothic style, laid out the present Sacred Heart Church in the traditional Latin cross, 275 feet long and 114 feet wide at the transept. Harding's basic sketch was largely followed in the church's construction and later expansions.

II–7. Church Interior, ca. 1876
When construction had to be halted because of budgetary limitations, the rear wall of the church was bricked up at the north end just behind the main altar in 1875. Almost a decade later, work began again to add the grand chancel and the apsidal chapels.

Ahuille in western France. Requiring more than fifteen years to complete, the present Sacred Heart Church's foundations were laid in 1870, its cornerstone in 1871, and by 1875, when the first Eucharist was celebrated, construction had proceeded to the first pillar inside the sanctuary (II–7). Only in 1886 were the apsidal chapels begun, with the Lady Chapel added in 1887.

Enter the front door of Sacred Heart Church (29) and stand in back of the main aisle.

The interior decor of the present church reflects the second major renovation that the structure has undergone in keeping with changing liturgical practices over the past century. Originally designed in the same year as the First Vatican Council, its interior (II–8) remained largely unchanged until 1931 when Wilfred Anthony, a New York architect, modernized the lighting and heating systems, repaired and cleaned Luigi Gregori's frescoes, and removed much of the rosewood ornamentation (II–9). The Second Vatican Council inspired the second

renovation (1967), particularly the addition of a contemporary altar (made from the church's original pews), which faces the congregation. The French Gothic altar, the main altar for almost a century, was designed in the ateliers of Froc-Robert in Paris for the Church of St. Étienne, Beauvais.

Walk left and proceed up the left aisle to the left of the pulpit.

The forty-two large stained-glass windows, containing 114 life-size figures and 106 smaller ones, were designed, crafted, and donated to Notre Dame by the Carmelite sisters at Le Mans, France (see Appendix II: Inventory of the Windows and Murals). Luigi Gregori (1819–96) (II–12), artist-in-residence at Notre Dame from 1874 to 1891, spent four years painting the church's numerous wall and ceiling frescoes. In the right transept as one faces the altar is the artist's version of *The Presentation of the Blessed Virgin in the Temple.* Gregori's rendering included himself (in grey), his wife, daughter, and a rejected suitor of his wife who is breaking a wand.

II–7

II–9. Church Interior, 1931
President Charles O'Donnell delivers the
funeral eulogy for Knute Rockne,
Notre Dame's most famous coach.

II–8. Church Interior, 1924
An impressive, elevated pulpit was added
in 1887; in the 1967 renovation, it was
lowered to the sanctuary floor and its
sounding board removed. The French
Gothic altar had been exhibited at the
Philadelphia Centennial Exposition in
1876, where it won a first premium for
design. Sorin bought it there duty-free
when the exposition closed.

II–9. Church Interior, 1931
President Charles O'Donnell delivers the
funeral eulogy for Knute Rockne,
Notre Dame's most famous coach.

II–9

II–10–13. Artists and Benefactors
Several centuries of creativity and philanthropy are represented in Sacred Heart Church: II–10, the baroque altar in the Lady Chapel, purchased by Sorin when he was in Rome in 1886, is believed to have been done by students of the Vatican architect Bernini (1598–1680);

II–11, the crown of gold jewels, an 1886 gift of Empress Eugénie, wife of Napoleon III, originally intended for the Virgin's statue above the golden dome, formerly hung suspended over the statue of Our Lady in the Lady Chapel; II–12, Luigi Gregori (1819–96), former Vatican artist who resided and worked at Notre Dame (1874–91), posed with his self-portrait; and II–13, *Descent from the Cross*, 1955, by Ivan Mestrovic, carved in Rome from a

piece of Carrara marble weighing nearly seven tons, the pietà is considered one of the Croatian sculptor's masterpieces.

II–12

II–10

II–11

Continue left and circle behind the French Gothic altar to the O'Hara tomb, the Lady Chapel, and the pietà sculpture.

In the several apsidal chapels behind the sanctuary are artifacts of nineteenth- and twentieth-century Notre Dame. In the first chapel to the left is buried Father John Francis O'Hara, prefect of religion, dean of commerce, University vice-president and president, bishop in the military ordinariate of World War II, bishop of Buffalo, archbishop of Philadelphia, and first cardinal from the Congregation of Holy Cross. An anonymous donor maintains a perpetual bouquet of red roses in memory of this dedicated, authoritarian, colorful Notre Dame administrator. The baroque altar that now stands in the Lady Chapel (II–10) in the church's extreme front was purchased by Father Sorin in Rome in 1887. This so-called Bernini Altar is believed to have been designed around 1720 by students of the noted Vatican architect. The three altars—baroque, French Gothic, and contemporary—depict a succession of liturgical designs in the eighteenth, nineteenth and twentieth

centuries. In 1955, Ivan Mestrovic (1883–1962), the Croatian maestro whom Rodin hailed as "the greatest phenomenon among the sculptors of the world," installed his famous group, *The Descent from the Cross.* Mestrovic (V–59), another artist-in-residence at the University (1955–62), has numerous works (see Appendix IV: Inventory of Campus Sculpture) adorning other parts of the Notre Dame campus.

B *Leave the church via the east (side) entrance and pause to view the World War I memorial entrance.*

Since the Civil War, the University's history has often been affected by American military conflicts. During World Wars I and II (IV–4–5 and V–4–7), the campus served as a base for officer-training programs. (Currently the University is one of the thirteen American institutions commissioning men and women in all four services.) In 1923, students who died in World War I. Francis W. Kervick (IV–26) and Vincent Fagan (IV–27), professors in the School of Architecture, designed a Gothic memorial entrance as a testament to the Notre Dame

II–13

II–14

II–15

II–14–15. Two Views of Presbytery and Gardens, ca. 1886 and 1890
Looking west from the Administration Building, figure II–14 shows the site of Phelan Hall behind Sacred Heart Church, the formal gardens below, and the presbytery; figure II–15, taken looking northeast from the eventual site of Corby Hall (27), shows Sacred Heart Church's added apsidal chapels, the gardens, and an additional sun porch on the presbytery.

The electric fixture inside the vestibule (look up as you leave) is constructed from the doughboy helmet worn by Father Charles O'Donnell (later president of Notre Dame, 1928–34) while serving as a chaplain in the European conflict.

C *Walk along the path beside Sacred Heart Church and pass between the church and the Administration Building to the front steps of the presbytery (35).*

Throughout its nineteenth-century development, the area behind the main church and the Main Building was known as the "French Quarter." It was a scene of constant and diverse activities. On the site now occupied by Sacred Heart's apsidal chapels and its crypt once stood William T. Phelan Hall (II–4), the first building named after an outside benefactor of the University. Built in 1850 and demolished in 1886, Phelan Hall, in addition to being an academic building (science department), also served as a temporary chapel for the University community when the main church was under construction. William Phelan, along with Sorin's heroes (Fathers De Seille, Petit, and Cointet) and Orestes A. Brownson (II–56), are interred in the church crypt.

As figure II–14–15 suggest, a formal landscape garden once graced the slope to the south of the presbytery (35), a building which is now a residence for C.S.C. priests and the offices of Sacred Heart parish. Throughout its history, the presbytery—a totally French building with its flat facade and mansard slate roof—has served Notre Dame as the provincial's house, an elderly men's home, the superior-general's headquarters during Sorin's tenure, and a priests' residence. The presbytery fronts on what was once a

II–16. Sister's Convent and University Kitchens, ca. 1905
The second-oldest buildings on campus are (l. to r.) the Holy Cross sisters' circular chapel (now earth sciences [77]), their convent (now Freshman Year of Studies [34]), and the University kitchens (formerly in front of Brownson Hall [34]).

little square formed by (l. to r.) the Sisters of the Holy Cross circular chapel (now earth sciences [77]), their convent (now Freshman Year of Studies [34]), their cloister, (now entrance to Brownson Hall [34]), and the University kitchens (now removed but formerly on a site in front of the present personnel department). This building complex with its circular garden, once dedicated to St. Joseph (whose statue has been replaced by a magnolia), can be seen in figure II–16.

Four sisters of the Holy Cross came at Sorin's request to Notre Dame from France in 1843. During the next 115 years, the women's religious community remained a significant, if unsung, part of the University's development. In 1958 their convent and buildings were converted to other uses. Upon first arrival, these women in sombre black habits with fluted French caps were a novelty on the northern Indiana frontier. So were their industry and dedicated service to the University. They staffed the laundries, infirmaries, kitchens, and St. Edwards' Minims School (III–10–18). There was hardly a facet of Notre

Dame life they did not influence. They set type in the University Press offices located just east of the rear of Brownson Hall, bound books and periodicals, and deciphered mysterious chirography in manuscripts which baffled the editors. They were tailors, nurses, gardeners, seamstresses, cooks, and charwomen for thousands of Notre Dame priests, brothers, lay faculty, and students. Beginning only with 4 sisters, their numbers grew to 140, then dwindled to only 14 in 1958.

Notre Dame students knew the sisters best in their role as University cooks. From 1849, when the first separate kitchen building was constructed, until 1927, when the South Dining Hall (IV–50) and its facilities were opened, the daily meals for all Notre Dame students were prepared by the sisters, with the assistance of the brothers as bakers and butchers, in a two-storey structure (now demolished) behind the Main Building (II–16). Often recognized by an anonymity which did honor to their acknowledged specialties—"Sister Pie" (Sister Bertina), "Sister Coffee" (Sister Lourdes), "Sister Steak" (Sister

II–16

II–17. University Cooks, 1906
Holy Cross sisters, who prepared the
University's multicourse cuisine daily for
over a century, here relax and provide
their own informal musical entertainment.

Martha)—the nuns prepared abundant meals from the meats, produce, and grains from the University farms (I–34–42; IV–38–44). Alumni still talk of their rectangular apple pie topped with cinnamon and sugar or the fact that steak was served twice a week—for breakfast.

The "Notre Dame bun," a culinary creation of Brother Willibrord, one of the University bakers (II–18), accompanied steak-and-gravy breakfasts and practically every other meal. Professor Richard Sullivan of the English department, who personally experienced the "buns," describes them as "inexpressibly excellent when fresh and piled with unsalted butter; but hardening gradually as they aged down the week; until they petrified finally into legend, and became formidable to dental fillings, and were universally cursed and celebrated, and addressed in ink, plastered with a stamp, and mailed–bare parcel post–to friends, parents, sweethearts, all over the country." The bakery's and kitchen's extensive food supplies were stored in granaries, root cellars, and ice houses in the area east of the rear of Brownson Hall (34).

II–18. University Bakers, ca. 1920
Brothers, hired men, and student workers turned out over three hundred loaves of bread and over three thousand each of the "Notre Dame buns" and cookies daily.

II–19. University Waiters, ca. 1910
A trio of student workers would use "hash carts" to deliver prepared food from the kitchens across a boardwalk to the refectories in the basement of the Administration Building.

D *Walk down the service road to the right to the stop sign, turn right, and walk along the lake road to a noticeable clearing on the bank of St. Joseph's Lake.*

Although the University expanded primarily eastward during 1850–80, the Holy Cross community continued to use the western shores of the campus lakes as appropriate settings for its religious houses (II–20). St Joseph's Lake, a twenty-five-acre, thirty-five-foot-deep body, also served as a topographical symbol separating the private religious lives of the priests and brothers from their apostolate of education to secular students. (Since 1967, when the Holy Cross community divested itself of legal ownership of the University, the lakes are the approximate boundaries between the landholdings of Notre Dame and the Indiana Province of Holy Cross.)

Across St. Joseph's Lake Sorin built a missionary's home (II–23) in 1862 on the site of the present Holy Cross House (47). When only a few clerics retired to the home, the building was converted into a novitiate, which was destroyed by

II–18

II–19

II–20. St. Joseph Lake and Environs, 1878
This lithograph map by Charles Shober of Chicago shows at the top, the missionary's home (40); between the lakes, a piazza (63) on which fronted Our Lady of the Holy Angels Chapel (64) beyond which was a cemetery (65); a statue of Our Lady (66); and then the brothers' (St. Joseph's) novitiate (68). St. Mary's College Road (62) bisected the former "Island." (Numbers correspond to this map's legend.)

II–21. Three Roads West, 1893
The roads of this intersection lead to (l. to r.) Holy Cross Seminary (I–32), St. Mary's College, and the brothers' novitiate and community buildings (I–33).

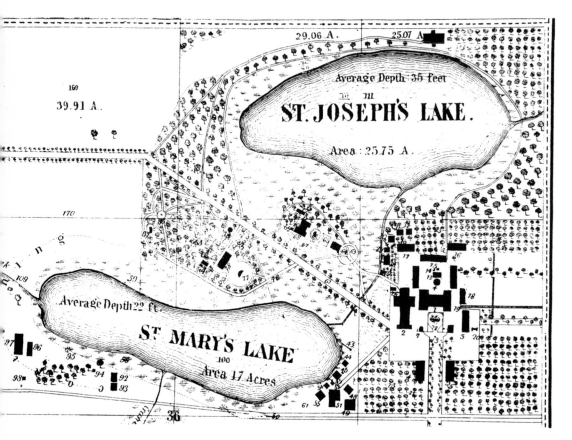

II–21

II–20

II–22

II–22. St. Joseph's Lake, ca. 1870
Students and faculty are seen at an
Independence Day outing on the lake.
President Auguste Lemonnier can be
seen in the bow of the first boat from the
right.

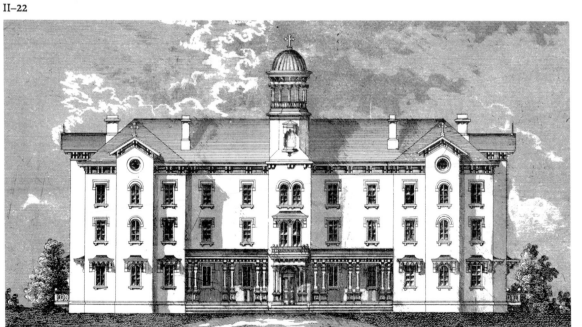

II–23

**II–24. Lady of Holy Angels Chapel and
Shrine, 1900**
A statue of Mary and the Christ Child
was enclosed in a glass shrine in front of
the chapel which, during the 1919 influenza epidemic, doubled as a quarantine
hospital.

II–23. Projected Missionary's Home, 1862
William Thomas's architectural drawing
of a three-storey structure containing
forty-eight private rooms for retired
missioners and diocesan priests from all
over the country.

II–25. Holy Cross Community Buildings, 1865
A view from the west shows (l. to r.) the priests' (St. Aloysius) novitiate, the brothers' (St. Joseph's) novitiate, the University infirmary (behind chimney of steam plant), Phelan Hall (at rear of Sacred Heart Church), and Main Building II.

II–25

fire in 1913 (III–24). Rebuilt that same year, it served again as a novitiate and then, from 1934 until 1961 (when Holy Cross House was constructed), was the Holy Cross community infirmary. To the left of this site are two Holy Cross community buildings: Moreau Seminary (32), built in 1958 to replace a building constructed in 1876 as an elderly men's home and con-

verted to a seminary in 1886; and St. Joseph's Hall (31), constructed in 1920 as another novitiate.

E *Turn left, walk across in front of Columba Hall (30), and stop in front of St. Joseph's statue.*

The Holy Cross brothers have occupied the land between St. Joseph's and St. Mary's lakes since 1843. Here have been their novi-

tiates, provincial headquarters, and community residences (II–25). The present statue of St. Joseph (the brothers' patron) roughly marks the site of the Our Lady of the Holy Angels Chapel (I–24), also known to Notre Dame students of the early 1920s as the "pest house." During the influenza epidemic of 1919, the University infirmary (III–4) could not accommodate all the afflicted,

so the second floor of this structure was divided into four wards where as many as eighty students were quarantined. Behind the "pest house" site and the present Columba Hall is another, less obvious historical marker—the last substantial remnant of the original Indiana forest that Sorin found in 1842. These woods of black oak, sassafras, sycamore, and burr oak, with

**II–26–27. St. Mary's College Students,
1870, 1920**

II–27

II–26

II–28

II–29

II–28. St. Mary's Academy, Bertrand, Michigan, 1845
The engraving shows the school's growth from its beginnings in a farmhouse donated by Joseph Bertrand to a 25' × 40' Main Building. Another of Father Badin's mission chapels was moved to the site, and a larger church was built.

II–29. St. Mary's College, Notre Dame, Indiana, 1890

a shrub cover of wild blackberry and honeysuckle, cover twelve acres which, ironically, was the approximate size of the original clearing in the forest when Sorin first arrived.

F *Walk left to the service road and face west toward St. Mary's College.*

Edward Sorin wanted to provide a Catholic education for young women as well as men. Hence he encouraged the Holy Cross sisters to establish a novitiate and a school near his college. He proceeded again without permission from the bishop of Vincennes, who, when he learned of Sorin's plans, refused to sanction the venture. An undaunted Sorin then requested the bishop of Detroit's approval to open a women's school in Bertrand, Michigan (I–12), only four miles across the state border and, conveniently enough, in another episcopal jurisdiction. Here, in 1843, began the Sister's School, later known as St. Mary's Academy (II–28). By April 1855 Sorin was able to move the Academy (due to a change in bishops and a fortuitous land purchase) onto the recently acquired Rush farmland, thereby

fulfilling his earlier desire of having a companion women's institution. The State of Indiana promptly granted an academic charter "for the education of young ladies in the various branches of the arts and sciences as usually taught in female colleges of the highest standards." By its charter, St. Mary's became the first legally authorized (fifth actually established) Catholic women's college in the United States.

Under the dynamic leadership of Mother M. Angela (1824–87), Sorin's female counterpart, St. Mary's taught the primary grades and high-school and college-level courses without granting degrees. In 1895 Mother M. Pauline assumed the office of directress of studies, whereupon she expanded the curriculum to include courses leading to a bachelor of arts degree, the first of which was granted to Agnes Ewing Brown in 1898. Mother M. Pauline became the first president of St. Mary's College in 1903 when the Academy designation was discarded.

St. Mary's and Notre Dame share a great deal of mutual history. Both campuses are heavily influenced by

II–30

II–31. Our Lady of Lourdes Grotto, 1898
A replica of St. Bernadette was later placed facing the Virgin, who is in the rock niche.

Sorin's French classicism and both shared his American architects. St. Mary's Bertrand Hall was designed by William Thomas in 1860–62, and Angela Hall was designed by Willoughby Edbrooke in 1892. As early as 1855 Sorin laid out a "road for the stage" (the present service road) that linked the two institutions, becoming on the west side of the Dixie Highway (U.S. 31-33) another "grand avenue" entrance, similar in conception to Notre Dame Avenue.

G *Turn around, walk down the service road, and cross the lake road to the Grotto of Our Lady of Lourdes (28).*

Father Sorin's devotion to the Virgin Mary pervaded much that he created. St. Mary's was one institutionalization of his piety; the Lourdes grotto (II–31) was another. Sorin had visited the Lourdes basilica in 1876, and by 1878 his local council began discussing the idea of duplicating the French shrine. A Notre Dame alumnus and priest of the diocese of Erie (Pennsylvania), Father Thomas Carroll (II–32), had the same idea and offered to finance

II–31

II–33. **South Bend Daily Tribune, April 27, 1879**

II–32. **Father Thomas Carroll**
A Notre Dame alumnus (1855), ordained a C.S.C. priest, Carroll later joined the diocese of Erie. His bequest helped finance the construction of the grotto.

its construction. Work began in the spring of 1896, using huge boulders to replicate the European shrine at one-seventh its scale.

H *Walk up the left steps and circle behind Sacred Heart Church (29) to the front of the Administration Building (36).*

Fire was undoubtedly the single most common cause of college failings in nineteenth-century America. Prior to 1879, Notre Dame had had its share of campus fires, some seven outbreaks, the most serious of which occurred in 1849, wiping out not only the new two-storey building which housed the orphans and apprentices, but also the tailor's shop, bakery, kitchens, and stables. Then, in the late morning of April 23, 1879, fire broke out on the coal-tar roof of the east wing of Main Building II (II–2–4). Three hours later that six-storey building—in reality the entire college plant—along with four other adjacent structures (the infirmary, music hall, minims' play hall, and St. Francis Elderly Men's Home) had burnt to the ground.

The exact cause of the fire was never determined. Theories abounded: some said students were smoking clandestinely in the dorm; others claimed that an ember from the steam plant's chimney ignited the blaze; and still others blamed it on spontaneous combustion. Workmen had been repairing the roof that morning, and the most probable explanation is that the sun or a spark ignited the sawdust and chips they had left on the pitch roof. In any event, the fire spread rapidly across the roof to the base of the dome which, when its supports burned away, collapsed under the weight of Sorin's beloved statue of Our Lady and carried the fire into the building's interior. Then the burning cornice and mansard roof fell—the cornice setting the building afire from the outside at its ground floor, the roof adding to its internal conflagration. By two o'clock that afternoon, only fragments of the outside walls tottered among the ashes (II–34–36).

Heroism, pathos, humor, and, of course, tragedy characterized the day. The University's fire-fighting equipment (water buckets) was woefully inadequate; South Bend's

Terrible Fire.

THE UNIVERSITY OF NOTRE DAME IN ASHES!

Three Hours Suffices to Destroy a Fifth of a Million Dollars.

SEVERAL FINE ADJACENT BUILDINGS BURNED TO THE GROUND.

The Magnificent Cathedral Untouched by the Flames.

INSURANCE, ABOUT $60,000.

Full Details of the Great Calamity.

At 10:30 o'clock this forenoon the university of Notre Dame was discovered to be on fire. The flames were first seen issuing from the roof near the dome of the building. Their origin is supposed to have been caused by the action of the sun on a portion of the roof recently repaired with coal tar.

II–34. 1879 Fire Aftermath
This photograph by South Bend photographer James Bonney gives a view from the east. Bonney, who prepared eight photographs of the fire's destruction, later marketed them as stereoscope slides.

II–35. 1879 Fire, Interior View
This artist's engraving was published in *McGee's Illustrated Weekly* (Philadelphia) in April 1879. Not only was the structure a total loss, but also the University library, museum, much of the institution's archives, and its interior furnishings were destroyed.

II–36. 1879 Fire Aftermath
Another James Bonney photograph, taken from the east, shows the burnt-out shell of Main Building II and some salvaged furniture. To the extreme right are the foundation remnants of the student infirmary, also destroyed in the fire.

II–34

II–36

II–35

steam pumper arrived two hours after the fire began. Students raced through the building, tossing out suitcases, files, stuffed animals from the museum, and books from the library only to see them catch fire when the cornice fell. Furniture, desks, and scientific apparatus were also thrown from the upper win- dows, shattering on the ground below. The rain of objects, in turn, endangered those trying to fight the blaze. Only the Holy Cross women remained calm, evacuating the infirmary and University Press with their usual efficiency. Miraculously, amid the chaos there was no loss of life and only minor injuries to the

FRONT ELEVATION OF NOTRE DAME UNIVERSITY
NOTRE DAME IND.

melange of students, faculty, staff, and townspeople who fought the fire.

The aging Sorin was in Montreal preparing to embark on his thirty-sixth trans-Atlantic crossing (he made fifty-two in his lifetime); he returned to Notre Dame immediately. Professor Timothy Howard described the old man's impact on his comrades: "He walked around the ruins and those who followed were confounded by his attitude. Instead of bending, he stiffened. He signalled all of them to go into the church with him. I was then present when Father Sorin, after looking over the destruction of his life's work, stood at the altar steps and spoke to the community what I have always felt to be the most sublime words I have ever listened to. There was absolute faith, confidence, resolution in his very look and pose. 'If it were ALL gone, I should not give up,' were his words in closing. The effect was electric. It was the crown-

II–37. South Elevation, 1879
This linen drawing was by Willoughby Edbrooke (II–40) of Burnham and Edbrooke, Chicago. It was Sorin's intent to have a similar grand facade on the north (rear) side of the structure that would then face, with a series of formal gardens, St. Joseph's Lake.

II–38. Architect's Sketch, 1879
Printed in *The Scholastic*, May 24, 1879,
this view accompanied an article outlining
the new building's specifications which
detailed its 320-foot length (including the
two wings to be added later) and 155-foot
depth; it was four storeys high with a
basement and a free-standing dome 250
feet high.

ing moment of his life. A sad company had gone into the church that day. They were all simple Christian heroes as they came out. There was never more a shadow of a doubt as to the future of Notre Dame."

The University would rebuild. Financial, moral, and physical help came from South Bend, Chicago (where eight years earlier Notre Dame students had staged a benefit for victims of the Great Chicago Fire), and the nation at large. Willoughby Edbrooke (II–40), a Chicago architect, was commissioned to design a "new Notre Dame" which, true to the Sorin pattern, was to be a more spacious, more grandiose, higher-domed building than the other two that had occupied the site. Its innovations included gas lighting (replaced with electricity in 1886), steam heat, indoor plumbing, and fireproofing. A construction marathon ensued during the summer of 1879: ground was broken on May 17th, and the stone foundation was in place by the 21st; three hundred laborers (among them fifty-six bricklayers) worked incessantly under the direction of Brother Charles Harding to com-

plete the building (II–39) for the students' return in September. Edbrooke called the finished product "modern Gothic"; a later University architect, Francis Kervick (IV–26), referred to the Victorian monument as "an eclectic and somewhat naive combination of pointed windows, medieval moldings and classical columns." Others have dubbed the building's riot of turrets, gables, angles, corners, and oversized dome and rotunda as pure and simple "modern Sorin."

Enter the Main Building's ground floor through the doors under the front porch stairs and walk north to the center of building.

Few campus structures except Old College (I–25–28) and Hoynes Hall (III–57) have a longer history of diverse and imaginative uses than the Administration Building. None are better cultural artifacts of late nineteenth-century and early twentieth-century Notre Dame. The building's basement (known in the French architectural tradition as a *rez-de-chausée*, or ground floor) initially housed trunk storage rooms (now the purchasing department),

II–38

II–39. Administration Building, 1879
Constructed in less than four months by
over three hundred laborers working
sixteen hours a day, the "modern Gothic"
edifice—minus its east and west wings
and dome—was finished in time for the
opening of the fall semester.

II–39

**II–40. Willoughby J. Edbrooke, 1843–
1896**
Architect of numerous courthouses and
other public buildings in Illinois, the U.S.
Treasury in Washington, the state capitol
in Atlanta, Edbrooke, in addition to doing
the Administration Building, designed
Notre Dame's Academy of Music (Washington Hall [44]), Science Hall (La
Fortune [43]), and Sorin Hall (26).

II–42–44. Main Building Ground Floor, 1880–1920
Before its conversion to University offices, the Administration Building's basement was a trunk storage area as well as the locale of student dining and lavatory facilities. Photo II–42, Brownson Hall refectory, 1893, also illustrates Jacob Ackerman's wall murals of European historical monuments; II–43 shows senior college students about to begin a noonday meal in 1916; II–44, student washrooms, 1900, shows communal facilities that afforded each student the "privacy" of a single metal locker for storing his toiletries.

student lavatories and washroom facilities (II–44; now the cashier's office), and student refectories (II–42–43). The two dining halls, each capable of seating up to 350 people, were located in the building's wings—the east portion (now the admissions office) allocated for the minim and prep students, the west dining room (the comptroller's office) for the collegians. A surviving menu of 1898 suggests that the fare served to the faculty and all students was ample and wholesome: oxtail soup, roast veal, dumplings, pureed rutabaga, yellow split peas, and grape pie.

Walk up the left stairs to the second floor, stop at the center of the rotunda (II–50), and face the front entrance.

Since the principal entrance to the building was via a broad, outside stairway to the second floor, the president and vice-president's offices, sleeping rooms, and parlors were first located in the area now occupied by information services. On the opposite side of the main hall (now the provost's office) was the main parlor (II–46), long pre-

II–41. Dome Regilding, 1920
Completed in 1882, the dome—brick foundation, iron skeleton, wood facade, topped by a nineteen-foot, four-thousand-pound cast-iron statue executed by Giovanni Meli to replicate a similar sculpure erected by Pius IX in the Piazza di Spagna in Rome—was regilded in 1920 by the American Rold-Gold Leaf Company. Regilding was done again in 1961.

II–42

II–43

II–45. Student Rules
During Corby's first administration (1866–72), the student regulations could be reduced to this single but comprehensive handbill of particulars.

II–45

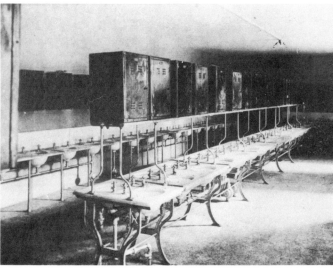

II–44

UNIVERSITY REGULATIONS.

SPECIAL RULES.

1. The Students of Notre Dame should at all times and everywhere behave like gentlemen. Therefore, good habits, gentlemanly deportment, politeness, neatness, order, application, respect for God and attention to religious duties are expected from them.
2. All the Students are required to attend the exercises of public worship with punctuality and decorum. They must be provided with books suitable for divine worship.
3. As soon as the bell announces the beginning or end of a College exercise, every one shall repair in silence to the discharge of that duty to which he is called.
4. The time of recreation excepted, silence must be inviolably observed in all places.
5. Students must show themselves obedient and respectful towards the Professors and Prefects of the Institution. They must never absent themselves from the place in which they ought to be, unless with permission from proper authority.
6. Students must carefully avoid every expression in the least injurious to Religion, their Professors, Prefects or fellow-Students.
7. Students are not permitted to visit private rooms.
8. Intoxicating liquors are absolutely prohibited.
9. **Compensation for all damage done to the furniture, or other property of the College, will be required from the person or persons causing such damage.**
10. No branch of study, once commenced shall be discontinued without permission of the Director of Studies.
11. Unless with parents and guardians, Students are not allowed to remain with visitors.
12. No one shall leave the University grounds without permission from the President, Vice-President or Prefect of Discipline.
13. Any breach of pure morals, either in word or action, must be reported forthwith to the President, Vice-President or Prefect of Discipline.
14. Students are not allowed to enter the playgrounds of the other departments without special permission.
15. No students are permitted to take private walks unless accompanied by a Prefect.
16. No one shall keep in his possession any money except what he receives weekly from the Treasurer, on Wednesdays, at nine o'clock, a. m. The College will not be responsible for any valuables, such as watches, money, etc., unless deposited with the Secretary.
17. Bulletins are sent to parents every month.
18. Bath-rooms, provided with hot and cold water, are fitted up for the use of the Students.
19. Stationery, etc., will be delivered to the Students daily, during the morning and the evening recess.
20. Students of low and vicious habits will not be retained in the College.
21. Students who have failed to give satisfaction in the class-room, or who shall have been guilty of misconduct or breach of rule, will be sent to the detention-room during the recreations or promenades, and required to prepare their lessons or perform such tasks as shall be assigned them, and will be excluded from all College exercises until such tasks be accomplished.
22. Every month the Students must write to their parents or guardians. All letters sent or received may be opened by the President, Vice-President or Prefect of Discipline.
23. No book, periodical or newspaper shall be introduced into the College without being previously examined and approved of by the Director of Studies. Objectional reading-matter found in the possession of Students will either be destroyed or withheld from them until their departure from the University.
24. Whether in class or in recreation, when permitted to converse at table, or during their walks, students should endeavor to improve the purity of their language and cultivate urbanity of manners. Bad habits and manners are sufficient to deprive a Student of Degrees and Honors.
25. The Students are reviewed on Wednesdays and Sundays with regard to their personal neatness.

W. CORBY, C. S. C., President.

II–46. University Parlor, 1911
This was the living room of the University until it was converted to the academic affairs office and then the provost's office (1970). The large public parlor was the scene of the annual faculty reception for seniors on President's Day.

II–47. Bookstore, 1914
Housed in a crowded room to the left of the student office was a small bookstore and magazine shop. Later this room became Coach Knute Rockne's athletic office and the ticket office for all varsity sporting events.

II–48. Student Office, 1893
Formerly located where the placement office (room 222) is now, this office served

as headquarters for the University registrar, accountant, admissions director, and cashier.

II–46

II–47

II–48

sided over by a succession of colorful University stewards, with the most famous, Brother Florian, even immortalized in fiction. Numerous other offices have come and gone behind the fifteen-foot-high oak transomed doors that line the corridors; these include classrooms, recitation rooms, a student office (II–48) and bookstore (II–47), and faculty private residences. Since 1890 the second floor walls have retained a series of twelve murals by Luigi Gregori (II–12), depicting the career of his fellow Italian, Christopher Columbus (II–55). Gregori, as he had also done in his church murals, utilized Notre Dame faculty for his models, particularly Father Thomas Walsh (president, 1881–93), whose likeness was used for Columbus in all the paintings except the deathbed mural, where Sorin was the model. (See Appendix III: Inventory of Murals in the Administration Building.)

Until Sorin Hall was built in 1888, Notre Dame students—collegiate as well as preparatory—prepared for their classes in two large study halls located in the right and left wings of the Main Building's

II–49

II–49. University Scrip, 1860–70
During its first decades, the University, caught in periods of acute deflation, issued its own currency which was negotiable in its internal accounting and also honored by various local merchants.

II–51. Commercial Department, ca. 1900
A large (40′ × 20′) classroom, adjoining the Brownson Hall study hall, was one of several specially equipped facilities for students enrolled in the commercial course.

II–51

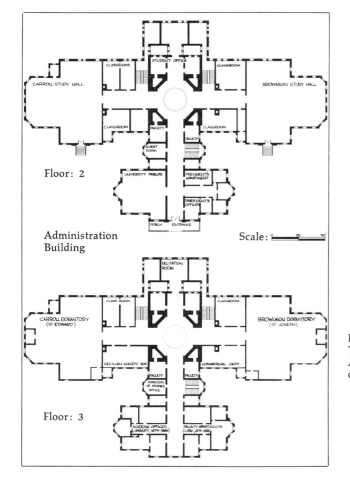

Administration Building

Scale:

Floor: 2

Floor: 3

II–50. Second and Third Floors
This map shows a reconstruction of the Administration Building's floor plan, ca. 1900.

II–52. Carroll Hall Study, 1880
All students studied in two long (77′ × 44′) halls. Each student had a desk wherein he stored *all* his books and academic materials.

II–53. Senior Lecture Room, 1893
In addition to being a classroom, this ornately decorated room was where student literary societies such as the Philodemics and Philopatrians held their meetings.

II–52

II–53

II–55. Discovery of Land, Friday, October 12, 1492, by Luigi Gregori
One of twelve murals done by Gregori in the Administration Building depicting the career of Christopher Columbus. Models for Gregori in this mural were Professor Arthur J. Stace and Joseph Lyons (foreground) and James F. Edwards (background). Columbus was painted in the likeness of father Thomas Walsh who became Notre Dame's seventh president in 1883.

second floor (II–52). Prefects such as Brothers Alexander (II–54), Paul, and Celestine presided on raised platforms and monitored communal study from 7 P.M. to 10 P.M., after which all students retired to their dormitories on the third and fourth floors. As late as 1909 the University president came personally to each study hall at the beginning of each semester and read the *University Regulations* (II–45) to the assembled students. The academic tone of the entire institution was still that of a French boarding school, definitely more a *collège* than a university. Father Auguste Lemonnier (1839–74), a lawyer and Sorin's nephew, tried to upgrade the school's intellectual credentials during his tenure as vice-president (1866–72) and president (1872–74). In what might be termed Notre Dame's first University priorities report, Lemonnier argued for more courses and faculty in mathematics, the natural and physical sciences, and law. He pressed for more scientific apparatus and began the University's library. As chief administrator he tightened graduation requirements in all programs, espe-

II–54. Brother Alexander, C.S.C. (1850–1926)
Like other famous Main Building rectors—Brothers Alphonsus, Bonaventure, Marcallius—Brother Alexander taught (algebra) in the prep department but was best known for his prowess as a disciplinarian.

II–55

II–56. Orestes A. Brownson (1803–76)
Transcendentalist, Owenite, editor of
Brownson's Quarterly Review, social
reformer, and author who became a
Catholic in 1844, Brownson was buried in
Sacred Heart crypt, and his papers are
part of the Catholic Manuscripts
Collection. In 1890 the University named
the collegians' residence as a memorial
to him.

II–56

II–57–60. The Brownsonites

II–57

cially in the commercial course (adding history and composition), and scrutinized the daily academic performance of faculty and students with a genuine interest in creating an intellectual atmosphere indicative of a university. Unfortunately this talented, erudite young Frenchman broke under the strain of overwork: he died in office in 1874, at the age of thirty-five.

Walk up the left stairs to the third floor, stop at the center of the rotunda railing (II–50), and face the front of the building.

Historically, student life at Notre Dame has meant residential hall life. Before separate halls were constructed (Sorin Hall [26] being the first built, in 1888), a student derived his campus identity from the dormitory in which he slept. The Administration Building was divided into Brownson Hall (collegiate division) and Carroll Hall (prep division), with the two third-floor wings further designated as St. Edward's dorm (now the advanced studies office) for Carroll students and St. Joseph's dorm (now the student affairs office) for Brownsonites

(II–56–64). In the dormitories each student had a bed and a chair, while his clothing was stored in lockers in the basement. Beds, arranged in long rows, had metal frames around them from which hung white drapes to create a limited degree of privacy. Two brother prefects had sleeping rooms adjoining each dormitory. Their responsibilities included extinguishing all lights at 10 P.M., rousting the students promptly at 6 A.M., and keeping pranks to a minimum.

II–58

II–59

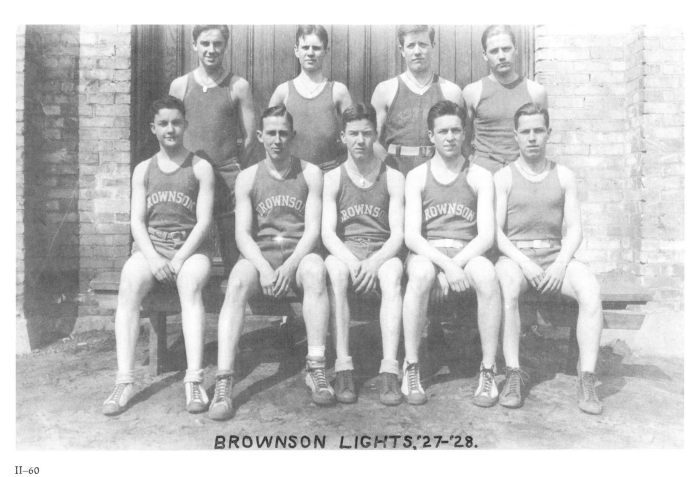

BROWNSON LIGHTS, '27–'28.

II–60

II–61, 63, and 64. The Carrollites

II–62. John Carroll (1735–1815)
First Roman Catholic bishop of the U.S.
(1790) and first archbishop of Baltimore
(1808), Carroll was active in founding
Catholic educational institutions in
America. Sorin named the residence for
preparatory students in his honor.

II–61

II–62

II–63

II–64

Twenty-two classrooms were scattered throughout the Administration Building's five floors. Several also served as assembly rooms (II–53) for student literary and musical societies: the Columbians, the Cecilians (now the dean of administration's office); the Philodemics, the Philopatrians, and the United Scientific Association. Where the current presidential and vice-presidential offices are now situated at the front of the third floor was initially the location of the college library until 1881 when it was moved to the fourth floor (II–72–73).

Walk up the right stairs to the fourth floor and note the historical marker (II–65) on the right stairwall.

Nineteenth-century Notre Dame inculcated religious and moral values in numerous ways. The Bishop's Memorial Hall (II–66) was one such didactic enterprise designed, in the words of its originator, James Farnham Edwards (II–70), to prompt "a special incentive to generous minded youths, who are by the presence of these memorials stirred to the emulation of the great dead." For Edwards the "great dead" were the Catholic bishops, missionaries, and lay men and women who had played a role in American religious history. An inveterate collector of every conceivable type of Catholic memorabilia (life-size paintings, busts, photographs, chalices, engravings, vestments, mitres, daguerreotypes, and funerary memorials such as figure II–65), Edwards displayed his collection in the Administration Building's third and fourth floor corridors (II–67). A combination of Catholic triumphalism, Edwards's historical interests, and Notre Dame's aspiration to become the center of American Catholicism, the exhibited artifacts of the Bishop's Memorial Hall stimulated a kind of religious pride and cultural identity for a minority group in an era that did not celebrate such a group consciousness. Of even greater importance from a scholarly perspective was the elaborate documentary collection of religious manuscripts and archival materials that Edwards amassed from all over North America and Europe. This amazing collection, once stacked between the joists of the dome because of a lack

II–65. Matthew Loras Funerary Marker
The only artifact of the Bishop's Memorial Hall still visible, it memorializes the first bishop of Dubuque, Iowa, for whom Loras College is named.

II–66. Handbill Description by James Edwards, 1885

II–65

of storage space in the library, is presently located in the University of Notre Dame Archives in the Memorial Library (72).

Walk to the center of the fourth floor and face the front of the building.

In addition to the Bishop's Memorial Hall, the fourth floor contained two additional student dorms (St. Patrick's, now the printing and publications office, and St. Aloysius, now storage), classrooms, private sleeping quarters for faculty and clergy, and the University library

Bishops' Memorial Hall,

NOTRE DAME, IND.

A NATIONAL Pantheon has been the dream of many visionary Americans. A much more practical, praiseworthy and Christian idea is that of the University of Notre Dame, Indiana, which has established a truly historic and suggestive monument to our illustrious dead in its "Memorial Hall of Our Bishops." Not many are aware that there exists at Notre Dame, Ind., a unique collection that commends itself to the interest of all who love and venerate the good men who have ruled over American dioceses. While a boy at college, Prof. J. F. Edwards conceived the happy idea of erecting a national monument to our prelates in the form of a Bishops' Memorial Hall. He immediately went to work, and after years of persistent search, he has brought together a large and valuable collection of life-size paintings, crayons engravings, photographs, rare old dageurreotypes, miniatures on ivory, busts and casts of all the bishops and archbishops who have held dioceses within the present limits of the United States. These have been placed in a large cruciform gallery, one hundred and fifty-five feet in length, one hundred and twenty at the arms, and a uniform width of sixteen feet. Besides the portraits, there is also an extensive collection of autograph letters and original documents written by the prelates; bound books, pamphlets and pastorals published by them; manuscripts relating to their histories, and printed volumes containing their biographies. In large, glass covered cabinets are displayed wonderful collections of mitres, crosiers, episcopal rings, gold chains, pectoral crosses and other articles used by our bishops, archbishops and cardinals. These cabinets, when placed in line, form a continuous stretch of one hundred and ninety-two feet by three in width. In a separate case are displayed manuscript sermons and letters written by Archbishop Carroll, a book from his pen—the first written and published by an American Catholic in the United States—a piece of the gold chain from which he suspended his pectoral cross, several rare engravings of the prelate himself, a picture of Pope Pius VI, who founded the American hierarchy, and a rare old bust of the Archbishop which stood for years on a mantle-piece in the private room of his kinsman, Daniel Carroll, of Duddington. Near by is shown a gold embroidered red velvet mitre, worn by Most Rev. Francis Patrick Kenrick, President of the First Plenary Council. A heavily embroidered and jewelled gold cloth mitre, worn by Archbishop Spalding when he opened the Second Plenary Council, stands surrounded by all his published works. In the section devoted to the Western dioceses is found a curious old crosier, of exquisite workmanship, made of tortoise-shell and silver. It was used by the venerable Garcia y Moreno, first Bishop of the Pacific Slope. Dioceses north, east, south and west are represented by *souvenirs* of their prelates.

This is the first attempt ever made in any country to illustrate a nation's whole episcopacy by a monument of this description. Many persons gave willingly of their treasures to assist in building this monument to our loved bishops. They deprived themselves of the pleasure of having relics at home in order to secure their greater safety in this collection, and at the same time to increase their value by making them parts of a systematic series. The hundreds of tourists and others who visit Notre Dame daily have their attention drawn by this Memorial Hall to the great work done by the American hierarchy, and a desire is excited to know more of the life and work of the truly apostolic men who planted and fostered the Faith in

our midst. No one can glance at the Indian dictionaries, grammars, prayer books and other works prepared for the Lake Superior tribes, without forming a high estimate of the services rendered religion by the sainted Baraga, who endured untold hardship to preach the Faith of Christ to the untutored savages of the North. In the same case with these works are displayed some manuscripts, a precious mitre and other *souvenirs* of the great Apostle of the Michigan Indians. It is the great desire of the originator of the Bishops' Memorial Hall to make it as complete and as national as possible. Any one who may have in his possession *souvenirs* of our deceased prelates, in the form of articles illustrating their pontifical dignity, locks of their hair, works published by them, and documents or old letters in their handwriting, can render a valuable service to the history of the Church by depositing them in the Bishops' Memorial Hall, where they will be religiously guarded for posterity, and preserved from danger—such as fire or robbery. A sight of the article will cause many a prayer to be said, not only for the persons whose memory it perpetuates, but also for all who assist in completing this monument already so well commenced and so solidly established. Attached to the Bishops' Memorial Hall is a large ecclesiastical museum containing *souvenirs* of missionary priests, Catholic laymen, and articles illustrating the different religious orders.—*Catholic Review.*

As an instance of the increasing interest in the history of the Catholic Church in this country, we may note the success which has attended Prof. J. F. Edwards in his establishment of the "Bishops' Memorial Hall" at the University of Notre Dame, Indiana. It has excited a general interest in his project of collecting in this place portraits of the Archbishops and Bishops of the United States, with some relic of each. The "Bishops' Memorial Hall" is already worth a pilgrimage to view it. The series of portraits is complete and authentic; the portrait of Bishop Egan alone being ideal. No portrait of Philadelphia's first bishop is known; and the portrait placed here was painted by the skilful artist Gregori, based on the description given by Father Jordan in the Woodstock Letters, and since generally copied and accepted. It is almost impossible to believe that Prof. Edwards has actually gathered all the precious mementoes that already enrich this hall. It is told of the witty Fontenelle, that once taking up a collection at the Church door, he held out a bag to a notorious miser, who put a donation in it. After going around, Fontenelle returned to the gentleman. "I have put something in it," he whispered to Fontenelle. "I saw it," retorted the wit, "but I do not believe it." So in this case, even the sight of the mitres, crosiers, chalices, pectoral crosses, rings worn or used by the Archbishops, and Bishops of this country, from the revered Carroll to our day, with books used and manuscripts written by them, so dazzle and astonish one, that though we see, we can scarcely credit that so much has been preserved and gathered safely into this noble hall. We see, yet we cannot believe. It is to be hoped that no other attempt of this character will be made, diverting other objects from being added to this precious collection. We trust that all having relics of any of our Bishops will render a service to Catholic history by presenting, or at least depositing them, in the "Bishops' Memorial Hall," at Notre Dame, Indiana.—*Dr. Gilmary Shea in U. S. Catholic Historical Magazine.*

II–67

II–68

II–69

II–70

II–67–69. Bishop's Memorial Hall Exhibited Collections
Photo II–67 shows rotunda view of third and fourth floors, 1893; II–68, fourth floor, west wing, 1893; and II–69, third floor, main corridor, 1893. In the nineteenth century, the Memorial Hall was a tourist attraction, and it formed a large part of the American Catholic church exhibit at the Chicago Columbian Exposition in 1893.

II–70. James ("Jimmy") Edwards (1850–1911)
Class of 1875, professor of history, director of the Lemonnier Library, founder of Bishop's Memorial Hall and the Catholic Archives of America, originator of the Laetare Medal, antiquarian, Beau Brummel who had his clothes tailored in Bond Street, Edwards was also faculty advisor to innumerable student organizations.

II–71. Fourth and Fifth Floors
The map shows a reconstruction of the Administration Building's floor plans, ca. 1900.

II–72–73. The University Library
Photo II–72, ca. 1882, shows a ground view with Director Edwards at the shelves to the left; II–73, ca. 1895, taken from the gallery looking west, shows an increase in number of volumes as well as Edward's memorabilia.

II–71

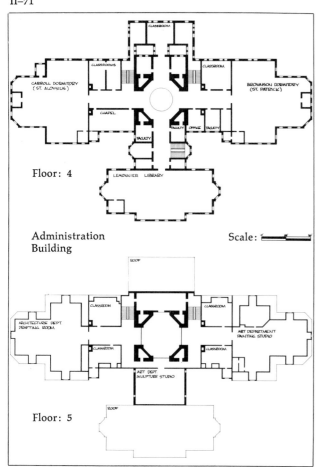

Administration
Building

Scale:

II–72

II–74. Art Department Logo, 1975
A visible remnant is shown of the former activity of the now-closed fifth floor. Notre Dame students received their artistic training here from 1879 until the I. A. O'Shaughnessy Hall of Liberal Arts and Sciences was opened in 1952.

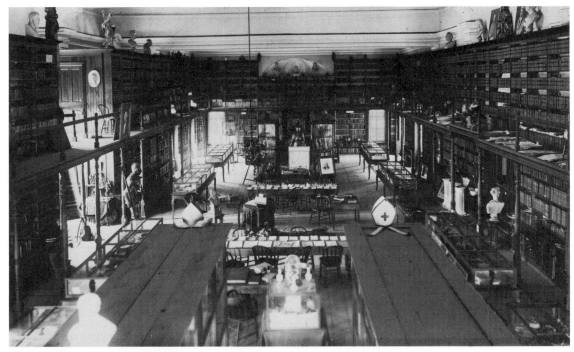

II–73

II–74

(now the counseling center). The library, begun by President Lemonnier in 1873 and subsequently known by his surname, had been only a large room in the east wing of the third floor of Main Building II. Its ten-thousand-volume collection was largely destroyed by the 1879 fire, but within a decade the indefatigable Professor Edwards had rebuilt the collection to fifty thousand volumes. Edwards was the library's first director, serving from 1874 until his death in 1911. The library's decor and organization (II–72–73) reflected his antiquarianism as well as Notre Dame's continual debt to European architectural models.

Glance up to the fifth floor and note the former logo of the fine arts department (II–74).

Architecture (II–77), along with painting, sculpture (II–76), mechanical drawing (II–75), and photography, were taught in the fifth-floor complex, now inaccessible to the public. The huge, double-storeyed classrooms and skylit spaces were also occupied at times by the music, speech, journalism, and geology de-

**II–75–78. Fifth Floor Departments,
1879–1959**
Although no longer used, the well-lit,
double-storeyed spaces of the building's
top floor have been employed for various
academic purposes: II–75, sculpture studio;
II–76, mechanical drawing classroom;
II–77, architecture drafting room; and
II–78, earth sciences classroom.

II–76

II–78

II–77

partments (II–78), and once housed
part of the University museum.
Hallways were lined with glass cases
which contained Civil War memorabilia such as General William Sher-
man's coat, Indian artifacts, and a
brocade chasuble of Père Marquette.
Above the cases hung huge can-
vases (still visible in the east and
west wings) painted by an itinerant
nineteenth-century cyclorama promoter who apparently ran out of
money or energy just after his lec-
ture-demonstration at Notre Dame.
He either sold or donated his canvas murals to the University. Gregori also had his studio on the fifth
floor, and it is his allegorical composition that adorns the inner dome.
The classical figures represent (l. to
r.) Religion, Philosophy, Poetry,
Law, and Science surrounding the
Virgin.

*Descend the stairs to the left of the
counseling center to the front porch.*

Notre Dame in the 1870s had expanded extensively following the
Civil War, suffered catastrophe in
the loss of its main physical plant,
only to rebuild and grow anew. Student life (II–79–84) remained

II–79. James Carbagal

II–80. Carroll Hall Cyclists, 1890

highly disciplined and supervised. Students were "given their trunks" for minor mischief (such as playing a cornet solo, "St. Patrick's Day in the Morning," at daybreak on March 17th from the top of the dome). There were few oustanding Catholic scholars in the country, and the $600 faculty salary Notre Dame offered satisfied only the most dedicated of laymen, most of whom, like Lyons, Edwards, and Howard (II–86, 70, and 83), were alumni. Such faculty, along with their clerical colleagues, were wont to take their evening pipe or cigar on the Main Building's handsome front porch, an area off limits to undergraduates until their commencement, when they walked down its stairs for the first time. Once an important rite of passage, the stairs regulation evolved into a tradition that is still observed by some students.

The year 1879 was assuredly a turning point in Notre Dame's history. Contemporaries and historians have argued that while Sorin founded the University on a cold winter afternoon in 1842, he also refounded it on a fresh April Sunday in 1879. His resolve to build

II–79

II–80

II–81. Andrew Rohrbach

II–82. James O'Reilly

II–83. Messrs. Dillan, McKennan, and Decker and Professor Timothy Howard

II–84. John T. Foxen

II–85. Auguste Lemonnier, C.S.C., Prefect of Studies and University President, 1872–74.

II–81

II–82

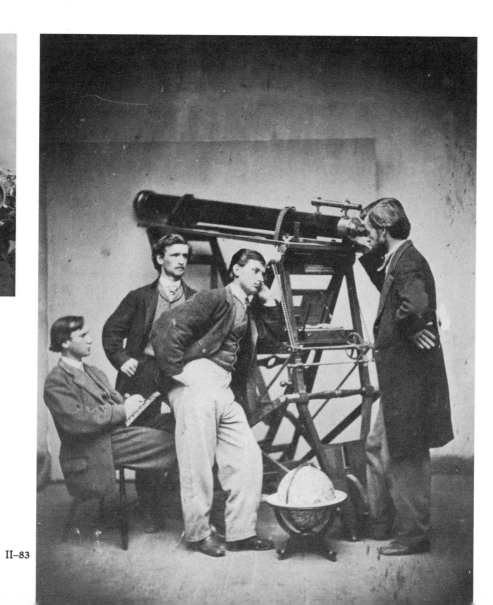

II–83

II–84

II–85

again inspired similar communal determination. Moreover, the extent of national sympathy and support that followed the fire indicated that Notre Dame had become more than a provincial midwestern college. The aging Sorin also decided that new and younger men (the plural was important) should begin to run Notre Dame. Hence, two years after the Great Fire, he appointed as president his protégé, Thomas Walsh, perhaps the first Notre Dame student ever deliberately recruited and educated to be the University's chief officer. Walsh was charged with expanding the faculty and improving the University's academic departments and its physical facilities. During the twelve years of his presidency (1881–93), Father Walsh would implement Sorin's directives as well as many of the ideas of Auguste Lemonnier, moving Notre Dame into a new era with many of its twentieth-century foundations either planned or established.

II–86

II–86. Joseph A. Lyons, Professor of English and University Historian

II–87. Notre Dame Faculty, 1874

II–88. Notre Dame, ca. 1888
This artist's engraving shows, with minor spatial distortions, the buildings of the Main Quad: (l. to r.) Sorin Hall, Sacred Heart Church, Administration Building, Academy of Music, and Science Hall.

II–87

III. The University in 1893

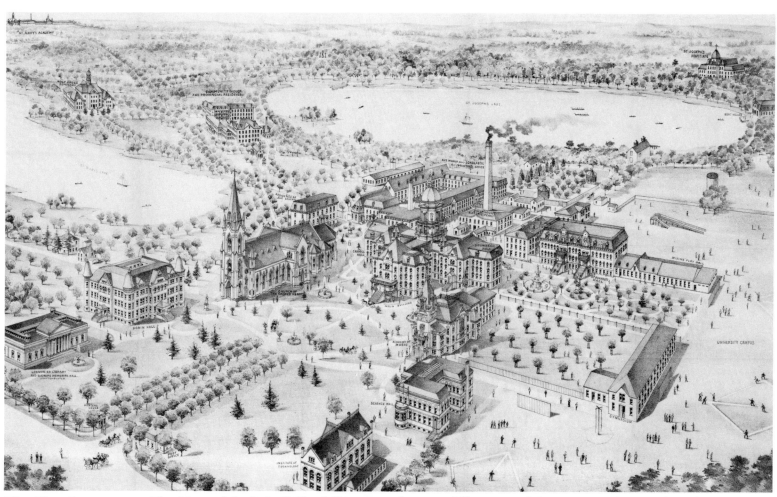

III–1. Notre Dame, ca. 1890. This lithograph by S. O. Childs of Chicago was done as a fold-out map of the campus in the *Annual Catalogue, 1890–91*. The contemplated Lemonnier Library and Bishop's Memorial Hall (lower left) were not built in the proposed location but on a site forty yards farther west.

Beginning at the front steps of the Administration Building (36), Walk III explores the growth of the University from the early 1880s to the turn of the century. A walk of 650 yards, it reviews the multiple activities in areas formerly located behind the Administration Building as well as those of St. Edward's Hall (45) and its Minim Department. Then, following the expansion of the University south along the Main Quadrangle, the walk proceeds by Washington Hall (44), the La Fortune Student Center (formerly the Science Hall [43]), and Hoynes Hall (42). The tour concludes, after crossing the quadrangle through the University arboretum and passing by Sorin (26) and Walsh (25) Halls, at the statue honoring Edward Sorin (98), founder and first president, who died in 1893.

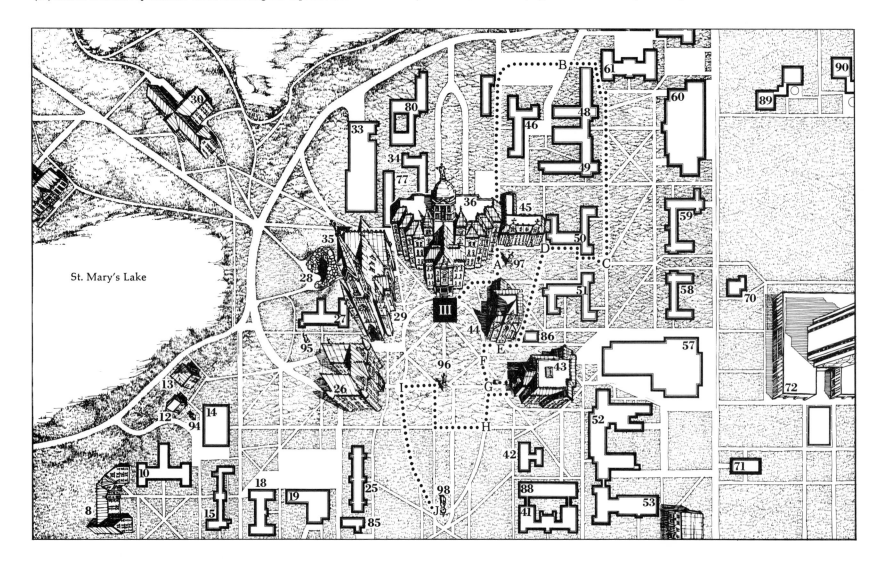

A Jubilee, an Uncertain Identity, New Horizons

THE ACADEMIC year 1892–93 should have been an occasion of great excitement at Notre Dame as the University prepared to celebrate a golden jubilee anniversary. Actually the year proved to be an important historical transition, a bittersweet time when Notre Dame experienced both serious internal losses and increased national prominence. The year 1893 marked the death of several of the institution's dynamic leaders and early guiding spirits: President Thomas Walsh and Father Alexis Granger both died in July; and in October, Edward Sorin succumbed to Bright's disease which had plagued him for several years. Three giants were dead within three months. In mourning, the University community postponed its anticipated golden jubilee celebration until 1895. However, Notre Dame did decide to proceed with its announced participation in the World's Columbian Exposition held in Chicago in 1893. The invitation to exhibit at the world's fair is evidence of the University's increasing national reputation, which, in turn, was enhanced by Notre Dame's displays of student publications, art work, and scientific research. Among the assembled artifacts and documents were 120 sepia views (14″ × 20″) of the University taken by Alexander Kirsch's classes in photography. Fortunately a number of these superb photographs (III–3) survive to afford us a visual benchmark of Notre Dame's self-image in 1893.

Father Thomas Walsh's unexpected death at the age of forty created a leadership vacuum that some historians argue was not really filled until 1906 when John W. Cavanaugh became president, replacing Andrew Morrissey. Walsh, a classics scholar who, even before his ordination in 1879, had been Corby's vice-president, had been named president in 1881 when he was only twenty-eight, the same age as his mentor Sorin when the latter founded Notre Dame. Walsh (III–2) upgraded the faculty with men like William Hoynes (III–53) in law, Albert Zahm (III–75) in science, and Maurice Francis Egan (III–73) in liberal arts. Walsh, like Sorin, was an energetic promoter of Notre Dame on a national scale. During his tenure the Laetare Medal (awarded annually to an outstanding American Catholic) was established. Sorin's fiftieth anniversary (1888) as a priest became a six-month international celebration at the University; and, under Walsh's guidance, Notre Dame made its first overtures toward limited participation in national intercollegiate athletics. Walsh, like Sorin, was a builder. His twelve-year presidency resulted in extensive expansion of the University's physical plant, especially in the erection of buildings clustered about the Administration Building.

A *Walk to the right of the Administration Building (36) along the walk to a point parallel with the St. Edward's statue (97).*

President Walsh continued to expand Notre Dame as a self-sufficient city. Many of the service facilities that made such independence and communality possible were located in the "back of Old Main" area (III–5). Infirmaries stood on a site west of the present St. Edward's Hall (30) as early as 1864 (see the outline of an 1879 infirmary retaining wall that abutted St. Edward's west wall and compare I–53 and III–4). The first infirmary was destroyed in the Great Fire of 1879; the second, rebuilt that same year, served Notre Dame students, faculty, and staff until 1934, when it was demolished. A third and still larger building (46), accommodating up to 125 patients, is now located to the northeast on the former site of the third (1899) steam plant. The student infirmaries, like the University kitchens and grade schools, were the special domain of the Holy Cross sisters, particularly Sisters Bethlehem and Cecila (infirmarian for thirty-four years), who saw most student patients through their illnesses with a ubiquitous prescription of calomel and salts.

Adjacent to the old infirmary was the site of numerous steam plants, which were enlarged or rebuilt to accommodate the succession of main buildings and the increasing student population. In 1900 a central plant (to heat all campus buildings) was

---

Notre Dame in 1893

Acreage: 1,300 Buildings: 24
Faculty: 52 Tuition: $170
Students: 542 Room/board: $200

III–2–3. Faculty and Students, 1888 and 1893
Photo III–2 shows, sitting among their colleagues (middle three), several important administrators during 1880–1900: (l. to r.) J. Zahm, T. Walsh, and A. Morrissey; III–3 shows, facing the Administration Building's front steps, the student body assembled, front to rear, in order of age: minims, preps, manual labor apprentices, collegians.

III–4. Infirmary and St. Edward's, 1882
Rebuilt in 1879 the student infirmary stood between St. Edward's Hall (shown here in original size before its several additions) and the Administration Building until 1934.

III–3

III–5. "Back of Old Main," ca. 1900

III–6. Steam House, 1893
The second of four power plants located behind the Main Buildings since 1844, this building served the University from 1876 until 1899, when it was converted into a natatorium (III–7).

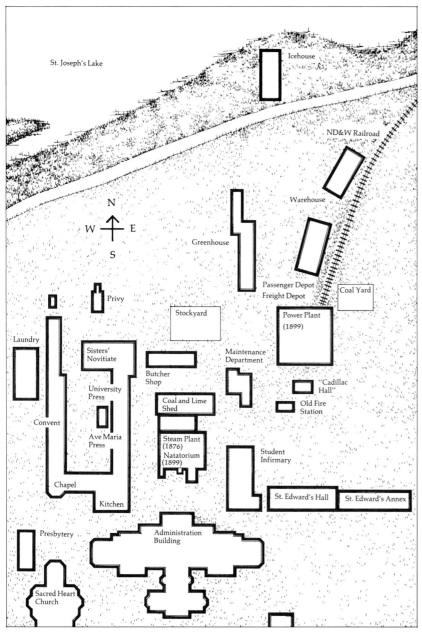

III–5

III–6

constructed on the approximate site of the present infirmary; the old steam house (III–6), located directly behind the Administration Building, was converted into a natatorium (III–7). "The building in which the swimming pool is located," reported *The Scholastic* in 1902, "is a commodious one, 90 feet long, 45 feet wide, two storeys in height, the upper storey of which is used for a trunk room. The swimming pool itself [III–8] is 57 feet in length, 27 feet in width, and 6 feet 6 inches in depth at one end and 7 feet 6 inches at the other." The pool in the Rockne Memorial Building (6) replaced the natatorium in 1937, but the structure was readapted by Father Bernard Lange (III–9) for weight lifting and other body-building exercises.

Father Lange's "gym" was a campus landmark to students who braved its forbidding entrance sign ("STAY OUT! THIS MEANS YOU!!") and paid their $5 membership fee to endure excruciating exercises, subtropical humidity, plus the verbal (often profane) invectives of the infamous Bernard Herman Benedict Lange (whose initials students

III–7. Natatorium, 1902
In addition to a swimming pool, the first floor of this structure had eighteen shower-baths. The second floor served as a clothes storage room for underclassmen.

III–8. Natatorium Interior
Steam-heated, electric-lit, the University pool (a mere fifty-seven feet long) indirectly added to the home team's

success in that only Notre Dame swimmers had sufficient practice to master the constant end-of-the-pool turns.

III–9. "B.H.B." Lange
Fourth strongest man in the world in 1922, Ph.D. in biology, founder and proprietor of "Father Lange's Gym," a body-and-muscle-building emporium first located in the abandoned natatorium and then in Brownson Hall.

transformed into "Build Healthier Bodies"). Father Lange was acclaimed to be the fourth strongest man in the world in 1922. A teacher of anatomy and biology, he was forced to resign his faculty position in 1935 due to his failing eyesight. Shortly afterwards he established himself in the abandoned natatorium where, for the next thirty years, he exhorted Notre Dame students with his notorious slogan: "One Man in Twenty Thousand Can Press His Own Weight—Are You A Man?"

Until 1927 the University kitchens (II–16) were located to the west of the natatorium (III–5) and in front of the present Brownson Hall (34), which then fronted along a road known as "printer's row." Here were the University and Ave Maria Presses. These offices, equipped with an Adams steam press and several hand presses, published scholarly and literary works, *The Ave Maria* and *The Scholastic* magazines (begun by Edward Sorin in 1865 and 1867 respectively), and all other publications (stationery, business forms, theatrical programs, advertising handbills, and so forth) of the University.

III–7

III–8

III–9

III–10–11. St. Edward's Hall and Gardens
Two views, taken respectively ca. 1888 and 1884, show (III–10): the hall's relation to the infirmary (far left); life-size galvanized iron angels representing Justice, Religion,

and Honor; and recreation hall (far right). View in III–11 shows heart-shaped garden plots containing twenty-foot floral displays defined in plantings of echeveria, pyrethrum, and achyranth identifying "St. Edward's Park" and, facing the hall, spelling out "Ave Maria."

III–10

III–11

Look to the right and in front of St. Edward's Hall (45).

Throughout its nineteenth- and early twentieth-century history, Notre Dame offered an educational program that extended from the elementary grades through graduate studies. The University's grade school, formally established in 1854, had its own building (III–4 and 10–11) by 1882 when St. Edward's House, or the Minim Department, was designed by Father Sorin and Brother Charles Harding. Over six thousand boys (ages six to thirteen) participated in the minims' program and a fair number continued in the University high school (preparatory department) and the undergraduate college, thereby becoming, in the parlance of the day, "lifers" at Notre Dame.

Reading, orthography, history, grammar, geography, mathematics, and penmanship, plus catechism and Bible history for Catholic students, formed the core of instruction for the minims. Special courses—vocal and instrumental music, languages, composition, drawing and painting, elocution, and physical culture—were also available and taught by the University faculty. The bulk of the teaching load, however, was assumed by the Sisters of the Holy Cross, one of whom, "Sister Al" (Sister M. Aloysius Mulcaire, III–13), was St. Edward's most-beloved principal (1875–1916). The Brothers of St. Joseph, especially "Brother Caj" (III–19), director of the Minim Department from 1881 to 1927, superintended the students' study and recreation time. Even the University presidents, beginning with Sorin, took an active interest in the elementary school by making a traditional monthly visit (III–18) to the St. Edward's classrooms.

Figures III–10–11 give some idea of the attention Sorin lavished on what he considered to be "a palace

III–12. St. Edward's Dormitory, 1916
Located on the hall's third and fourth floors, these communal quarters were provided for the minim students.

III–13. "Sister Al" (1845–1916)
St. Edward's principal from 1875 to 1916, Sister M. Aloysius Mulcaire taught over half the six thousand minims who went through the University grade school.

III–14. Minim Classroom, 1902
A typical third-floor classroom in St. Edward's Hall.

III–12

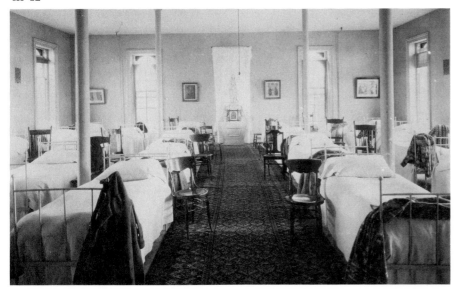

III–13

III–14

for his princes." In close proximity to the University infirmary, the hall had ornate iron dual-staircase entrances, religious murals, and a large recreation facility. The entire complex—a self-contained community for 150 boys—was fronted by a formal four-hundred-foot Victorian garden complete with water fountains, a statue of St. Edward (97), and a ground-level floral display (III–11) that identified St. Edward's Park.

On the building's *rez-de-chaussée* were located the lavatories, toilets, and several clothes storage rooms. The second floor was comprised of St. John's Chapel, a parlor, study halls, classrooms (III–14), clubrooms, and a reception hall. Students rose at 6:40 A.M. and retired at 8 P.M. in dormitories on the third and fourth floors such as that pictured in figure III–12; also on the third floor were classrooms, recitation rooms, and the music hall. The minims ate in a basement refectory of the Administration Building.

University officials claimed that St. Edward's was "a complete school within itself." The institution published its own sixty-page catalogue that outlined the extensive academic, social, athletic, spiritual, and disciplinary advantages of sending a young boy to board at Notre Dame (III–15–18). Cost per ten-month year in 1902 was $250, which included tuition, board, laundry, books, gymnasium fees, and tickets for all University lectures and concerts. Piano lessons and

rental were extra at $35 per year, while similar arrangements could be made to learn the violin, guitar, or mandolin at $25. A summer school and camp was established by the Brothers of St. Joseph at nearby Paw Paw, Michigan, for pupils who remained at the University during the vacation period (July and August). Parents could send their child to the brothers' camp-school for an extra $40. (For a brief period in the late 1910s both the prep and collegiate divisions also offered sum-

III–15

III–16

III–17

III–18

III–15–18. The Minims
In addition to academics, minim life had other facets: III–15, military drill as a Sorin Cadet; III–16, reception of Holy Communion (posed in front of St. Edward's statue); III–17, Wednesday afternoon bicycle outings; and, III–18, Father Sorin and his "little princes."

III–19. "Brother Caj" (1855–1928)
As director of the Minim Department, Brother Cajetan Gallagher was in charge of the brothers who, in turn, superintended the students' study and recreation time.

III–20–21. University Crew, 1893
Posed ready for a daily workout and also at a studied informal moment, the Notre Dame teams were headquartered in a charming two-storey boathouse (III–21) built in 1890. In the background of figure III–20, along the far shore, can be seen (l. to r.) St. Edward's Hall, the Administration Building, the 1876 power plant, and one of the University's ice houses (far right with ice ladder extending into the lake).

mer camp courses in Michigan.) Hence, it was possible that a student could come to Notre Dame at age six and never leave its confines until he completed his bachelor's degree.

B *Walk to the left of St. Edward's Hall along the sidewalk that is left of the infirmary (46) to the edge of the parking lot overlooking St. Joseph's Lake.*

The University could accommodate students in such familial surroundings because of its multifaceted physical facilities and services. The Notre Dame lakes, particularly St. Joseph's, have been employed for their recreational (III–20–21), religious (III–23), and even culinary potential. The local council minutes in 1847 note that "Brothers Vincent, Lawrence, Basil and Francis de Sales will fish the whole day on Wednesday," and throughout the University's early decades fresh fish from its lakes was part of the student diet. Ice houses (III–21) were built as early as 1853 on the southeast shore of St. Joseph's Lake, and ice was harvested (III–22) as late as 1916. Throughout

III–20

III–22. Cutting Ice, 1916
In addition to fish for its kitchens, the
Notre Dame lakes provided ice which
was stored in lockers. From 1853 to 1916
two such ice houses stood on the lake's
southern shore, both later being
destroyed by fires.

III–21

III–22

III–23–24. St. Joseph's Novitiate, 1913
Originally the site of the missionary's home (II–23) which was converted to a novitiate only to be destroyed by fire in 1879, this structure (III–23) was rebuilt that year. In the spring of 1913, fire broke out again (III–24). Rebuilt a third time in 1913, it served as a novitiate until a new one was constructed at Rolling Prairie, Indiana, in 1934. The building then became the C.S.C. community infirmary until the present Holy Cross House (47) was built on its site.

III–23

III–24

the nineteenth century, this lake was the course for several annual summer regattas sponsored by the Lemonnier Boat Club.

Turn around and face the student infirmary and the area in back of the Administration Building.

The "back of Old Main" area (see map, III–5) also contained the University train station and freight depots (III–28–29), which formed the terminus of the Notre Dame and Western Railroad, a private spur line of the former Michigan Central (now Penn Central). The ND&W's tracks, which now only extend up to the University's fourth and most recent (1932) power plant (63), were laid in 1902 and came up to the earlier steam house (III–6) behind the Administration Building. At various times coal yards, warehouses, ice houses, and a stockyard were located along the tracks. The passenger depot served students traveling to and from the campus during vacations. This was especially the case for the special student trains (III–28) that John Zahm brought each year from the western United States. Passenger trains chartered by

alumni clubs throughout the Midwest steamed on to the Notre Dame campus via the ND&W's tracks on home football Saturdays. John Gould, '02, and his "Power House Special" from Chicago achieved a notoriety still remembered by actual and "subway" (railway?) alumni.

Former students also recall structures such as the picturesque but inadequate firehouse and its neighbor, "Cadillac Hall" (III–25). Fire was probably the most menacing physical threat Notre Dame faced in its history. Up to 1920 there were over thirty blazes in addition to the 1879 catastrophe; yet the University remained content with antiquated equipment, limited facilities, and valiant but volunteer student firemen (III–26). "Cadillac Hall," the first University garage, was the twentieth-century replacement for the University livery (IV–41) and an inauspicious building except for its famous inhabitant, John "Johnny" Mangan (III–27). Coming to Notre Dame from Ireland in 1910, Mangan stayed on as the University chauffeur for forty years, beguiling administrators, berating faculty, and befriending students.

III–25–26. "Cadillac Hall" and Firehouse, 1957
The Notre Dame garage was erected in 1916 to house the first automobile (a Cadillac given to J. W. Cavanaugh) that the University owned. The campus fire department (built in 1896) and its volunteer staff, ca. 1899 (III–26), was replaced in 1946 by professional equipment, a modern building (62), and trained personnel.

III–27. John "Johnny" Mangan
Notre Dame chauffeur for forty years, overseer of "Cadillac Hall," self-styled advisor to University presidents, Irish campus character who hoped to be buried (and was) in the C.S.C. Community Cemetery because he knew the seminarians prayed daily for those interred there.

III–25

III–27

III–28

III–26

III–28. The Zahm Special, 1885
John Zahm had a special palace car built by the Worcester Excursion Car Company for use of the western students, their parents, and friends traveling to and from the campus. The car contained sleeping berths and a special diner with a private *chef de cuisine*, formerly of Delmonico's in New York. Excursions were made from Mexico City, the Pacific coast cities, and Denver before and after each school vacation.

III–29. The Minims' Campus, ca. 1899
Behind the Administration Building can be seen (l. to r.) the boathouse on the lake, N.D.&W tracks leading to the passenger station and freight depots, the 1899 power plant, the eight-acre minims' playing field, and beyond, to the north and east, the University farms.

C *Walk to the right along the path between Stanford-Keenan Halls (48, 49) and Haggar Hall (61); then bear right and walk in front of Stanford-Keenan and Zahm (50) Halls and come to the mailbox between Cavanaugh (31) and Zahm Halls. Face east with the mailbox at your back and look out on the North Quadrangle.*

From the 1880s until the 1930s the land east of the "back of Old Main" was largely devoted to student playing fields and agricultural purposes (III–29). The North Quadrangle, now enclosed (viewing l. to r. around the rectangle) by Zahm, Keenan-Stanford, and Haggar Halls, the North Dining Hall, Farley and Breen-Phillips Halls, the Fieldhouse (57), and Cavanaugh Hall, was largely the minims' campus, an eight-acre field north and east of St. Edward's Hall. As illustrated by figures III–29–31, the area was the scene of diverse activities. Several baseball diamonds and three football and rugby gridirons were encircled by a track used for both foot and bicycle racing; also included were a tennis court, swings and turning poles, a toboggan slide and

III–29

III–30–32. St. Edward's Annex and Playing Fields, 1893

Figure III–30, an 1893 engraving, depicts the two-hundred-foot east annex (added in 1888 and torn down in 1937 to permit the construction of Zahm Hall), which contained, in addition to more dormitory space, a gymnasium, handball and basketball courts, a library and reading room (III–32), a roller-skating rink, game room, and armory. Playing fields (III–31) to the east adjoined the annex. The iron railing (lower foreground, III–30) delineating St. Edward's Park survives on the present campus as a historical vestige of the park's southern boundary.

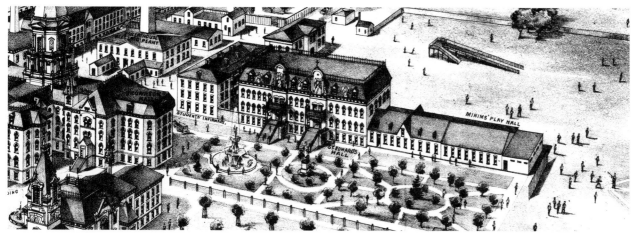

III–30

III–32

III–31

**III–33. "Brother Leep's Rec Store,"
ca. 1914**
Sole proprietor of the famous campus
snack shop located in the partition
between the Brownson and Carroll gyms,
Brother Leopold Kaul provided Notre
Dame students with confections for
over forty years.

**III–34–36. "Rockefeller Hall" and
University Gymnasium, 1893**
Located on a site directly adjoining the
present band building, the University
privies were also called "Rockefeller Hall"
because their second storey was often a
temporary dormitory for drifters. The
gymnasium, built perpendicular to the
privies in 1882, had the latest gymnastic
apparatus (III–35–36), a hardwood
interior, a barbershop, and "Brother
Leep's" shop. This building remained the
main gym until replaced by the Fieldhouse (57) in 1899.

III–33

III–35

III–36

III–34

III–37. First Varsity Football Team, 1887

III–38. Lacrosse Squad, Including Brother Hugh and Father "Daddy" Reagan, 1896

III–39. Varsity Baseball Team, 1888

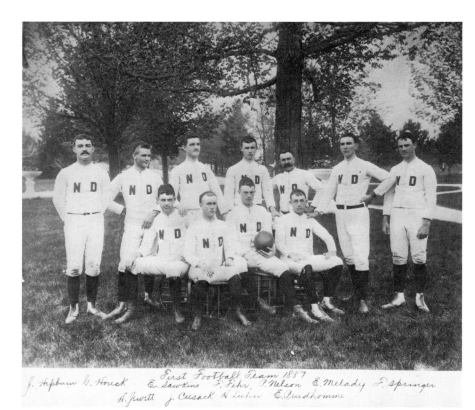

III–37

III–38

III–39

ice rink for winter sports, and the adjacent St. Joseph's Lake for summer water recreation. Every minim was required to participate in light military drill as one of the Sorin Cadets (III–15) whose three companies tramped these fields two hours every week, replete with miniature Remington rifles and navy-blue uniforms.

D *Turn around and walk west (straight on the path to the right) beside Zahm Hall to the southeast corner of St. Edward's Hall.*

The cadets' rifles were stored in an armory in the St. Edward's Hall east annex (III–30), a two-hundred-foot, one-and-one-half-storey addition, also known as the minims' play hall. (Look up at St. Edward's Hall east wall to see the former roofline of the annex depicted in the different brick coloration.) In addition to the armory, the play hall (which was torn down in 1937 to permit the construction of Zahm Hall) contained more dormitory space, a gymnasium, handball and basketball courts, a library and reading room (III–32), a roller-skating rink, a game room, and storage area for the

minims' bicycles. Expanded in 1884, in 1888, and again in 1914 (the northwest annex), St. Edward's Hall continued as the Minim Department until 1929 when the University phased out the program. Vincent Fagan, a member of the architecture faculty, then converted the building to a collegiate dormitory.

E *Turn right, walk south along the path between Cavanaugh and Washington Halls (44), and continue to the right of the small band building (86) to the front of Washington Hall.*

Since the 1840s students (III–37–39) have used the recreational areas that have been largely located east of the Main Quadrangle. Various wooden gymnasiums have occupied the site where the band building (86) is now located. In 1866, a two-storey (160′ × 45′), red-brick structure (III–34) was erected and equipped with the latest gymnastic apparatus (III–35–36); it remained the main gym until 1899, when the present Fieldhouse was constructed. Within this first main gym, Brother Leopold Kaul, a typesetter for the University and teacher

of violin in the music department, also ran a confectionary and soft drink shop. "Brother Leep," as he was known to generations of students, ran his store from 1864 to 1917, when it was superseded by the Badin Hall cafeteria. He stocked his 15′ × 40′ shop with pretzels, candies, and over twenty varieties of cakes. On a board nailed to the wall behind the counter, he displayed and numbered his wares. Customers could see at a glance what was for sale and order what they wished by its number. "Number four," a chocolate-covered marshmallow-and-vanilla confection, topped with a toothsome pecan, was the leading favorite. Hence, "lemonade and fours" became a campus legend. Three "fours" and two pints of lemonade cost a nickel in 1902.

West of the first main gym were two adjoining buildings on a site now east of the band building. One was used as an indoor baseball practice room and an armory for the Hoynes' Light Guards (III–53). The other was the University privy. The second floor of the 30′ × 60′ communal privy was euphemistically

known as "Rockefeller Hall," where Brother Hugh Clark (III–38) housed homeless drifters who came to the campus seeking employment. Brother Hugh, also a Brownson Hall rector for thirty years and an avid athletic fan, arranged lodging and meals for men in exchange for their maintenance work on the campus grounds.

F *Walk to the intersection of the Main Quadrangle road; turn around and face Washington Hall.*

Nineteenth-century Notre Dame, given its French cultural tone and its Catholic liturgical tradition, was highly supportive of the fine, dramatic, and musical arts. Since 1846 a structure primarily devoted to instruction in, and performance of, these arts has been located on the approximate site of the present Washington Hall. The first music hall was a two-storey, clapboard building equipped with classrooms, practice rooms, and sufficient instruments for both an orchestra and a marching band (III–44). The University's annual closing exercises (III–41), first known as "exhibitions," were also held in this hall,

III–40–41. Exhibition Hall, 1874
Located on approximately the site of
Washington Hall (44), the first University
theatre (III–40 illustrates its cast of
William Tell) also served as a music
building. Figure III–41 shows its interior
decorated for the 1876 commencement
exercises.

III–40

III–41

III–42. Interior, Washington Hall, ca. 1900
Although completely painted over in 1956, the present University theatre was once an ornately decorated hall. Frescoes and murals done by Luigi Gregori and Signor Rusca included four emblematic figures (Tragedy, Comedy, Music, Poetry) in the four corners atop which were four portraits of exponents of these arts (Shakespeare, Molière, Mozart, Dante). Over the proscenium, Washington's presence loomed, flanked by orators Demosthenes and Cicero on each side of the stage.

III–43. Washington Hall, 1890
This structure, like most of Notre Dame's French-inspired buildings, was initially entered on the second floor by a front staircase. Such an architectural detail can still be seen at the building's rear entrance. Removed from the modern campus are the ornamental water fountains that flanked the Administration Building and the hitching post in front of it.

III–43

III–42

III–44. Notre Dame Band, ca. 1905
One of the oldest university bands in continual existence in the U.S. (founded in 1846), the Notre Dame musical unit poses here in front of the John Harry "Shilly" Shillington monument, formerly located in the yard between Washington and Science Halls. Students erected this war memorial for Shillington, a Brownson Hall student killed in the U.S.S. *Maine* disaster in Havana harbor in 1898. The memorial is now located to the right of the Administration Building.

as were lectures, concerts, and campus assemblies; the Exhibition Hall's front portico served as a favorite backdrop for numerous student group photographs (III–40).

When this structure was destroyed in the Great Fire in 1879, Willoughby Edbrooke was commissioned to design a new music building to replace it. His creation, the present Washington Hall (III–43), was completed in 1881 and done in his "modern Gothic" mode. The placement, facade, and proportions of this Academy of Music parallel those of Sacred Heart Church and served to define further the beginning of a central quadrangle constructed on the two sides of what was then the terminus of Notre Dame Avenue.

Washington Hall, so named because the first president was Edward Sorin's greatest American political hero, was really two buildings. The main theatre component (III–42) was octagonal in shape. Its gallery, traditionally reserved for the student body in the nineteenth century, had a seating capacity of three hundred, while the main floor accomodated another four hundred. Sophocles'

Oedipus Tyrannus, performed entirely in Attic Greek, was the theatre's opening night offering in 1882; its stage was soon a forum for speakers such as Henry James, William Butler Yeats, and William Jennings Bryan. Beginning in 1916 the theatre became the locale for free, feature-length Saturday matinees and evening movies for students who could not afford downtown shows. Behind the theatre, but still part of the building, was the music hall which, in addition to housing performing rooms and classrooms, also contained the recreation and reading rooms of Brownson and Carroll Halls (the present band room), plus the dressing rooms of the bicycle club and the student athletic association.

Campus apocrypha has long maintained that Washington Hall's Gothic architecture is appropriately haunted. Doors are claimed to slam on windless nights, footsteps are heard on the roof. One legend claims the ghost is that of George Gipp (IV–31), famous Notre Dame All-American who supposedly once lived on the upper floors and slept on the steps of the hall the night be-

III–44

III–45. Science Hall, ca. 1890
John Zahm's testament to the role that science should play in Notre Dame's curriculum, this structure, built in 1883 with occasional neoclassical touches, housed various scientific departments

until it was converted, in 1953, with the assistance of Joseph La Fortune, '16, into the present La Fortune Student Center (43). A short-order restaurant, The Huddle, along with public lounges, is in the rear of the building and open to campus visitors.

III–46. John A. Zahm (1851–1921)
Priest, physical chemist, evolutionist, publicist, Chautauquan and lecturer, University vice-president, Holy Cross provincial, explorer, author, and American Catholic intellectual.

III–45

III–46

fore he became fatally ill in 1920; others insist the ghost is that of a steeplejack who fell to his death while working on the fly loft in 1886.

G *Walk down the quadrangle road to the front of La Fortune Student Center (43).*

Science at Notre Dame became the first academic discipline to occupy separate research and instructional quarters with the opening of Science Hall (III–45) in 1884. This structure, the only example of neoclassicism on campus other than the present Architecture Building (14), was also a monument to the academic orientation that John Zahm (III–46) envisioned for the University. Designed by Zahm in concert with Edbrooke of Chicago, the building contained classrooms (III–50 and 52), laboratories (III–49), and apparatus rooms (III–51) for the developing divisions of chemistry, botany, mathematics, physiology, geology, physics, and mechanical engineering.

Father John Zahm, assuredly one of the most brilliant minds Notre Dame ever had the opportunity to

III–47. Physics Class, 1897
Undergraduate science majors, along with their mentor John Zahm, posed in front of the double staircase formerly on the east wall of the present lobby of the student center. Among them is Julius Nieuwland (front row, third from the right, with hat and coat in hand).

III–47

nurture, had intellectual aspirations for the University that exceeded the less ambitious plans of Father Andrew Morrissey (III–2), University president from 1893 to 1906. Historians of this period in Notre Dame history rightly juxtapose the different objectives of these two men and see the last decade of the nineteenth century as a period when the University experienced an intensive, although largely internal, debate over its future direction. The principals in the debate could not have been more different: Zahm—German, aloof, intellectual, urbane, cosmopolitan, a theologically progressive scientist whose literary interests prompted him to amass one of the greatest Dante collections in the United States; Morrissey—Irish, talented, clever, gregarious, warmhearted, politically astute, a financial conservative whose own academic career had been thwarted when administrative responsibilities were thrust on him shortly after his ordination.

More than personalities collided, however, during the years when Morrissey was president and Zahm was provincial. The future identity of the University—a question first raised by Auguste Lemonnier and Thomas Walsh and later to be re-argued with increasing vigor and seriousness in the 1920s and 1960s —was at stake. Briefly summarized, Morrissey felt that Notre Dame had already achieved a solid reputation as a prep school and that it should not expand rapidly in physical plant, personnel, or academic programs; it simply could not, in Morrissey's estimate, "compete with all those schools so heavily endowed." Zahm, on the other hand, envisioned Notre Dame as potentially "the intellectual center of the American West"; an institution with large undergraduate, graduate, and professional schools equipped with laboratories, libraries, and research facilities; Notre Dame should strive to become the University that its charter claimed it was.

Walk up the stone steps to the front door of the La Fortune Student Center and enter the first floor lobby.

Although Zahm insisted on academic excellence in all the University's departments, he quite naturally encouraged development of his own specialty. Science Hall and the research conducted within it are ample testimony to his success. Here the expanding University museum (III–48), one of Zahm's pet projects, was housed in the two-storey center of the building (now the lobby of La Fortune); here future Notre Dame scientific pioneers (Fathers Alexander Kirsch, Francis Wenninger, and Julius Nieuwland) were trained; here Jerome J. Green (III–74), guided by the findings of Marconi and Decretet in Europe, was the first American to send a wireless message (from Science Hall to Hoynes Hall in 1895); here Albert Zahm (III–75), John's younger brother, designed the first successful helicopter, the first wind tunnel, and launched the first man-carrying glider from the building's roof.

In 1893 at the First International Aeronautics Congress, held in Chicago, Albert Zahm presented a paper, "Stability of Aeroplanes and Flying Machines," wherein he explained for the first time in America the method of launching an aircraft. Zahm conducted such experiments in the Science Hall throughout the 1880s. Late one evening his shop

III–48. Science Museum, ca. 1900
The lobby of the present student center formerly housed various geological, biological, and chemical collections. This view, taken facing the curator's office (now student activities), shows some of the wall displays, exhibit cases, and the mezzanine (now enclosed as the second floor).

III–49–50. Science Hall Classrooms
III–49, biology lab; III–50, electrical engineering class.

III–49   III–48

III–51

III–52

III–51–52. Science Hall Interiors
III–51, dynamo room in the basement;
III–52, botanists at work.

assistant tested part of their research on aerodynamics in a model glider that Zahm had built and had suspended by a fifty-foot cable from the ceiling of the museum. The technician left numerous shoeprints high on the walls of the museum where he put out his foot to save himself from crashing while rapidly banking around in the limited air space. When Brother Benedict, the Science Hall curator, found the scuff marks the next morning, he attributed their existence to a supernatural rather than a scientific cause and sprinkled the entire building with holy water to expurgate the Devil, who alone could walk on walls.

H *Exit the student center lobby by the front entrance, walk to the left along the quadrangle road, and face toward the front of Hoynes Hall (42).*

Engineering education at Notre Dame began as part of the science program and was originally taught in the basement of Science Hall. With the addition of civil engineering to the curriculum in 1873, Notre Dame became the first Catholic university in America to establish a

III–53. William J. "Colonel" Hoynes (1846–1933)

The self-promoted "Colonel" for whom Hoynes Hall was named and his student officers of Company A of the Hoynes Light Guards are seen before a Memorial Day dress parade in 1886. Hoynes, in addition to serving as faculty commander of this military unit, also achieved fame as a journalist, G. A. R. soldier, fastidious campus Beau Brummell, law dean, Republican politician, interminable pep-rally speaker, and eccentric bachelor-don who lived in Sorin Hall for forty-four years.

III–53

formal course of study in engineering. Later, mechanical (1886) and electrical (1891) engineering departments were created, and by 1889 John Zahm was pressing for another building to house these new areas of concentration. Zahm initially tried to buy the Machinery Hall at the Chicago 1893 World's Fair, intending to have it dismantled, transported to Notre Dame, and reassembled on campus. Although the idea failed, he was able to convince the University administration to build a new structure, now known as Hoynes Hall (42), to house what was first called the Institute of Technology (III–54).

A three-storey, 40' × 100', utilitarian brick building designed by Brother Charles Harding, the institute provided students (III–55) with several classrooms, two mechanical drawing rooms, a machine shop, a gymnasium, a vertical-engine room, a foundry, and a forge. The School of Engineering, largely under the direction of Professor Martin McCue, outgrew these facilities, and in 1905 it was moved to a new Engineering Hall (IV–53) which stood approximately on the site of the present

III–54. Institute of Technology, 1890

Originally Hoynes Hall was designed to house the expanding mechanical engineering department (III–55). In 1902 the chemistry and pharmacy departments took over the building, while the engineers moved to the newly built Engineering Hall (IV–53–54).

III–56. Hoynes Afire, 1916
A phosphorus fire broke out on the third floor of the hall on September 13, 1916. Although the blaze was extinguished, the chemical spread throughout the building. The dried phosphorus ignited a week later and the resulting fire, fed by a southwest wind, did $70,000 damage to the interior. Sparks from the exploding chemicals at one point even set St. Edward's Hall (45) afire.

III–57. Hoynes Rebuilt, 1918
With its third floor removed and its roof line and window treatment altered, the hall was used as a recreation center for military students during World War I. In 1919 it was dedicated as the Hoynes College of Law.

Dillon (20) and Alumni (23) Halls. This marked the beginning of Hoynes Hall's long history of versatile renovation: it housed every college in the University, except Business Administration, for some period during the next seventy years.

The chemistry and pharmacy departments, long the domain of Father Joseph Carrier, took over the building in 1902. Its interior was rearranged to accommodate three research labs, a chemical library, the University drugstore, a museum, and classrooms. In 1916 a dramatic chemical fire (III–56) gutted the hall, but the University and the Knights of Columbus Council raised funds to restore it (III–57). In 1919 it became the Hoynes College of Law in honor of William J. "the Colonel" Hoynes (III–53), the energetic military commander, flamboyant law dean, and professor of law for over fifty years.

The Law School, formerly housed in the Administration Building and then Sorin Hall, had the interior of Hoynes Hall redesigned to suit its expanding educational programs, adding a large moot

III–55. Mechanical Engineering Students, 1893
Undergraduate engineers, formerly taught in the basement of the science building and first occupants of Hoynes, posed here with their tools and examples of their work in one of a series of 125 photographs taken for the University's exhibit at the Columbian World's Fair held at Chicago in 1893.

III–56

III–57

III–58. Law Library, ca. 1924
Equipped with a mere five thousand volumes in 1914, the law library had no librarian until 1925, and its holdings increased slowly until a new building (37) was built in 1931.

III–58

courtroom on the first floor, a new law library (III–58), classrooms, and faculty offices. When the School of Law outgrew these facilities and moved to its present building (37) in 1930, the School of Architecture departed its crowded quarters on the fifth floor of the Administration Building (II–77) to take possession of Hoynes Hall. In 1963 the psychology department was added to the arts and letters curriculum, and it assumed (and redesigned) the offices and classrooms vacated by the architects, who had gone to the remodeled Lemonnier Library (IV–21). Psychology was shifted to Haggar Hall (61) in 1974, and by early 1976 Hoynes had a new occupant—the music department.

Turn around and observe the diversity of tree species in the University arboretum.

Hoynes Hall was one of the final nineteenth-century buildings deliberately placed to define the Main Quadrangle and enclose its arboretum. As is evident in early lithographs (II–1 and 89), formal gardens, sculptured foliage, and ornamental fountains were once a part of a park

III–59

III–60. Brother Philip Kunze (1844–1926)
In addition to teaching penmanship and German in the preparatory department, Brother Philip, custodian of the campus grounds for sixty-five years, endeavored to plant his arboretum with every tree indigenous to the U.S. that would grow in the northern Indiana climate.

III–61. University Arboretum, 1912
Looking directly south toward Notre Dame Avenue can be seen the central quadrangle flag stanchion as well as Brother Philip's famous yucca-plant collection, two hundred of which were exhibited at the St. Louis Exposition in 1903.

III–60

III–61

that was the terminus of Notre Dame Avenue. Brother Peter (I–63) and his surveying class laid out this attempt to transplant a bit of the French Renaissance tradition to northern Indiana in 1886, but it was Brother Philip Kunze, a Silesian, who planted the Main Quad's marvelous arboretum (III–59) with its fifty-tree species. Brother Philip (III–60), a talented calligrapher whose work in German and English script was widely published, also spent sixty years landscaping the Notre Dame campus. Many of the 306 species, identified in Peter E. Herbert's *Trees, Shrubs, and Vines on the Notre Dame Campus* (Notre Dame, 1966), survive as living monuments of European horticultural formality and romantic landscape design (III–61).

I *Walk directly across the Main Quadrangle on the path that leads to the front of Sorin Hall (26).*

Until the late 1880s most Notre Dame students slept in communal dormitories and studied in communal study halls. Occasional exceptions were made for senior students who occupied a few, select

III–62. Sorin Hall, 1893
Upperclassmen of Notre Dame's first
dormitory with private rooms purchase
local and hometown newspapers from a
vendor who visited the campus daily.

III–62

III–63–64. **Student Rooms, ca. 1893**
Victoriana prevailed in Sorin's student
quarters in the nineteenth century.

III–63

III–64

private rooms in the Administration Building. These students so distinguished themselves academically that John Zahm and President Walsh argued for a new residence hall composed entirely of private rooms. Although many faculty members and even more parents thought the idea excessively permissive, if not immoral, Walsh commissioned Edbrooke and Burnham of Chicago to submit plans for a "Collegiate Hall." On May 27, 1888, Father Sorin blessed the cornerstone as part of the student celebration of the fiftieth anniversary of his ordination. The hall, by popular accolade, was named for him.

Sorin Hall, done in Edbrooke's eclectic modern Gothic (one wag called it an "English Tudor sideboard turned upside down"), originally contained sixty private rooms (12' × 14'), supposedly "large enough to encourage study and at the same time small enough to discourage visiting." On the first floor was the chapel of St. Thomas Aquinas and the law department's lecture rooms, reading rooms, and library. The now famous "subway," partitioned into student quar-

III–65. Sorin Subway 'Rec' Room, 1912
Known as the "subway" because its
eighteen rooms were eight feet underground, the Sorin basement—long the
residence of student athletes—had a
recreation room where students such as
Knute Rockne (front right) spent
free hours.

ters in 1924 and so named because
all of its rooms were at least eight
feet underground, was first a trunk
room. A later addition (1897) expanded Sorin to its present size. "A
desk, chairs, a book case, a bed and
other necessary articles are provided
by the college," noted *The Scholastic* in 1890, and "the rest of the
garnishing of the room is left to the
taste of the student. Some of the
men in Sorin Hall go in for aesthetic
embellishments. *Chacun a son
metiér.* Here you find the baseball
gloves quartered, as it were, with a
physiological chart and a microscope
nestling among back numbers of
Scientific American, all shaded by
Turcoman curtains sent by some
loving mamma."

A comparison of Sorin Hall's furnishings (III–63–64) with those of
more recent Notre Dame halls and
their residents (VI–43–44) offers insight into the changing American
social history of the past century.
The Hall's contemporary plaudit—
being the first Catholic college dormitory in the United States with
individual rooms—likewise suggests
the building was an important symbol in the University's historical de-

III–65

III–66. Law Classroom, 1893
Colonel Hoynes held his contracts class
on the first floor of Sorin Hall until 1917.
Hoynes's own rooms and offices, as well
as the diminutive law library, were also
located on the hall's first floor.

III–67. Byron V. Kanaley

III–68. Jubilee Mandolin Orchestra

III–66

III–67

velopment. Two years after its completion, English professor Maurice Francis Egan (III–73) wrote an evaluation of Notre Dame's social experiment entitled "A New Departure in Catholic College Discipline" (*The Catholic World*, February, 1890). Egan argued that if Catholic colleges were to become genuine undergraduate colleges instead of mere prep schools, they would have to abandon antiquated residential requirements for their collegians. Egan, however, saw no necessity for any relaxation of discipline: "The rules of order and cleanliness are not more stringent or more scrupulously enforced at West Point than in Sorin Hall." No visiting in the rooms was allowed; lights went out at a fixed hour; noise, liquor, and women were strictly prohibited. In Egan's words (and in the University's estimation), "a college ought to stand *in loco parentis*. If it seeks to divest itself of all responsibility for the morals of its students, it fulfills the lesser part of its mission." Professor Egan also saw Sorin Hall as an architectural embodiment of Notre Dame's entrance into "successful competition for students with the growing number of nonsectarian colleges throughout the nation." The hall was reserved for upperclassmen, admission to it limited to students of high academic standing.

Legend and lore about Sorin Hall —as with all of the other nineteen residence halls subsequently erected —continues to be a large part of Notre Dame history. In Sorin, William Hoynes held forth as a professor of law for over forty years. Hoynes was but one of the numerous bachelor-dons (others include Professors Edward Maurus, Paul Fenlon, Charles Phillips, and Paul Byrne) who have had their rooms in this hall. Hoynes is also indirectly responsible for Sorin's front porch. Making his exit one evening attired in his usual sartorial plummage, "the Colonel" was unexpectedly doused with gallons of ice water by a student prankster at a third floor window. Construction of the present porch followed shortly after this incident. Later, Rector John "Pops" Farley distributed student mail from this porch three times daily with constant badinage about the correspondence's potentially amorous

III–69. **Edward E. Bereman**

III–70. **Warren A. Cartier**

III–71. **L. C. M. Reed**

III–72. **Raymond G. Malley**

III–69

III–70

III–71

III–72

contents. In a room on the first floor, one of the most famous of all school songs, "The Notre Dame Victory March," was written by two students, Michael and John Shea, in 1906. From another room, ever open for student visitation, Father John O'Hara, prefect of religion and later University president, founded and wrote *The Religious Bulletin* and counseled students about their spiritual lives.

In one sense Sorin Hall's original facilities were soon overshadowed by the construction of Walsh Hall (25), where no expense ($100,000) was spared to implement and advertise the private-room dormitory concept. Notre Dame's only hall with built-in closets, originally designed suites, and its own basement bowling alley, Walsh's rooms and corridors were also first decorated with an expensive burlap wall-covering. The luxurious wall-covering unfortunately became infested with bedbugs shortly after installation. Burlap and pests removed, Walsh was claimed to be the campus "gold coast" by its residents until students in Howard-Morrissey-Lyons argued for similar recognition.

J *Turn left and walk south on the quadrangle road past Walsh Hall (25) and to the front of the Sorin statue (98).*

Walsh Hall, named in honor of President Thomas Walsh, is appropriately adjacent to Sorin Hall and also faces the Sorin monument (98) in the center of the Main Quadrangle. Both men, Sorin the patriarchal founder and Walsh his energetic protégé, died within three months of each other in 1893. The memorial to Edward Sorin was the idea of John Zahm, another Sorin disciple who, in 1905, wrote to alumni and friends soliciting contributions for a monument to the priest who literally made Notre Dame. The bronze statue sculptured by Ernesto Biondi was unveiled the following year.

Other historical markers were added to the campus in 1906. A replica of Badin's original Log Chapel (I–22) was constructed, and Badin's last wish to Sorin, that he be buried at the University, was fulfilled when his remains were transferred from Cincinnati to the reconstructed Log Chapel. The Founders' Monument (I–1), placed in 1906, is adjacent to Badin's chapel.

III–73. Maurice Francis Egan, Professor and Holder of the first "Chair of Literature"

III–74. Jerome Green, Professor of Electrical Engineering

III–75. Albert Zahm, Professor of Mathematics and Aeronautical Researcher

III–73

III–74

III–75

III–76. William H. Taft and University President John W. Cavanaugh

III–76

III–77

III–78. Sorin and His Faculty
Assembled lay and religious faculty of
the University, 1876.

III–79–82. **Edward Sorin, 1814–1893**
The University's first president through
the decades and a variety of hirsute styles:
III–79, ca. 1865; III–80, 1872; III–81,
1881; III–82, 1892.

III–79

III–80

The year 1906 also marked the first full year of the John W. Cavanaugh (III–76) presidency, a tenure (1905–19) wherein Notre Dame slowly began changing from a prep-school-and-a-college with eight hundred students (III–67–72) to a college-and-prep-school with sixteen hundred students. By Cavanaugh's ascendency to the presidency, departments in journalism and political economy had been added to the expanding curriculum. The University had also celebrated its fiftieth year anniversary, self-advertised as "an epoch in the history of educational work in the West." Despite this hyperbole and despite its momentary identity crisis as to its future direction, the University did aspire to a new maturity. Notre Dame, under John W. Cavanaugh and the faculty (III–73–75) he recruited, decided to take the beginning steps toward achieving university status in fact as well as in name.

No one would have applauded the new aspirations more than Edward Sorin. His statue (III–83) was fittingly placed at the heart of the campus he had envisioned, designed, and built. Zahm deliberately had his figure facing outwards so that, in Zahm's words, "the majestic form and features of the venerable founder will thus be the first to meet and welcome students and alumni returning to their alma mater and to all who visit Notre Dame." The position of Sorin's statue, his campus behind him and the larger world in front, was also indicative of what manner of man he was—outgoing, future-oriented, enterprising, always anxious not only to be *in* the center of things but to *be* the center of them.

Sorin, of course, was more than a weathered bronze statue, the name of a campus residence hall, or a street in South Bend. He was more than the memorial's Latin inscription (see III–83) said of him. Sorin (III–79–82) was a man, a priest, a character of amazing contradictions and delightful extremes. In business transactions he could exhibit all the traits the French have in mind by the term *sangfroid*. Bishops and even his own religious superior knew his wrath and, on occasion, his defiant disobedience. Shrewd, opinionated, adventuresome, by 1893 he had parlayed the 524 acres,

$300, and a line of limited credit that Bishop Hailandière had given him in 1842 into an extensive portfolio of landholdings and investments so complex that it took eighteen years finally to settle his estate.

Yet there was another Sorin. A man of almost childlike religious faith, he loved children, especially the minims of St. Edward's (his "little princes"), with the extravagance of a doting grandfather. To these youngsters he could be suprisingly tender; he was not above lugging a bushel of fresh peaches to their study hall, shooting marbles with them in their dirt play yard, or sending them a new velocipede while on one of his expeditions to Paris. Savior faire with adults was also a Sorin forte. He could charm a faculty member into staying on another year despite a proffered meager salary, play social lion to the South Bend gentry with private dinner parties *à la Parisien*, and keep good press relations with an annual New Year's Day gift to the local newspaper's staffs: "a huge pyramidal cake, flanked by bottles of Bordeaux of the vintage '75 and California wines of 1878 and a good flagon of Chartreuse."

III–81

III–82

Notre Dame has usually had a rather good press but never another presence quite like Sorin. He was part confidence man, part visionary, part paterfamilias. A man of salt and savvy, of great heart and great hope, Sorin's influence dominated Notre Dame even after his death when, as one religious periodical eulogized, "the Western Church lost its 'grand old man.'" Like his statue, Sorin has become larger than life in Notre Dame history, but the excess is not without its truth. John W. Cavanaugh, another Sorin man who would personally perpetuate many of the founder's traits (dictatorial governance, personal charm, visionary leadership), characterized Sorin's legacy in his florid but accurate peroration at the Sorin memorial's unveiling: "Threescore years and more have passed since a young missionary first looked in hope and affection on the wilderness where now blooms this beautiful garden. . . . Rich only in the zeal of his soul, strong only in the courage of his heart, he labored on, til today the work he directed is the pride of America and the glory of the Church. . . . Notre Dame is Father Sorin's monument."

III–83

III–83. Edward Sorin Memorial
Erected in 1906, the monument's translated Latin inscription reads:

For God, the Greatest, the Best In memory of Edward Sorin, superior general of the Congregation of Holy Cross, founder of the University of Notre Dame, who was renowned for his apostolic virtue and devoted to American Catholic education. Born February 8, 1814, he lived

for 78 years. As a token of their respect and gratitude, students, alumni, and friends erect this monument.

May his soul find salvation, 1905

III–84. Notre Dame, ca. 1912
This view from atop the Administration Building shows the perimeters of the South Quad: left, Science Hall and Hoynes Hall; right, Sorin Hall and Walsh Hall. In the background can be seen the fields

of the University farms, an unpaved Notre Dame Avenue, and to the far left, the farm buildings along Dorr Road, then also known as St. Joseph's Avenue.

III–84

IV. The University in 1920

IV–1. Notre Dame, ca. 1912–16. This engraved drawing executed by Darnel and Beckman of Philadelphia shows some of the projected (but never built) structures planned for the front of the campus. Walsh Hall replaced the projected engineering shops (lower left), and the Hurley School of Commerce was built on the site of the proposed Lemonnier Library (lower right).

Beginning at the Sorin statue (98) in the middle of the main Quadrangle, Walk IV explores pre– and post–World War I Notre Dame. A walk of 700 yards, it reviews—while moving along the perimeter of the west wing of the South Quad—the curricular, administrative, and financial changes effected during President James Burns's tenure, 1919–22. It also explores the increase in residence halls and academic facilities, notes Notre Dame's national football fame (symbolized by the Rockne Memorial of the 1920s), and visually reconstructs the University farms of the early twentieth century. Continuing up the quadrangle past the South Dining Hall and the site of the former Engineering Hall, the walk ends at "the circle" in the front of the campus.

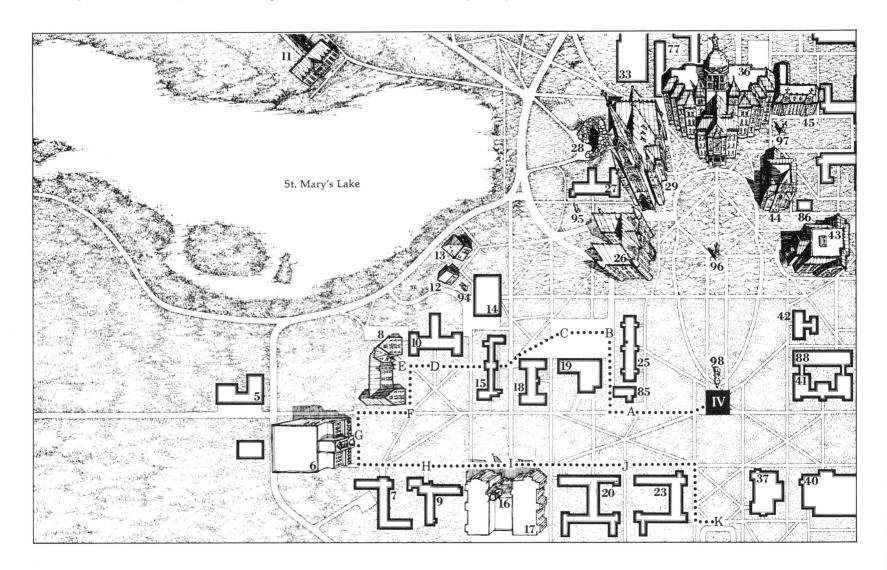

Burns's Innovations, Kervick's Plan, Rockne's Teams

HISTORIANS USUALLY portray the years immediately preceding and following America's involvement in World War I as a critical watershed in the national history. Within the brief span of a few years, crucial changes occurred in the political, economic, social, and intellectual life of the United States. Similarly, the University of Notre Dame underwent a transformation during the years 1917–20. Changes occurred or were set in motion that had important ramifications for the institution's twentieth-century history.

Changes took place at Notre Dame in presidential governance, in the traditional relationship between the University and the Holy Cross community which controlled it, and in the involvement of laymen in new positions of authority and influence. Changes were also evident in the school's spectacular physical and demographic growth such that, from

Notre Dame in 1920

Acreage: 1,550 Tuition: $170
Faculty: 67   Buildings: 28
Students: 1,207 Room/board: $404

1919 to 1933, fifteen major building projects transformed the campus, and the size of the student body and faculty nearly tripled. During this period, the institution engaged in its first nationwide campaign for endowment funds and organized its alumni for an annual contribution program. Furthermore, major changes took place in academic organization. Elementary and preparatory programs were phased out, and an increased emphasis was given to college-level instruction and the development of graduate studies. Football evolved from a Saturday-afternoon diversion, played before an average Cartier Field crowd (V–18–20) of six thousand, to a national mania witnessed by an average of fifty thousand fans a game.

In 1920 the recently inaugurated president James Burns appointed a Board of Associate Lay Trustees whose principal duty was to raise a million-dollar endowment. In the fall of 1920 Knute Rockne's "Rockmen" won the unofficial Western Football Championship a second time with the stellar playing of All-American George Gipp. That year also marked the publication of Professor Francis

W. Kervick's comprehensive plan for future campus development. Kervick's projection of an appropriate campus architectural style and land use influenced the physical development of Notre Dame for the next thirty-five years.

University expansion came in the wake of World War I but not before Notre Dame also played its role in the war effort. The 1917 Selective Service Act, as amended, required all men (aged eighteen to forty-five) to register for the draft. This legislation, when coupled with the enlistments concomitant with the declaration of war, caused colleges —especially all-male institutions— considerable financial difficulties due to decreased enrollments and consequent tuition losses. Congress, however, authorized the Students' Army Training Corps (SATC), which enabled students to receive their military training while still attending college. In this program, men of freshman status or higher volunteered for induction into the army (see IV–4). If accepted, they continued their undergraduate studies at the expense of the government while learning military science, tactics, and

drill (IV–5). Every three months the student soldiers were evaluated and, if found inadequate as potential officers, mustered immediately into the regular army as privates.

As in the Civil War (I–45), Notre Dame responded to the national mobilization by sending eight priests into the armed services as chaplains. The University was also awarded a government contract for an SATC enrolling over seven-hundred students in September 1918. Heartley "Hunk" Anderson, '18, described a typical day in the life of Notre Dame recruits: "We got up at 5:50 A.M., drilled until 7:00 A.M., after which we went to the mess hall [formerly the old main gym, III–34] to eat. After that we went to class. At 3:00 P.M. we went back to the drill field except on those days when Rockne got us excused for football practice. We wore Army uniforms to class." The SATC's brief tenure (September 1918 to the November armistice) brought the assurance of enrollment, government subsidies, and federal rental of University facilities. Nonetheless, faculty carped at students leaving classes for drills, formations, and work details; civilian students

IV–2

IV–3

IV–2–3. Notre Dame, 1914
These two panoramic views taken by
Spencer of Battle Creek, Michigan, show
the Main Quadrangle (IV–2) when it was
the main terminus of Notre Dame Avenue

and the assembled faculty (IV–3): (l. to r.)
W. Maloney, J. Tiernan, J. Ryan,
F. Verhusen, E. Burke, W. Benitz,
W. Bolger, J. Maguire, J. Drury, P. Hebert,
M. Quinlan, Col. Campbell, C. Doremus,
W. Lavin, R. Green, J. Worden, J. Burke,
M. Walsh, J. Cavanaugh, M. Schumacher,
Bro. Philip Neri, L. Carrico, R. Kaczmarek,
J. Caparo, P. Hagerty, W. McInerney,
F. Ackerman, E. Maurus, W. Hoynes,
J. Hines, F. Kervick, J. Plante, J. Cooney,

T. Crumley, J. Nieuwland, Capt. Stogsdall,
E. Davis, G. Farabaugh, J. Quinlan,
E. Burns, J. McGinn, F. Derrick,
J. O'Donnell, Bro. Cyprian, C. Hagerty,
M. McCue, J. Riddle, T. Burke,
C. O'Donnell, and E. Eggers.

IV–4. Notre Dame SATC, 1918
Seven hundred students pledge allegiance and are inducted (October 1) into the U.S. Army on the upperclassmen's (Brownson) campus behind the science building (43) that lacks its 1924 rear addition.

IV–5. Target Practice, 1918
SATC students prepare for European trench warfare on a rifle range constructed in front of the Old College (13).

IV–4

IV–5

thought the new recruits disrespectful of campus customs and discipline; administrators, particularly President Cavanaugh, who periodically clashed with the unit's commanding officer over academic priorities, worried about the conversion of a place of learning into a military barrack. Tensions were further exacerbated when the Spanish influenza epidemic struck the campus in October–November 1918, killing one sister-nurse, nine students, and hospitalizing over two hundred others.

The SATC only temporarily disrupted Notre Dame's traditional academic routine. James Burns (IV–6), however, elected president in 1919, permanently altered the University through his reorganization of its management structure, finances, curricula, and his raising of its educational standards. Thomas McAvoy, Notre Dame archivist and historian, called Burn's drastic innovations nothing less than "a major revolution in the academic development of the institution."

James Burns was the first president to earn a doctorate, first president to be elected to the office while not actively engaged at the University (he had been superior at Holy Cross College, Washington, D.C., from 1900 to 1919), and the first president to be professionally trained away from Notre Dame (at Cornell and Catholic University). A national leader of the Catholic Education Association, Burns authored three histories of American Catholic education. Along with his assistant and confidant, Father Matthew Schumacher (IV–7), Burns valued scholarly research and academic excellence. Both men wanted to push Notre Dame in these directions as expeditiously as possible.

The Burns-Schumacher innovations can be catalogued under three general categories: 1) improving academic standards (recruiting faculty with doctorates, upgrading of the Law School, and standardizing college entrance and graduation requirements); 2) revamping the administrative structure (establishing an academic council with authority "to pass on all major academic matters and to make policies and regulations," appointing individual deans to govern the newly created colleges of arts and letters, science, engineer-

IV–6–7. The Innovators
Photo IV–6 shows James Burns (1867–1940), ninth University president and oldest priest (fifty-two) ever elected to the office. A chemist, then religious superior, Burns greatly changed Notre Dame with the assistance of Matthew Schumacher (1879–1966) (IV–7), professor of philosophy-theology, director of studies, 1907–19, and then president of St. Edward's College (Austin, Texas) and St. Thomas College (St. Paul, Minnesota).

ing, law, and commerce, and appointing individual chairmen to set academic policy in specific departments); and 3) strengthening financial support (creating a twelve-man Board of Associate Lay Trustees, securing outside endowment support from the General Education Board of the Rockefeller Foundation ($250,-000) and the Carnegie Foundation ($75,000), and overseeing the University's first major fund-raising drive among alumni and friends).

A *Walk to the right along the path leading west down the South Quadrangle to the front of the Knights of Columbus building (85).*

Burns's brief but brilliant administration is rightly remembered for academic expansion rather than physical development. Yet the financial resources that Burns amassed during the early 1920s enabled his successors—Fathers Matthew Walsh, Charles O'Donnell, and John O'Hara—to expand the campus with new structures such as the Gothic post office (now the Knights of Columbus building [85]), built in 1934. To a rural, isolated residential college such as Notre Dame, mail service was

IV–6

IV–7

IV–8–9. University Post Offices
Located to the right (east) of the Sorin statue (98), this first post office (IV–8) was built in 1856, and the second (IV–9) was constructed in 1914. The second structure was converted into a library and moved to the back of Chemistry Hall (V–27; 53) in 1934. The third post office (present Knights of Columbus chambers) (85) served the University until 1967, when a still larger substation (24) was built along Notre Dame Avenue.

IV–8

IV–9

practically as important as meal service. Edward Sorin knew this, as well as the fact that the establishment of a U.S. postal station at Notre Dame would put his campus on all official government maps. As early as 1851 Sorin petitioned for an appointment as postmaster of Notre Dame du Lac, a position he secured later that year through the intercession of Senator Henry Clay. A post office, varying in size and architectural idiom (IV–8–9), has subsequently been located at the front of the campus for over 125 years.

B *Walk down the South Quadrangle to the intersecting path that runs between the Knights of Columbus building and the Hammes Bookstore (19); turn right and walk to the first basketball court behind the bookstore.*

Although Sorin held the office of Notre Dame postmaster, most of the actual work was done by the Holy Cross brothers and the apprentices in the University's Manual Labor School (IV–10). The Manual Labor School, another campus institution created by Sorin in 1843 and chartered by the state of Indiana in 1844,

was a vocational school initially established for orphaned youngsters entrusted to Sorin's care. The trade school was soon open to any boy aged twelve to twenty-one. Although the Manual Labor School remained a separate and distinct organization from the college (the apprentices had their own campus, teachers, masters, prefects, and shops), Sorin always viewed the vocational school as another integral aspect of his imperial plans to make Notre Dame a center for all types of Catholic education.

During its more than sixty years of existence, the Manual Labor School occupied three different campus sites and was known by several different names. The first shops and dormitory (1848) were located at the rear of the present Administration Building (36), approximately on the site of Brownson Hall (34). Destroyed by fire in 1849, this complex (IV–11) was rebuilt (1850) at what was then the front entrance to the campus on the west side of Notre Dame Avenue, approximately where Walsh Hall (25) is now located (see I–53). Expanded in the 1860s, the main structure

IV–10. Manual Labor School Campus, ca. 1898
This engraving insert by E. A. Wright of Philadelphia shows at the left, the Manual Labor School; behind it, the farm buildings; and to its right, a projected Walsh Hall and a porter's lodge. On the other side of Dorr Road was the Engineering Hall, which also housed the apprentices' shops.

IV–11. Manual Labor School, 1844–65
The earliest extant engraving locates the apprentice's quarters, complete with its adjoining recreational area, on the west side of Notre Dame Avenue. In 1865 this building was moved some ten yards, remodeled, and expanded into the structure shown in IV–12.

IV–12. St. Joseph's Industrial School, 1886–97
Moved westward from the front of the main campus to the farmyard complex (see I–41), the school was also given a more pretentious title. This three-storey, cream-colored, clapboard building (120' × 40') was located parallel to the present Corby Hall (27), shown at the extreme right.

IV–10

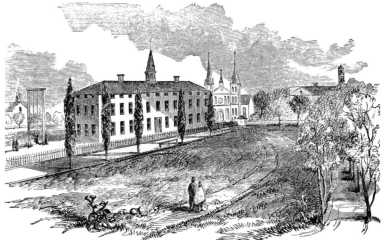

IV–11

IV–12

IV–13. Prospectus, 1872

IV–14–15. "Badin Bog"
A view (IV–14) from Sacred Heart Church steeple depicts activity on the south end of the "bog" in 1914, whereas IV–15 shows the famous 1915 Herricks-Rockne marble championship in progress in front of Corby Hall (27). Figure IV–15 also illustrates the Sorin bathhouse and privy (the one-storey structure with the wood tower between the hall's two rear, or west, wings) that students used until indoor plumbing was installed in 1923.

IV–13

MANUAL LABOR SCHOOL,
NOTRE DAME, INDIANA.

I.--ITS OBJECT.

THE Manual Labor School at Notre Dame, Indiana. is established with a view to afford boys of moderate means and sound morals an opportunity to learn some useful trade, and to acquire the elements of an English education, together with a knowledge of their moral and religious duties, and to protect them from the contagion of the world at a period in their lives the most difficult to preserve faith and morals; under all circumstances they are expected to behave themselves as youths fearing God, to lead pure and innocent lives, and to show at all times a deep reverence for everything connected with religion. They work from nine to ten hours a day, during which time they are required to use diligence; in order that the end for which they come to the Manual Labor School may be accomplished by them.

Boys once admitted are expected to remain until they are twenty-one years of age, unless a dismissal becomes absolutely necessary. They go to school for three months in the winter, during which time they are free from all other occupation, except the ordinary work to be done about the house; they end the classes for which they are fit in the University. They should endeavor to appreciate and profit by the advantages offered them to lay the foundation of a useful and honorable career.

The School is dedicated to St. Joseph, the glorious patron of Christian laborers; the inmates, therefore, should honor him with great fidelity. Hence it will be readily perceived that this School must be one of Morality, Piety and Industry.

II.--ITS MEANS.

In order to carry out the preceding principles, the following trades are established under the direction of competent and experienced masters, viz.: Boot and Shoe Making, Tailoring, Carpentering, Blacksmithing, Masoning, Printing, and also Agriculture.

III.--ITS REQUIREMENTS.

Boys for the Shoe Shop must not be under twelve nor over fourteen years of age, and for the Tailor Shop the same; for the trades of Carpenter, Blacksmith and Mason, boys must not be under fifteen nor over sixteen years of age; for Printing it depends on their smartness.

With regard to those who are to be admitted to the Manual Labor School; each boy is required to give satisfactory testimonials relative to sound morals and capacity to learn the trade which is specified in his letter of proposal; to bring the Certificate of his Baptism; to pay a fee of one hundred dollars ($100); and furnish good and sufficient clothing for one year.

ORDER OF THE DAY.

Rising, 5:30, A. M.; Breakfast, 6; Work, 6:30; Recreation, 11:30; Dinner, 12; Work, 1, P. M.; Recreation, 6; Supper, 6:30, followed by Recreation; at 8, Recitation of the Beads and Night Prayer; then all retire to rest; all must be in bed before nine o'clock, and silence must be observed until after Breakfast next morning.

SUNDAYS AND HOLIDAYS.—Rising, 5:30, A. M.; Study of Catechism, 6; Breakfast, 7; Recreation; Catechism, 8:30; Inspection, 9:30; Mass, 10.

W. CORBY, S.S.C.

IV–14

IV–15

(IV–12) was moved on wheels in 1886 to a site where the intramural basketball courts behind the bookstore are now located. Here it stood until 1897 when it was replaced by a brick building (IV–16), first called St. Joseph's Industrial School and then, in 1903, St. Joseph's Hall (IV–17). In 1917, with the addition of two wings, its name was changed to Badin Hall (IV–18).

Apprentices who lived, worked, and learned in these buildings were required to pay an entrance fee, have sufficient clothes for two years, and sign an indenture binding them to remain in the institution until they were twenty-one. They wore a uniform ("satinet of gray color for the coat and black for their pantaloons") and worked at any number of trades: printing, blacksmithing, carpentering, cabinetmaking, bricklaying, tailoring, shoemaking, and farming. As its 1872 prospectus (IV–13) indicates, the apprentices also had opportunities for a common-school education. After an eight-hour day in the shops, the students attended evening classes where, as early as 1845, they were taught "Writing, Linear Drawing, Bookkeeping, Purity of Language, Public Reading, Music, French, Reading, Spelling and Arithmetic."

St. Joseph's Industrial School and its shops manufactured the diverse goods (shoes, tools, furniture, and clothing) that were used by the personnel at Notre Dame and its numerous nineteenth-century satellite institutions. Besides adding to the University's self-sufficiency, for a brief time the apprentice shops even brought in a limited revenue when salable items were marketed in local South Bend stores. The school's boom years were the early 1860s, when sixty-two apprentices worked at eight trades. By the 1870s the program was no longer economically feasible. Until 1917, however, the University continued to operate the trade school in order to provide vocational training for poor young men. This was fortunate, since several of its students—Joseph Lyons, John Zahm, and James Burns—went on to distinguished academic careers at Notre Dame.

C *Walk to the center of the intramural courts and face the Architecture Building (14).*

IV–16–17. St. Joseph's Industrial School and St. Joseph's Hall, 1898 and 1917
Designed and built by Brother Columkille, this central portion (IV–16) of present Badin Hall (18) first housed the apprentices and some of their shops. In 1917 it was converted to a residence known as Badin Hall (IV–17).

IV–18. Badin Hall, ca. 1937
The first separate residence solely for freshmen, this dormitory, along with Walsh Hall, was the first residence hall for undergraduate women in 1970.

IV–16

IV–17

IV–18

IV–19

IV–19. Badin Bookstore
Initially housed in a crowded room to the left of the student offices (II–48) in the Administration Building, the bookstore was later moved to Badin's first floor where it sold Notre Dame souvenirs as well as texts.

IV–20. "Badin Caf," 1920
The University leased space for a basement cafeteria in Badin, first to an outside food chain and then, in 1920, to O. A. Clark, a South Bend restaurateur. Until 1927 when the South Dining Hall was opened, all students had the option of paying $350 a year for food in the Administration Building's refectories (II–42–43) or buying their meals individually in the cafeteria.

IV–20

IV–21. Lemonnier Library, 1920
Designed by Edward Tilton, a New York architect who researched numerous American library facilities in order to prepare his drawings, the structure was placed on the site of the first Notre Dame farm complex (I–34) that had been moved in 1900 to the southeast corner of the present South Quadrangle (see IV–38–39).

IV–22. Library Interior, 1920
In addition to two main reading rooms, the library also housed a School of Library Science, Zahm's famous Dante Collection, the Wightman Art Gallery, the Catholic Manuscripts Collection, and the Medieval Institute.

Apprentices had their own recreation area (IV–14–15), a dirt field with poor drainage, on the site now occupied by the present bookstore and the intramural basketball courts and later called the "Badin bog." Over the years the "bog" was used for tennis courts, a makeshift golf course, and various pickup athletic events by the vocational students and collegians. At one time the University attempted to create another lawn quadrangle, which would have eliminated the "bog." Campus gardeners plowed and seeded the area. Students, in subtle protest, surreptitiously planted it with beans and corn. When the students' crop blossomed, the University gave up its lawn idea, plowed everything under, and returned the "bog" to the students.

The "bog" took its name from its proximity to Badin Hall (18). In 1917, when the Manual Labor School (known then as St. Joseph's Industrial School) was phased out, President John W. Cavanaugh fortuitously received a $10,000 gift from a benefactor to expand Notre Dame. The University raised another $10,000, two wings were added to the former apprentices' building (IV–18), and its name was changed to Badin Hall. With an increasing student population, additional dining-hall facilities were required, and a 200-person public cafeteria (IV–20) was installed in the first floor of Badin that same year. It, along with the refectories in the Administration Building (II–42), served the University community until the new South Dining Hall (IV–50–52) was built in 1927. Badin's first floor has housed the University bookstore (IV–19), the C.S.C. community's recreation commons, and various campus services such as the barbershop, travel bureau, and laundry pickup.

In the same year that Badin's two wings were added, the University celebrated its seventy-fifth anniversary with the dedication of the Lemonnier Library (IV–21–22) which now houses the architecture department. The library building, a two-storey, neoclassical edifice of Indiana limestone, was purposely situated in its present location for two slightly contradictory reasons. Placed away from other buildings to the west in order to make it less

IV–21

IV–22

susceptible in case of fire, it was also designed to be the focal point of a new interior quadrangle (for which the "Badin bog" had been futilely landscaped). This quad was to be enclosed by (moving clockwise) a new dormitory (never constructed) overlooking St. Mary's Lake, Corby Hall (27), Sorin (26) and Walsh (25) Halls (both of which would have front entrances added to their western elevations), another new dormitory on the site of the present bookstore, and Badin Hall. Such a formal quadrangle was never built, but the Lemonnier Library (see IV–22) served the University until the Memorial Library (72), the only other stone building on the campus, was opened in 1963.

D *Walk through the archway of Howard Hall (15) to the front entrance of Morrissey Hall (10) and take note of the architectural detail on these Gothic buildings.*

Despite newly converted facilities such as Badin Hall, Notre Dame in the early 1920s continued to face a serious housing shortage. Maintaining a residential campus had always been a University objective. Halls were an essential part of Notre Dame life. They were miniature parishes, each with a chapel, several resident pastors, and a daily schedule of religious services. They were cloisters, providing the quiet atmosphere for the three-hour mandatory evening study period. They were training camps, fielding teams for an extensive intramural athletic program.

By 1919, given the influx of students in the post–World War I college boom, 250 students were forced to live in South Bend; by 1921 that number grew to over 600. The increasing off-campus population distressed University officials, especially Father Matthew Walsh, who, when he assumed the presidency, vowed to "bring the boys back on the campus." President Walsh felt that off-campus living weakened student "spirit," hindered religious training, accentuated disciplinary problems, and encouraged class absenteeism. In 1921 campus students had an 11-percent failure rate, but the figure for off-campus residents was 17 percent. On many college campuses the fraternity movement helped solve the student dormitory crisis, but such organizations were soundly rejected in Notre Dame's discussions of its housing difficulties. In 1924 President Walsh even dismissed the suggestion that the University seek a chapter of Phi Beta Kappa on the grounds that "our policy is not open, even in a remote manner, to any form of fraternity."

Walsh solved the dormitory shortage by commissioning the constsruction of new buildings. During his administration (1922–28), two temporary residences (Freshman and Sophomore Halls, see V–39–40) and three permanent dormitories (Howard, Morrissey [IV–23], and Lyons Halls) were constructed. Several of these projects had already been discussed or authorized during the Cavanaugh and Burns administrations, but it was Walsh's term that coincided with the events (an endowment campaign, postwar enrollment increases, and football income) that greatly facilitated the physical expansion of the University. Francis Kervick (IV–26) and Vincent Fagan (IV–27) of the School of Architecture designed the present enclave formed by the three halls named for Timothy E. Howard (dean emeritus of the Law School, chief justice of the Indiana Supreme Court, Laetare medalist), Andrew Morrissey (University president, 1893–1905), and Joseph A. Lyons (professor of English, 1847–88, and author of the University's first published history).

E *Walk to the Lyons archway for a view of St. Mary's Lake and Vincent Fagan's waterspout (IV–24) at the bottom of the archway stairs.*

The Kervick-Fagan group remains an impressive testament to their sensitivity to human scale and their attention to individual details. Fagan's masonry carvings (IV–24–25) delight the eye and stimulate the imagination. Kervick's Lyons-Hall arch frames St. Mary's Lake, providing a delightful vista as well as a picturesque entrance to the hall. The arch was so sited that from several vantage points on the western half of the South Quadrangle (for example, from the front entrance steps of the South Dining Hall, IV–50) a walker, while surrounded by buildings, could still have a view of the lake.

The arch was but one of the ways

IV–23

IV–23. Morrissey Hall Facade, 1930
Designed by Francis Kervick, the Morrissey tower entrance has all the elements of the Gothic form: skeletal quality, additive asymmetry, and stunning vertical proportions.

IV–24

IV–25

IV–24–25. Fagan's Ornamentation
Beginning with the simpler forms that he first executed for Howard Hall, Vincent Fagan elaborated his penchant for decorative details in every other campus building he helped design throughout the 1920s and 1930s.

IV-26-27. Notre Dame Architects
Figures IV-26 and IV-27 show Francis
Kervick (1883-1962) and Vincent Fagan
(1898-1951) respectively. Both taught in
the School of Architecture for over thirty
years. Kervick, a bachelor-don, generous to
a fault, directed the architecture school
from 1914 to 1950 and wrote its first history, *Architecture at Notre Dame* (1938).

Fagan—raconteur, wit, radio personality,
doggerel poet—collaborated with his
brother-in-law, Joseph Cassasanta, to
write two of the school's fight songs,
"Hike, Notre Dame" and *"Down the Line."*

IV-26

IV-27

by which Kervick sought to harmo-
nize the academic classicism of
Sorin's original campus, Kervick's
own English quadrangle system, and
the landscape potential of St. Mary's
Lake. Implementation of Kervick's
plan for the campus's development
would have allowed a walker to
journey from a symmetrical quadrangle (the South Quad) into an
English collegiate courtyard (the
Howard-Morrissey-Lyons group)
and then, by way of the carefully
placed archway, into a formal public space (see IV-29 for the location
of a classical open-air theatre that
Kervick proposed to place behind
Lyons Hall). An arboretum patterned after a model nineteenth-
century English park would have
surrounded the amphitheatre. The
leisurely informality of the lake,
with its patches of forest and mean-
dering paths, would have climaxed
a walk that began in the controlled
formality of a structured quadrangle.

F *Walk to the intersection of the
South Quad path and face toward
the center of the quadrangle.*

Francis Kervick's completion of

the Howard-Morrissey-Lyons residential group was the first tangible
result of his detailed campus plan
(IV-28-29). President Cavanaugh
had commissioned Kervick to draw
up a plan for the future development of the campus. In April 1920
Kervick submitted his sketches to
then President Burns with an accompanying letter explaining the
plan's rationale and objectives. Kervick's basic idea was to stop building along Notre Dame Avenue and
locate future structures along the
east-west county road (then called
Dorr Road by the county and St.
Joseph's Avenue by the University;
in Kervick's plan, it was to be called
University Road) that bisected the
campus in front of the Sorin statue
(98). A fragment of this road can
still be seen extending from the rear
of the Rockne Memorial (6) to U.S.
31–33. Kervick saw the possibilities, once the county road was
closed, of creating a long east-west
quadrangle. The academic and residential buildings sited there would,
in his estimation, create a campus
environment "as Hawthorne describes Oxford, 'The air of a sweet,
quiet, sacred, stately seclusion.'"

While several of Kervick's ideas
were implemented—Howard-Morrissey-Lyons Halls and the commerce (41) and chemistry (53)
buildings were built on his proposed
locations—many other Kervick innovations were never actualized.
The "open air theatre where one
may hope to see a revived interest
in mystery and Elizabethan plays"
was never built; nor were the proposed executive offices and lay
faculty residences built that were
projected to flank a hugh memorial
arch entrance gate (IV-28). Likewise, the proposed pharmacy, geology, architecture, music, and
museum buildings were also never
constructed.

In his report to President Burns,
Kervick insisted that "the wonderful beauty of the lakes should be
emphasized by placing buildings in
closer relation to them, giving vistas
so that visitors to the University
may not leave without knowing that
lakes exist here." Frank Lloyd
Wright also recognized the landscape potential of Notre Dame's
lakes. Through the efforts of an
alumnus, Wright came to Notre
Dame in 1923, met President Walsh,

IV–28

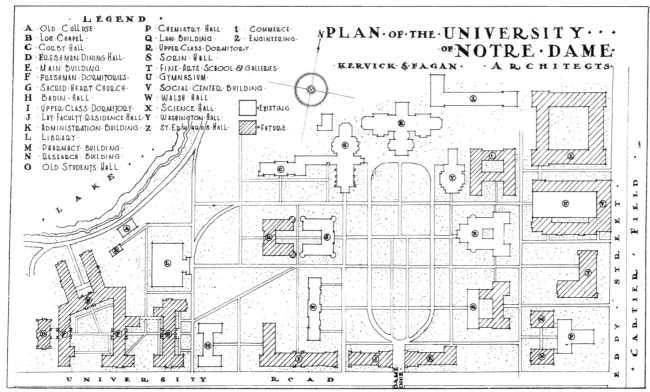

IV–29

IV–28. South Quad Projection, 1922
Kervick's sketch of his proposed elm-lined quadrangle that he hoped would be characterized by "that sequestered peace one feels on the common of an early American village."

IV–29. The Kervick Plan, 1920
Kervick's grand scheme would have created two east-west axes of the campus (one extending from the Lemonnier Library to a proposed fine arts school and the one that became the South Quadrangle). This plan was used throughout the 1920s for the endowment campaigns and to suggest to potential donors the University's projected expansion.

IV–30. Rockne Memorial, 1937
This athletic facility contains a swimming pool, handball and squash courts, a solarium, apparatus rooms, basketball gyms, the golf shop, various athletic offices, and, recently, the Institute for Urban Studies. Over the buildings front entrance are two stone bas-relief plaques honoring Robert de La Salle and Leopold Pokagon (I–11); over other entrances are the seals of the United States and the University, the coats of arms of Norway (Rockne's home), France (origin of the C.S.C.), and West Point and Annapolis (traditional Notre Dame athletic opponents). Inside is a Gothic foyer, dedicated to "the Rock." Here, in glass-enclosed cases displaying the numerous athletic trophies won by Rockne, are other artifacts of Notre Dame's football prowess in the 1920s. Over the shrine broods a bronze bust of Rockne (IV–35) done by Nison Tregor in 1940.

IV–30

IV–31

IV–31. George Gipp (1895–1920)
Native of Laurium, Michigan, varsity basketball, baseball, and football superstar, pocket and three-cushion billards champion of South Bend, womanizer, laconic, aloof, troubled young man who became a tragic hero.

and was extremely impressed by the campus topography. He saw the lakes as a natural unifying element of future development and as a social and recreational focal point. Walsh was also impressed with Wright. The president wrote an associate in the fall of 1923 that Wright had "already indicated his interest in Notre Dame to the extent of offering his services gratis should we wish him to make a survey of our future plans." It is not known if Wright ever did prepare any architectural drawings. In any event, it was Kervick's "collegiate Gothic" idiom, not Wright's organic architecture, that prevailed at Notre Dame for the next thirty years.

G *Walk to the right down the South Quadrangle to the entrance of the Rockne Memorial (6) and enter by the right side door.*

The pervasiveness of the collegiate Gothic revival, much in vogue in America as an appropriate architectural style for collegiate building during the early twentieth century, can be seen in such unlikely structures as the Rockne Memorial (IV–30), designed by M. Carroll and

C. E. Dean of Kansas City, Missouri, and built in 1937–38. Notre Dame's colorful football history and Knute Kenneth Rockne are synonymous in the popular mind. In the 1920s, Rockne, along with his superstars—George Gipp (IV–31) and the Four Horsemen (IV–37)—became household words in an era that sports historians still nostalgically refer to as the "golden age." When writing about the Rockne era (1918–31), it is easy to lose perspective. As D. C. "Chet" Grant rightly points out, pre-Rockne Notre Dame football teams had won 145 games while losing only 40 against more formidable competition than most early collegiate squads. Rockne's statistics, of course, are more impressive: 105 games won, 12 lost, 5 tied, five teams were undefeated and six lost only one game, and two teams were national champions. Yet the whole ambience he created—his half-time exhortations delivered in a staccato voice, his sense of the histrionics of college football, and his insight into the competitive drives of young men—made Notre Dame football and Rockne into national legends.

Rockne came to the University from Chicago's Scandinavian northside in 1910 after saving money to underwrite his education by working for the U.S. postal service. During his undergraduate years he was a top student in the science school (IV–32), a middle-distance runner, and a pole-vaulter (IV–33). He acted in campus theatrical productions, helped edit *The Dome*, earned pin money as a paid amateur boxer in South Bend, and played varsity football under Coach Jesse Harper. After graduating *magna cum laude* in chemistry, Rockne was asked to stay on at Notre Dame as a chemistry instructor and as Harper's assistant. In 1918 he moved up to athletic director and head coach (IV–34). For the next thirteen seasons his personal charm, salesmanship, shrewd scheduling, and immense knowledge of football technique propelled the University into the national limelight of spectator sports; the ascendancy of such sports has constituted a cultural phenomenon that, since the 1920s, has been one of the great common denominators of the American public.

More books have been written about Knute Rockne than any other Notre Dame personality. Assuredly a legend in his own time, he was a tough, ambitious, flamboyant, self-confident, and self-motivated man who loved the dramatics of collegiate football coaching as much as the physical contest itself. Even as a young man Rockne looked appropriately sagacious, like Everyboy's surrogate father. His battered fedora, a self-cultivated trademark as familiar as Walter Winchell's, and his rumpled, ill-fitting gray and blue suits (Westbrook Pegler thought he always looked like "a beaten up tin can") only added to his stature as an American folk hero. There can be little doubt that Rockne's tragic death at age forty-three in a 1931 airplane crash in Kansas helped broaden and perpetuate his legend. His campus funeral (II–9), given nationwide coverage by CBS, was practically a national day of mourning. Rockne coached in the only era in which Frank Merriwell of Yale could have been created in fiction; it was an age of unique heroes—Ruth in baseball, Dempsey in boxing, Jones in golf, Tilden in tennis—and one in which Notre Dame contributed its share in Rockne, George Gipp, and the Four Horsemen.

George Gipp, who had come to Notre Dame on a baseball scholarship in 1917, was dropkicking on one of Brownson's practice fields (V–23) one afternoon when Rockne happened to be passing by. Rockne recognized Gipp's potential and invited him out for the football squad. A year later Ring Lardner, who served his newspaper apprenticeship covering South Bend sports, wrote: "Notre Dame has one signal: pass the ball to Gipp and let him use his own judgment." By 1920 Gipp had led Rockne's varsity for three years in rushing, passing, and scoring, and in that year he was named the University's first official All-American.

The "Gipper," despite his penchant for gambling at poker and at pocket and three-cushion billards and despite his indifference to football publicity, became a campus and national idol. After the final game of the 1920 season he contracted a strep-throat infection and died at age twenty-five that December. On

IV–32–35. Rockne at Notre Dame, 1910–31
IV–32, chemistry major and Sorin Hall resident, 1914; IV–33, varsity middle-distance runner and pole-vaulter, 1912; IV–34, head coach and athletic director, 1924; IV–35, campus icon and national legend, 1931–?

IV–32

IV–33

IV–34

his deathbed Gipp was supposed to have made a last request of Rockne which has survived as a bit of perdurable Notre Dame lore. Rockne's only poor team was the 1928 eleven, that had lost four games. As this squad faced a seemingly impossible task against a powerful, undefeated Army team, the coach concluded his famous pep talk: "Before George Gipp died, he said to me, 'Rock, some day when the going is real tough, ask the boys to go out and beat Army for me.'" In a 12–6 upset, Notre Dame did just that and gave birth to the chant: "Win One for the Gipper."

Rockne's 1924 team, undefeated in ten games with a Rose Bowl win over Stanford, achieved a fame similar to Gipp's when sportswriter Grantland Rice began his account of another Notre Dame victory over Army (13–7) with a now famous paragraph: "Outlined against the blue-gray October sky, the Four Horsemen rode again. In dramatic lore they are known as Famine, Pestilence, Destruction, and Death. These are only aliases. Their real names are Stuhldreher, Miller, Crowley, and Layden. They formed

IV–35

the crest of the South Bend cyclone before which another fighting Army football team was swept over the precipice of the Polo Grounds yesterday afternoon."

Football was a mixed blessing for early twentieth-century Notre Dame. There were the nuisances of the University president being plagued by constant demands for choice tickets and fervent demands for scheduling games with other schools wishing to share in Notre Dame's gate receipts. Of greater importance to the University were the attacks on its intregity and academic standards that resulted from its football success. Occasionally the allegations were ludicrous. A story in a Kansas paper began: "Virgil H. Evans, a well-known football star, released from the Kansas State Reformatory, June 18, 1924, and parolled to the faculty of Notre Dame, South Bend, Indiana, to play the 1924 season on the college team, has been returned to the Kansas State Penitentiary to complete his sentence." In 1922 the American Association of Colleges and the recently formed NCAA requested the Carnegie Foundation to investigate

intercollegiate football's impact on American educational life. Seven years later the Carnegie Report was published, citing Notre Dame in both complimentary and critical terms.

Of the three chief charges against the University's football program, one certainly appears justified; its athletic department did not abide by the economic restrictions that governed the rest of the institution's operations. For example, in 1929 football uniforms cost $15,400, nearly the same amount which was budgeted for library book acquisitions. Two other major allegations —that Notre Dame athletes were unduly subsidized and that the school allowed constant violations of academic regulations and eligibility requirements—appear to be distortions of the facts. Athletes as well as other students merely had campus jobs that paid part or all of their tuition and board. A faculty Board of Athletics, reorganized in 1924, monitored the academic standing of all players according to Western Conference standards and frequently suspended players when it deemed necessary.

IV–36. Notre Dame–Stanford, 21–10, Rose Bowl, 1925

IV–37. Four Horsemen, 1924
The most famous backfield in Notre Dame football history: (l. to r.) Don Miller, right halfback; Elmer Layden, fullback; Jim Crowley, left halfback; and Harry Stuhldreher, quarterback.

IV–36

IV–37

IV–38. University Farms
The University farms as seen from the northeast.

In spite of the public controversies and hostile allegations, University officials, alumni, and students argued that football made certain positive contributions to the institution: educational opportunities for the poor, a unifying cause for school spirit, a character-builder for young men, an acceptable outlet for excess energy, and promotion of intramural competition were reasons offered in defense of continuing the sport. Complimentary national publicity, despite the embarrassment of charges of professionalism and commercialism, was judged a favorable benefit to the University. Notre Dame teams since the 1920s were thought to provide a cultural symbol with which thousands of priests, nuns, and laity could identify. One historian has observed that "in some manner, the 'Fighting Irish,' who were neither all Irish nor all Catholic, represented the effort of the predominantly immigrant and poor Catholic group in this country to get ahead." And, of course, besides raising religious and ethnic consciousness, Notre Dame football brought the University a substantial monetary return. From $235 in 1919, the annual profits grew steadily, reaching $529,420 in 1929. This income bolstered faculty salaries and built academic facilities and residence halls.

H *Exit Rockne Memorial and walk up the right (south) side of the South Quad to the front of Fisher Hall (9).*

The University received revenue from ancillary sources other than football. Its farms, under the direction of Brother Leo Donovan (IV–42), achieved almost as widespread a reputation regionally as its athletic teams did nationally. At the turn of the century most of the Notre Dame farm buildings—formerly located east of the Old College (I–34–42)—came to be concentrated in the southwestern corner of the present South Quad as well as a larger tract (St. Joseph's Farm [V–54] in Granger, Indiana) eight miles northeast of the campus. The Brothers of Holy Cross staffed these various University farms which, at their greatest extent, covered over 3,500 acres and produced everything from peat for fireplaces to tobacco for faculty cigars.

IV–38

IV–39. University farms
The University farms as seen from the southwest.

IV–40. Notre Dame Farmholdings, 1902
This manuscript map, allegedly drawn by Brother Donovan, suggests the plantings and land use of outlying University property in the early twentieth century.

IV–39

The Notre Dame farm consisted of approximately 1,100 acres that in 1900 practically ringed the campus on all sides (IV–40). By that date most farm buildings were located on a site now occupied by Fisher (9) and Pangborn (7) Halls, the South Dining Hall (17), and the current ninth, tenth, and eleventh holes of the W. J. Burke Memorial Golf Course. The farm complex (IV–38–39) included several farmhouses for the brothers and hired hands (IV–43), the University horse barn and livery (IV–41), a dairy barn with a large Holstein herd, a circular barn (IV–46) and surrounding sties for raising over 700 Hampshire hogs (IV–47), a hennery, and several grain-storage buildings. Fields of corn, alfalfa, and wheat stretched beyond these structures to the South Bend city limits.

When Brother Donovan took over as director of the farm in 1900, this land's fertility was practically exhausted due to a lack of knowledge as to the benefits of rotating crops, planting legumes, or using fertilizers. Donovan, a local Lakeville farmer before joining the brothers' community in 1897, eventually per-

suaded John Zahm to permit him to take courses at the Universities of Iowa and Illinois in order to find a solution to the farm's declining productivity. After learning new agricultural techniques, which he coupled with his own experimentation, he began to apply manures, limestone, and huge amounts of rock phosphate (twelve freight carloads went on the present golf course) to his fields. Yields increased tremendously. A thirty-acre field (formerly extending south of the present Law Building) produced 300 bushels of potatoes before Donovan's experiments and 8,200 bushels after his fertilizing. A record for wheat productivity in the state was set in 1918 when the harvest (IV-45) yielded 6,000 bushels per 200-acre plot.

Brother Donovan, who supervised the Notre Dame farms from 1900 to 1940, also excelled in breeding livestock. By 1910 he had introduced hog and cattle feedlots to the campus. His increased corn yields enabled him to feed beef cattle, which, in turn, produced manure for his fields. In 1912 he first took his beef to the International Stock

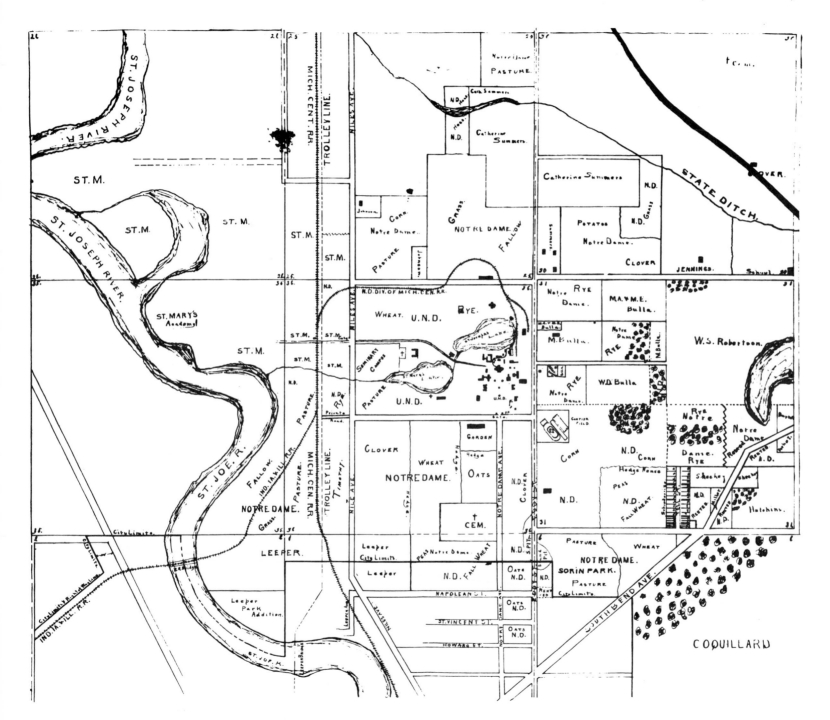

IV–41. University Stables
The campus horse barn, a testimony to the former status of agriculture at Notre Dame, was erected in 1902. Really a livery stable, it housed forty horses to work the surrounding fields and to draw wagons and carriages. Located on the site now occupied by the west wing of the South Dining Hall and Fisher Hall, it, along with three tons of hay, was destroyed by fire on October 13, 1925, with an estimated loss of $65,000.

IV–42. Brother Donovan and Champ, 1910
An astute husbandman, Leo Donovan loved breeding horses, especially great draft animals such as the Belgian stock horses he used to cultivate his fields.

IV–43. Farmhouses
Fronting along Dorr Road, these simple structures served as sleeping, eating, and recreation quarters for the brothers and hired hands who worked the farms.

Show in Chicago, winning first prize for the best grain-fed cattle in the Hereford class. For the next thirty-five years he exhibited prime beef, Hampshire hogs, and Belgian stock horses at state fairs and stock shows. Named Indiana State Champion Feeder in 1937, he supplied and slaughtered (in structures formerly behind Moreau Seminary [32]) all the beef and pork for the University kitchens and shipped the surplus to the Chicago stockyards.

Donovan became such an expert on cattle breeding and Indiana soils that he was invited to lecture at agricultural institutes and schools as well as contribute to agricultural journals. He was a major force behind Notre Dame's establishment of an agricultural school in 1917. The first Catholic university to offer two-year and four-year degrees in agriculture, Notre Dame's program was expanded in 1919 to award a bachelor of science in seven agricultural areas. Although the "Aggie" school never reached its anticipated 300-student enrollment, it did continue in a modified form until it was discontinued in 1932.

As demands for other uses of

IV–41

IV–42

IV–43

IV–44. Stock Raising, 1922
In the 1920s, the University's School of Agriculture used its various herds to teach animal husbandry and dairying. A bachelor of science could also be secured in the fields of agronomy, horticulture, farm mechanics, and agriculture and commerce (foreign and domestic).

IV–45. Wheat Harvest, 1918
A bumper crop necessitated harvesting assistance from the University faculty and local C.S.C. community. Working among them, fifth from the left, is Father "Pops" Farley.

IV–46

IV–46. Hog Barn
This distinctive circular barn used to house over 700 Hampshire hogs. Hogs and beef cattle were either butchered in a slaughter-house behind Moreau Seminary (32) or sold at the Chicago stockyards.

IV–44

IV–45

IV–47. Swine Herds, 1920
Beginning in 1844 when Father Sorin designated that the University would "mark its stock of all kinds with a square crop off the right ear and a slit in the same," Notre Dame engaged in, and for a time taught, animal husbandry. Brother Donovan, Indiana State Champion Feeder in 1937, exhibited livestock such as these at state fairs and the International Stock Show in Chicago.

IV–49. Spring Plowing, 1924
In addition to using its extensive horse-power, the Notre Dame farm was mechanized by the mid-1920s. Here a field northeast of the campus is prepared for planting.

IV–47

IV–48. "Notre Dame Bull"

IV–49

University land increased in the late 1920s, the farms were moved from the South Quad to land along Bulla Road (V–1) and then entirely to Granger, Indiana, where the brothers' community still operates a 1,900-acre dairy- and beef-cattle farm on land purchased by Edward Sorin in 1867. When Brother Donovan moved his farm complex to the Bulla Road site, Notre Dame officials could continue to execute Kervick's 1920 plan. The University was also able to implement a proposal of William J. Burke, a Ports-

mouth, Ohio, industrialist, who felt the school should have a golf course. Burke offered to develop the land at his own expense if the University would provide the real estate. Although Burke died before all the arrangements were finalized, the present eighteen-hole course, complete with its own tree nursery, was named in his honor and opened to golfers in 1929.

I *Walk to the front of the South Dining Hall (17).*

Ever since Mistress Eaton, wife

of Harvard's first president, was ac-cused of putting goat dung in the hasty pudding in 1639, it has been an American tradition for students to complain about the food served in college dining halls. Notre Dame students were no exception. With the post–World War I increase in the student population, the Admin-istration Building refectories and the Badin Hall cafeteria could no longer provide adequate or accept-able food service. As early as 1922 University officials began planning a new central dining facility.

In 1924 the University awarded an honorary degree to Ralph Adams Cram, distinguished Boston ar-chitect and leading proponent of Gothic campus and ecclesiastical ar-chitecture. On his visit to Notre Dame, Cram, who had redesigned West Point, Rice, and parts of Princeton in the Gothic style, ex-pressed his willingness to assist Notre Dame in any of its future building projects. President Walsh, who had apparently neglected Frank Lloyd Wright's similar offer a year before, took advantage of Cram's

IV–50

proposal and asked him to design a new dining hall. Cram responded with a Gothic design (IV–50) that he felt demonstrated "the incorporation of Western Christian culture into the modern American educational process."

The only extant English-vermilion brick campus building, the South Dining Hall, as it came to be called after the North Dining Hall (60) was built in 1957, originally contained two large dining halls (each seating over a thousand) with a two-storey structure between

them housing a cafeteria, basement lounge, faculty dining room, and the kitchens.

Enter the dining hall's front entrance and view one of its dining rooms (IV–51–52) and the public cafeteria.

The building is purposefully reminiscent of a medieval guildhall. The two great refectories (IV–51–52) that flank the public cafeteria (now called the Oak Room) are identical in size (206' × 60' × 35'), decoration, and structure. Oak-beamed

ceilings, tall lancet windows, dark oak paneling, glass chandeliers, oak furniture, terrazzo floors, limestone fireplaces, and orchestra balconies combined to create an atmosphere of dignified formal dining. The cafeteria, with its red-tile flooring, its walls and pillars wainscotted with multicolored Bemidji tile, and its oak tables, can serve 300 persons. Augustin Pall, a Hungarian artist, executed the wall murals to the east (John Zahm's expedition with Theodore Roosevelt to South America and Julius Nieuwland's discovery

IV–50. South Dining Hall, 1928
This magnificent Gothic building (232' × 204') constructed of English-vermilion brick and Indiana limestone was designed by the Boston firm of Cram and Ferguson, with Kervick and Fagan as associate architects.

IV–51

IV–51–52. Dining Hall Interior, ca. 1930
Until World War II when the west hall
changed from family-style dining to a
cafeteria line, mealtimes at Notre Dame
rivaled "mess formations" at West Point
and Annapolis. Each meal, from start to
finish, lasted exactly twenty-five minutes.
At the sound of the first bell, the students,
dressed in suit jacket and tie, marched in
formation through specifically designated
hall entrances and proceeded to take their
seats at tables set with silver and china.
They stood there in silence until grace
before meals was said by the presiding
official. The University president held this
position in the east hall, and the dean of
discipline bore this title in the west hall.
Another bell rang, all sat down, and the
waiters brought on the soup. At the next
signal, the dinner was served. Finally, the
closing grace was said, and the students
quietly left the halls in orderly lines.

IV–52

IV–53–54. Engineering Hall, 1909
Two views, east (IV–53) and west (IV–54), show the engineering college, which fronted on Dorr Road. In the first-floor window (see IV–53) the sign, "Brother Francis, Undertaker," denotes the University's embalming and coffin-manufacturing shop run by the former University steward and cabinetmaker (I–19).

IV–55. University Hearse, 1911
Housed in a small garage behind the wing of the Engineering Hall (see IV–53–54), this hearse was used in the burials of anyone associated with the University; burials were either in the C.S.C. Community Cemetery or in Cedar Grove Cemetery. The horse-drawn hearse was part of the University mortuary that was sold in 1911 to I. W. McGann, who continued the business in South Bend.

of synthetic rubber) and to the west (a panorama of Notre Dame history from its pioneer years, through its centenary during World War II, and on to future construction and growth). In 1944 Pall finished a third mural that portrayed Notre Dame's contemporary history. Several members of the faculty and administration were depicted and, in their estimation, in most unflattering poses. The mural was never hung.

J *Exit the dining hall and walk east along the quadrangle path to a point between Dillon (20) and Alumni (23) Halls.*

As figure IV–39 indicates, a two-storey, 140′ × 40′ Engineering Hall (IV–53–54) had been built in 1905 approximately on the present site of Dillon (see IV–76) and Alumni Halls. The Engineering Hall, in addition to housing that college's various departments, also contained the workshops for students of the Manual Labor School. Here were located tailor, tin, carpentry, machine (IV–56), and steam-fitting shops as well as the University's mortuary (see IV–55). In the predawn hours of June 29,

IV–53

IV–54

IV–55

IV–56. Machine Shops, 1902
Apprentice students from the Manual
Labor School at their metalworking lathes.

IV–57. Ornamentation, Dillon Hall, 1931
Maginnis and Walsh, Boston architects,
continued Fagan's proclivity for Gothic
masonry details.

IV–56

IV–57

1928, an electrical storm struck a high-tension line leading to the building's top floor, setting the floor afire and causing over a hundred thousand dollars damage. The partial destruction of this building, never considered adequate by its faculty, caused William Benitz, professor of civil engineering, to comment, "Isn't it too bad that the fire department got here too soon." While the University constructed a temporary roof over the building's first floor, engineering classes were held in the basement of Badin Hall until the present Cushing Hall of Engineering (40) was constructed in 1933.

K *Walk to the middle of "the circle" between Alumni Hall (23) and the Law School (37).*

When Alumni Hall (1931) and the Law building (1930) were erected on the respective sites of the old Engineering Hall and one of Brother Donovan's potato fields, Francis Kervick's South Quadrangle became further defined. The two buildings, along with "the circle" between them, created a new main entrance to the University. Al-though this movement of the institution's front entrance was but a few hundred yards further south (compare IV–64 with IV–65), this expanded orientation toward the city of South Bend coincided with the increasing involvement of Notre Dame students in the surrounding local community during the 1920s. During that decade almost a third of the student body was forced to live off campus due to increased post–World War I enrollments. Notre Dame officials, however, were highly restrictive in their rules and regulations regarding off-campus behavior. Students were forbidden to drive automobiles or to visit certain monitored areas in the city (for example, the Tokyo Dance Hall on South Michigan Street), which were patroled by the prefect of discipline in the "Skive Wagon" (IV–61).

Despite such vigilance, Notre Dame students made forays into the city on foot or via the yellow, Hill Street streetcar (IV–60), which they once set afire in 1916 in a fit of pique. A more violent student disturbance occurred in the spring of 1924 when an estimated 2,000 Notre Dame students, local resi-

IV–58–61. Notre Dame Off Campus
The Hill Street streetcar, seen here about
to depart for South Bend (IV–58–59), was
set afire (IV–60) by the students in 1916.
Photo IV–61 shows Fathers Eugene Burke
and "Pops" Farley in the "Skive Wagon"
they used to patrol city streets for Notre
Dame students frequenting the declared
off-limits areas.

IV–61

IV–58

IV–59

IV–60

IV–62

dents, and undergraduates from Catholic colleges in Chicago skirmished with 35,000 members of the Ku Klux Klan. The Imperial Klan of Indiana purposely assembled in South Bend, intent on holding a parade in order to demonstrate their strength in a traditionally Catholic area. City fathers denied the Klan a permit to march, and Notre Dame students promised to "aid the police" in preventing the illegal parade and to keep "adequate law and order." A Klan member, in turn, volunteered "to blow up Notre Dame if the KKK would furnish the dynamite." A weekend of taunts, threats, and occasional rioting resulted in surprisingly few injuries and little property damage.

During the Klan confrontations, Notre Dame men operated out of Hullie and Mike's (IV–63), a favorite city gathering, eating, and watering spot for students during the 1920s. The combination cigar store, three-cent restaurant, poker parlor, and billards room was run by Irishmen George Hull and Mike Calnon. Outside their multipurpose emporium, students also assembled to watch the progress of Notre Dame

IV–63. Hullie and Mike's, 1916
Perhaps the first of a long line of student meccas (Sweeney's, the Philadelphia, Guiseppe's, Corby's, Frankie's, Fat Wally's Electric Beer Joint, and so forth), Hullie and Mike's, 112 South Michigan Street, hosted Notre Dame's first football banquet, and, at one time, everything served at its lunch counter—sandwiches, pie, cake, ice cream, coffee—could be had for three cents a serving.

IV–63

away-football games as it was relayed by Western Union and translated to the electric light bulbs of the "Gridgraphie" outdoor scoreboard. Naturally, students celebrated or mourned the outcome of the afternoon's contest in the streets (and taverns) of South Bend and were usually on hand to welcome back their compatriots at South Bend's Union Station (IV–62).

Turn around and face the Administration Building.

The years 1917–34 have been correctly characterized by historian David Arthur as "a critical period in Notre Dame's history." The era extending from the eve of World War I to the depression of the early 1930s is filled with both unprecedented change and fundamental continuity. Formerly an institution with extensive grade, vocational, and preparatory school programs, Notre Dame by 1934 had abandoned these aspects of its educational scheme and was concentrating on upgrading its undergraduate and recently created graduate schools. Although the master of arts degree had been awarded throughout the

nineteenth century, only in 1918 was a formal program in graduate studies established, and that operated principally only during the summer. Originally intended to provide an opportunity for religious teachers to finish their baccalaureates in order to meet certification requirements then being imposed by many states, the summer session became the core of the University's Graduate School which was officially established in 1932. The summer programs offered undergraduates a chance to make up lost credits, and it opened the University to women, particularly nuns and lay teachers. The University-trained teachers, in turn, actively recruited for Notre Dame among their high school students. Notre Dame's graduate program in the 1920s was at best a promising start. Father J. Leonard Carrico, director of studies in the 1920s, felt that the advanced programs grew too quickly and lacked sufficient research faculty and resources. Father Philip Moore (V–63), historian of the University's academic development, noted in 1960: "looking back today upon the library resources and

IV–64

IV–65

IV–66. John Meyers

IV–67. Grover Miller

IV–68. Michael R. Pomis

IV–69. Breen McDonald and Fred McHaffery

IV–69

IV–66

IV–67

IV–68

other conditions essential to genuine graduate work, especially at the doctoral level, we must conclude that in the 1920s Notre Dame was over-ambitious and over-extended in most of the fields in which advanced programs of study were offered."

Nonetheless, Notre Dame did continue, if but hesitantly, toward the intellectual goals that James Burns had given it during his brief administration. Burns, as C.S.C. provincial, sent many talented young priests on to secular universities for advanced degrees. Eventually these men returned to teach at Notre Dame. The University's lay

faculty (IV–72–73 and IV–75) increased in quantity and quality. In 1919 laymen and religious were almost equally represented on the faculty; by 1932 laymen outnumbered religious nearly three to one. During this period, laymen with doctorates rose from fourteen to twenty; those with the masters degrees, from twenty-three to forty.

Before World War I, Notre Dame had no endowment. The University's only income, apart from tuition, fees, and room-and-board charges, was a few hundred dollars interest from funded scholarships. Of course, the institution benefited from the "living endowment" of

priests, brothers, sisters, and the low salaries of dedicated lay professors and staff members, plus the calculated use of auxiliary enterprises such as farms, missions, and astute real estate transactions. The 1920s endowment campaigns, coupled with the support received from the Rockefeller and Carnegie Foundations, marked a new era in the school's financial history. Part of the income raised by Burns, plus football revenue, enabled his successors to expend over $5 million on campus construction. This was more than four times the amount spent in the first eighty years of Nore Dame's development, and it

built four academic buildings, seven residence halls, a dining hall, a basketball gymnasium, and a football stadium.

Presidents Walsh, O'Donnell, and O'Hara were campus builders. They, along with Cavanaugh and Burns, were also the first C.S.C. leaders subject to a new code of canon law which had gone into effect in May 1918 and precipitated John W. Cavanaugh's retirement from the presidency. By custom, the president of Notre Dame also served as the religious superior of the Holy Cross priests and brothers who lived and worked at the institution. Canon 505 of the new code

IV–70

IV–71

IV–72

IV–73

IV–74

IV–75

IV–70. Duke Riley

IV–71. The Night Watchman

IV–72. Austin O'Malley, Professor of Literature

IV–73. Notre Dame Litterateurs. Seated are (l. to r.) President Charles O'Donnell, William Butler Yeats, and Professor Charles Phillips. Standing are Yeat's secretary and former president John W. Cavanaugh.

IV–74. Brother Florian, University Treasurer and Steward

IV–75. Jacques Maritain, Visiting Professor of Philosophy

limited the term of a superior to six years in the same house. Cavanaugh could have remained president by relinquishing the office of superior to another priest, but he rejected this solution because he viewed the affairs of his congregation and those of the University as too interwoven to permit harmonious governance by separate leaders. The next six University presidents also maintained this dual authority and for this reason each of them was limited to six-year presidential administrations.

Limited presidential terms did not diminish the intimate, familial, paternal environment of Notre Dame in the 1920s and 1930s. President O'Hara in 1934 could still identify every graduating senior by name. A fourth of the lay faculty lived permanently in the campus residence halls. Francis Kervick's plan, by his own account, endeavored to give "to the architecture of Notre Dame much of the charm and homelike hospitality that one sees in the customs of the University."

Student life reflected this familial philosophy. A strict schedule of religious and academic activities pre-vailed. A student's day began at 6:30 A.M. with morning prayer, followed by morning Mass (which was optional except on Saturday and Sunday); class or study periods lasted until 3:30 P.M., after which outdoor recreation was encouraged; at 7:30 P.M., night prayer was recited, followed by compulsory study until lights-out at 11:00 P.M. (10:00 P.M. for freshmen). A prefect of discipline and a prefect of religion enforced this order of the day as well as dormitory and dining hall regulations, a dress code, and restrictions governing off-campus behavior.

In the 1920s extracurricular life centered around the resident halls and the intramural playing fields, but students were also involved in dramatics, oratory, debate, the glee club, orchestra, band, and publications (*The Notre Dame Juggler*, originally a humor magazine, eventually became a literary journal and ended *The Scholastic*'s monopoly of campus journalism). With the expansion of the University's course offerings, academic societies increased, and with the increase in the student population, the number of clubs for those from distinct geo-graphical regions proliferated. Student government and increased social activities probably constituted the most notable changes in student life during the 1917–34 period. When Father Burns, an innovative rector in Sorin Hall, became president, he established the Students Activities Committee (SAC), an organization composed of faculty and student leaders charged with the responsibility of exercising "general supervision over student activities, organizations, traditions and customs" and making "more effective the sanest undergraduate opinions." Among its first projects, the SAC attempted to expand the number of social activities. Previously only one campuswide social function was permitted each year, with each of the upper classes having a formal dance limited to class members and their dates. By 1934 there were dances after each football game; they were held weekly in the spring.

As a national depression continued to plague the United States, Notre Dame, for once in its history, had a modicum of financial stability. In 1934 the University gained a new executive, when John O'Hara, who had been prefect of religion, vice-president, and then acting president during Charles O'Donnell's lingering illness, assumed the institution's highest office following O'Donnell's death after the 1934 commencement. The University that O'Hara was to lead was quite different from the one from which Cavanaugh had resigned in 1919. Its student body had tripled, and its faculty had grown in size, excellence, and number of laymen. The administration was no longer as tightly controlled by the Holy Cross community and was more receptive to ideas from alumni and the Board of Associate Lay Trustees. Extensive physical growth transformed the campus, and the increased revenue (net income rose from $16,500 to $800,-000) opened many new options for implementing the University's academic programs. In brief, Notre Dame was finally a totally collegiate institution with the foundation laid for the expansion of graduate instruction and research and a strengthened tradition of unique residential undergraduate education.

IV–76. Notre Dame, 1936
In place on Kervick's South Quadrangle
were: (l. to r.) the Lyons-Morrissey-
Howard group, remodeled Badin Hall,
South Dining Hall, Dillon-Alumni group
with an Oxford inner court, "the circle,"
the Law School, Hurley School of Commerce, Cushing Hall of Engineering, and
Chemistry Hall.

V. The University in 1942

V–1. Notre Dame in 1934. This rather rare air photograph, taken from the northwest, shows the South Quadrangle nearing completion, especially the Hurley School of Commerce, the Law School, and the Cushing Hall of Engineering. Also in place are the stadium and, to its left, Cartier Field. Farmland still surrounds the campus perimeters.

Beginning at the statue of Our Lady of the University (99) in the center of "the circle," Walk V explores pre– and post–World War II Notre Dame. A walk of 1,200 yards, it traces the expansion of the campus to the northeast under the aegis of two builder-presidents, John O'Hara (1934–40) and John J. Cavanaugh (1946–52). The walk delineates the development of the eastern half of the South Quadrangle, reviews the construction of the stadium (73) and the uses of Cartier Field, proceeds by Chemistry Hall (53) and Nieuwland Science Hall (52), and retells the history of the Fieldhouse (57). The diverse activities of the North Quadrangle are noted as one walks across this quad between Breen-Phillips (58) and Farley (59) Halls and on to the Vetville historical marker at the rear of the Memorial Library (72). The walk ends, as it began, exploring the impact of the military occupation of the campus in the 1940s.

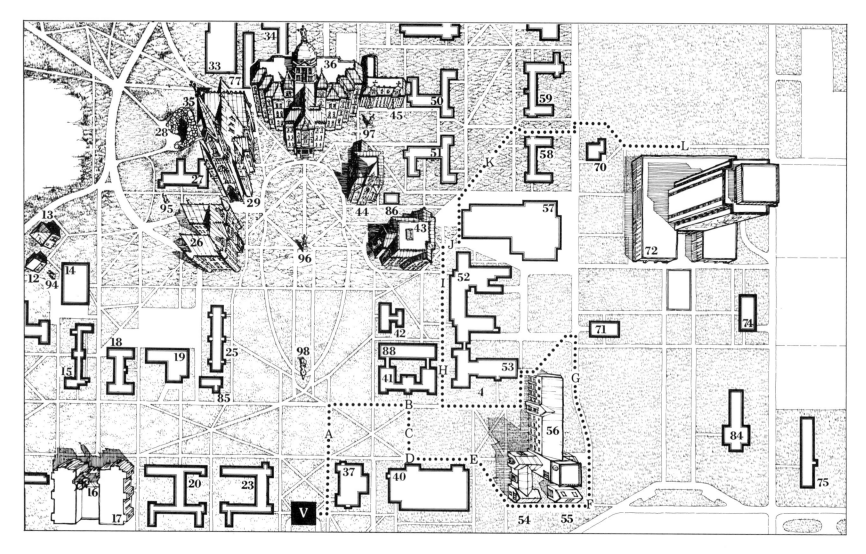

Centennial Celebration, Military Occupation, Renewed Expansion

CERTAIN HISTORICAL eras are often neglected or dismissed as uneventful simply because preceding and subsequent decades appear more colorful in the contemporary imagination or in later historical scholarship. Such is the fate of the period 1934–52 in Notre Dame history. Compressed between the University's national fame of the 1920s and the continuing dynamism of the Hesburgh administration beginning in the early 1950s, these eighteen years—the presidential tenures of John O'Hara, Hugh O'Donnell, and John J. Cavanaugh—are, nevertheless, a time of considerable growth, academic diversification and continued national prominence.

The University's 1942 centenary, as with every other official institutional anniversary except the fiftieth, took place when the United States was at war. The celebration, subdued though it was because of the war, prompted historical reflection on

---

Notre Dame in 1942
Acreage: 1,700   Buildings: 45
Faculty: 337   Tuition: $330
Students: 3,055
Room/board: $459

---

what Notre Dame had been, was, and could become. Extensive display of the new University seal and coat of arms (V–2) symbolized this historical consciousness, as did the publication of an official University history, *Notre Dame, One Hundred Years* (Notre Dame, 1942), by Father Arthur Hope. Although most campus construction was halted by the war rationing of materials, the eastern half of Kervick's South Quadrangle (V–1) was largely completed by 1942, as was the outline of a new North Quadrangle. The now demolished Navy Drill Hall (V–42), built a year later, in addition to being a tangible artifact of the military presence on the campus in the 1940s (other such structures include the ROTC Building [5], the Aerospace Engineering Lab [75], and Vetville [V–48–52]), also represents the growth of the modern campus eastward.

A *Walk to a point parallel with the flagpole in the center of the South Quadrangle and face north toward the Administration Building (36).*

Economic depression and war mobilization are hallmarks of both

the national history and the University's development during the period 1934–45. The financial crisis begun in 1929 did not affect the University until after 1930–31, when there was still a peak enrollment of 3,227. Throughout the remainder of the 1930s, the student population declined steadily. The University, which did not dismiss any lay faculty members or reduce their salaries, was kept afloat by its traditional financial parsimony, by the prudent investments of its Board of Associate Lay Trustees, and by government subsidies from federal agencies such as the National Youth Administration. The decline in enrollment due to the depression was suddenly accelerated by America's military mobilization and conscription in 1941–42. Once again the economic viability of all-male institutions such as Notre Dame was threatened by the nation's involvement in an international conflict.

Even before America declared war, President Hugh "Pepper" O'Donnell thought it wise to offer University facilities to the armed forces. O'Donnell first approached

the army, which had set up the SATC program (IV–4–5) on campus in 1918 and which had been the Notre Dame student's favorite service since the formation of the Continental Cadets (I–55), the Notre Dame Zouaves, and the Hoynes Light Guards (III–53). Although the army showed little interest in O'Donnell's offer, the navy established a unit of the Naval Reserve Officers Training Corps (NROTC) on campus in September 1941. In this program, current and incoming Notre Dame students (approximately 150 a year) who passed physical, mental, and aptitude tests remained at the University, completing their college work in the normal eight semesters. Along with this NROTC program, the University also began a Civilian Pilots' Training Corps and arranged adult evening training courses for defense workers.

Early in 1942 the campus, particularly the expanse of the South Quad (V–4–5) and the surrounding athletic fields (V–6), took on the atmosphere of an armed camp with the establishment of the naval V–7 Program. The V–7 Program, also

V–2. University Seal

Designed by Pierre de Chaignon la Rose of Harvard in 1931, the armorial seal consists of a shield with a clear blue field and a cross of gold. The heraldic colors, gules and azure (gold and blue), are symbolic of the Mother of God, to whom Father Sorin first dedicated Notre Dame. At the shield's base are two wavy lines of silver (indicating the *a Lacu,* "of the Lake," in the University's official title), and above them to the left is a silver star, another emblem of the Virgin, Star of the Sea. The cross represents the Congregation of Holy Cross, which founded Notre Dame; an institution of learning is denoted by the open book. The phrase "Vita, Dulcedo, Spes," taken from the ancient prayer to the Virgin, the Salve Regina, celebrates her as "life, sweetness, and hope."

V–2

called the Midshipmen's School and composed mostly of men already graduated from colleges other than Notre Dame, was divided into two groups: four-month deck officer trainees and two-month trainees being prepared for special assignments. In 1943 still another naval program, the V-12, which also included the marines, occupied the campus. These men were billeted in Dillon, Alumni, Zahm, Cavanaugh, and Breen-Phillips Halls, while the V-7s were quartered in Lyons, Morrissey, Howard, and Badin, and the NROTC in Walsh. Civilian undergraduates, approximately 250 men, were confined to Sorin and St. Edward's Halls and to a definite second-class-citizen status during the military occupation. Although exact figures of the number of military personnel trained at Notre Dame have never been released by the Pentagon, Thomas McAvoy, the former University archivist, estimated that 11,925 men completed their officers training between 1942 and 1946.

The war years inextricably changed Notre Dame. Contracts came for government research. A speedup cafeteria system in the South Dining Hall replaced the former family-style dining, feeding twice as many men in half the time, with much less than half the former intimacy and civility. The public "caf" overflowed with military brass, WAVES, and recruits whose campus stay often extended only four months rather than the usual four years. Vacation periods were abbreviated, classes accelerated, semesters shortened, and one year there was no Christmas holiday. Women appeared all over the previously all-male, semicloistered campus, replacing the undergraduates who formerly had done part-time jobs in offices, dining halls, laboratories, and the library. Sentries patrolled the campus perimeters at night; long blue, white, and khaki lines tramped the quadrangles by day (V–4–5).

B *Walk across the South Quadrangle to the front of the Hurley College of Business Administration (41).*

World War II involved the United States in the foreign affairs of the twentieth century. Prior to

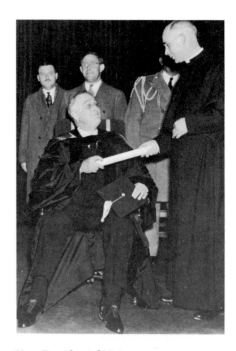

V–3. Presidential Visit, 1935

At a special convocation honoring the new commonwealth status of the Philippine Islands, Franklin Delano Roosevelt, the first American president to visit the campus while in office, received an honorary doctorate of laws, presented here by University President John F. O'Hara.

V–4. Navy at Notre Dame, 1943
A class of the University's Midshipmen
School is seen assembled with their
officers on the South Quadrangle facing
the front of the Rockne Memorial (6). To
the right is the South Dining Hall,
which served as the military mess hall
throughout the war years.

V–4

V–5. Navy at Notre Dame, 1944
The complete University naval training units (NROTC, V-7, V-12) fill up the west half of the South Quad from Dillon Hall (20, lower left) to the Rockne Memorial. To the left of the Rockne building is the golf course's old first tee, and to the right is the ROTC Building (5), first built by the Navy along Dorr Road during World War II.

V–6. Cartier Field Drill, 1942
Navy recruits are seen on parade beyond the confines of Cartier Field's famous wood fence. Signal towers can be seen along the area's perimeter, and behind the Fieldhouse (upper left) is the new Navy Drill Hall (V–42) under construction.

V–8. Flag Raising, Main Quad, 1942
The presentation of an American flag by the senior class, a traditional commencement ceremony, is here enacted at the old tripod flagpole formerly located in the Main Quad west of the Hurley School of Commerce (41). The two Civil War cannons, gifts to the University for its service to the Union cause, were donated as scrap metal for the war effort later in 1942.

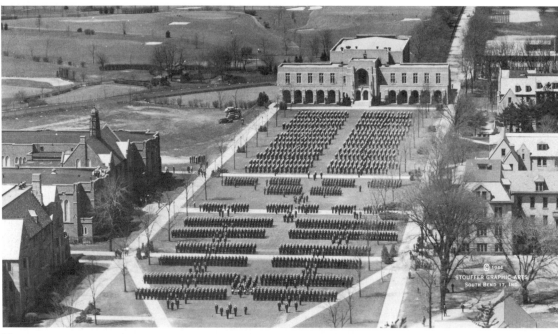

V–5

V–6

V–7. Drill Hall Interior
V-7 trainees learned signal language required of a deck officer in the Drill Hall (V–42) built by the navy to house its various activities.

V–8

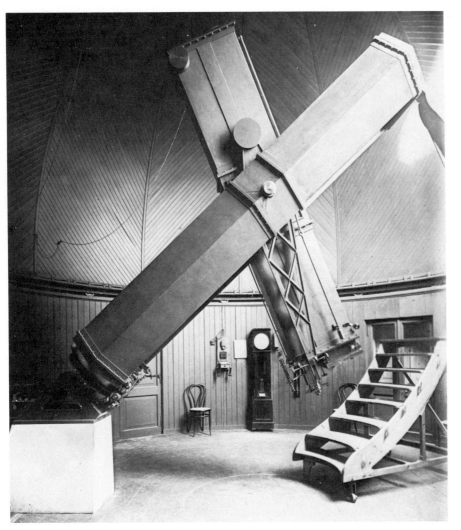

V–10

V–9

V–9–10. University Observatory, 1891–1937

Designed by Arthur J. Stace (I–62) of the engineering department, the observatory (V–9) was located on the present site of the Hurley School of Commerce (41). Its interior (V–10) consisted of a revolving dome; an east wing, or transit room, in which was mounted the main telescope; and a north wing, or computing room, which contained small instruments and a reference library. Removed to the east campus (V–1), the observatory was demolished in 1937.

V–11. Hurley Globe, 1931
In the memorial foyer of the Hurley College of Commerce is located an eight-foot, aluminum, revolving, hydraulic terrestial globe documenting the world trade routes. Other world trade patterns are depicted on three illuminated wall maps that hang in the foyer.

this, Edward Nash Hurley, chairman of the United States Shipping Board during World War I and University Laetare medalist in 1926, felt that Notre Dame's newly created (1921) College of Commerce should be international in its course offerings and degree programs. To foster this end he personally contributed $200,000 in 1930 for the erection of a new building to be known initially as the College of Foreign and Domestic Commerce. Built approximately on the site of the former University observatory (V–9–10), the structure, now called the Hurley College of Business Administration (41), finally afforded a permanent academic home for the programs in business studies known variously since 1853 as the mercantile department, the commercial course, the commercial school, and the commerce department. Since 1913 when the commerce department was subsumed under the School of Arts and Letters, commercial classes were taught in random buildings spread about the campus. Father John O'Hara (V–3) attempted through the 1910s to remedy this deficiency and to create an autonomous com-

merce college. In the Burn's reorganization of the University in 1921, O'Hara became the first dean of a separate commerce college.

Hurley's gift in 1930 fulfilled O'Hara's other objective of an academic building for the college. Designed at Hurley's request by fellow Chicagoans Graham, Anderson, Probst, and White, the two-storey, E-shaped, Gothic structure utilized the same materials and architectural idiom that were later employed by Maginnis and Walsh in their Law School building (37), built across the quadrangle in 1930 and the Cushing Hall of Engineering (40), designed by the Kervick-Fagan partnership in 1933. (When the business school was expanded in 1968 with the addition of Hayes-Healy Center (88), Graham, Anderson, Probst, and White again designed the building, which turned out to be an extremely successful and harmonious use of the Gothic in a contemporary mode.) The architects emphasized Hurley's and the University's concern for international business by creating a two-storey memorial hall and foyer in the building's center. Therein was mounted, in a recessed

pit, an eight-foot terrestial globe (V–11), depicting the world's historic trade routes. A miniature, copper, three-masted clipper ship in full sail was placed atop the building's exterior tower to dramatize further the school's interest in foreign trade and not, as some undergraduate wags from other University colleges are wont to claim, to symbolize a men's yacht club.

C *Walk to the center of the quadrangle and face the Cushing Hall of Engineering (40).*

President Charles O'Donnell, with the assistance of John O'Hara and O'Hara's successor as dean, James ("Mac") McCarthy, had persuaded Edward Hurley to build the commerce school in part by promising to name the structure in his honor. "The University would be happy to perpetuate the name of the donor of any building," wrote O'Donnell in the alumnus monthly in 1931, "by naming the structure after him." Subsequent Notre Dame presidents would employ the promised dedication with considerable success in financing future construction projects. While this common

V–11

V–12. Notre Dame Builders, 1952
Two key men in the post–World War II
Notre Dame campus expansion—Father
Theodore Hesburgh, fifteenth president,
and Ignatius A. O'Shaughnessy,
president of Globe Oil and Refining of
Minneapolis. Over a twenty-year period,
O'Shaughnessy gave the University over
$5 million plus a large stock portfolio.

V–12

technique of fund-raising introduced
a new factor in Notre Dame's campus architectural planning (the impact of the donor's desires had not
been an issue in the architectural
design, siting, or construction of
previous buildings), it did bring
considerable income for new construction to the University.

The academic or east wing of the
South Quadrangle is an architectural testament to the generosity of
Edward Hurley, John F. Cushing,
and Ignatius A. O'Shaughnessy
(see V–12). It was also an attempt
to create an interdisciplinary environment, with the O'Shaughnessy
Hall of Liberal and Fine Arts acting
as a link between the business and
physical science areas (Hurley
School of Commerce, Chemistry
Hall, Nieuwland Science Hall) on
the north and engineering and legal
studies areas (Cushing Hall of Engineering and the Law School) on
the south.

D *Walk to the front of the Cushing Hall of Engineering.*

John Cushing had been on the
verge of withdrawing from the University after his third year as a

student in 1905 because of financial
difficulties. President Morrissey,
however, allowed him to complete
his engineering degree without
charge. Twenty-five years later,
Cushing repaid that generosity with
a gift of $300,000 to construct a
new engineering building to replace the old hall (VI–53–54), destroyed by fire in 1928. The present building, built in 1933 and
about to be renovated, contains
classrooms and drafting rooms, laboratories, machine shops, academic
and faculty offices, and a 600-seat
auditorium. Francis Kervick designed it in the collegiate Gothic
style. His partner, Vincent Fagan,
never completed the projected exterior bas-relief panels of eminent
Catholic scientists such as Ampère,
Volta, Ohm, and Roentgen, but his
deft touch can be seen in his char-
acteristic ornamentation on the
building's front and side elevations.

E *Walk along the quadrangle to the
northeast corner of the engineering
building and stop to face the
O'Shaughnessy Hall of Liberal and
Fine Arts.*

Until 1952 the College of Arts

and Letters, the University's oldest and largest collegiate division, had no academic facility except the multipurpose and overcrowded Administration Building. Classroom space had to be pilfered from practically every other campus building; faculty offices were almost nonexistent. In the early 1950s, I. A. O'Shaughnessy contributed $1.5 million and his own architects, Ellerbe Associates, to erect a building for the liberal arts college. The structure was sited to terminate the east end of the South Quad and to close old Juniper Road (V–15). The hall, perennially ridiculed by architectural students because of its asymmetrical main entrance, its ill-proportioned clock tower, its narrow, low-ceilinged corridors, and its poorly ventilated classrooms, was constructed in 1952. There is no truth to the persistent legend that its architectural plans were actually those drawn for a Minneapolis parochial grade school.

O'Shaughnessy Hall is actually a complex consisting of the dean's offices, classrooms, language labs, a computer terminal, departmental offices, and the studios (in the tower) of WSND, the student-operated AM-FM radio station. The University Art Gallery (54), open to the public from 10:00 A.M. to 4:45 P.M., Monday through Friday, and from 1:00 P.M. to 5:00 P.M. on the weekends, adjoins O'Shaughnessy Hall and contains over 4,000 objects including fine collections of old masters, eighteenth-century paintings (V–13), religious art (V–14), as well as good Near and Far Eastern and primitive collections. A separate sculpture studio (55) was built for Ivan Mestrovic (V–59), noted Croatian artist-in-residence at Notre Dame from 1955 to 1962; an outdoor court (directly behind the Art Gallery) displays some of his work.

F *Walk across the diagonal path to the south corner of the Art Gallery (54). Proceed east along the path to the right of O'Shaughnessy Hall, observe the Mestrovic pieces in the sculpture courtyard, and stop at the back of O'Shaughnessy. Face toward the stadium (73).*

Notre Dame's 59,074-seat stadium (V–15), the "house that Rockne

V–13

V–14

V-15. East Campus, 1936
Looking directly north along old Juniper Road, this airview shows, looking right of the road from bottom to top, the MacNamara residence (subsequently a faculty residence, religious house, student dorm, faculty club, and senior bar), the stadium, Cartier Field (V-18-20), and the University farms of 1930-50.

built," has been a campus landmark and symbol of the University's football prowess since it was built in 1930. Constructed by the Osborn Engineering Firm of Cleveland (builders of such sport palaces as Yankee Stadium in New York and Comiskey Park in Chicago), the Notre Dame Stadium, 670' × 480' × 45', measures one-half mile around and is faced with both Belden brick and white-limestone trim. The original sod of Cartier Field (V-20), venerated because Notre Dame did not lose a home game there in twenty-three years, was moved to the stadium's field in 1930. Southern Methodist University played the first game in the new facility that same year, losing to Notre Dame 20-14. The Naval Academy lost the dedication game the following week, 26-2, to Rockne's last, and his second straight national championship, team.

Rockne's teams appear to have been the first to adopt consciously the ethnic nickname of the "Fighting Irish." In the late nineteenth and early twentieth centuries, Notre Dame's athletic teams were assortedly called "the Catholics," "the

Irish," "the South Benders," "the Catholic Collegians of Indiana," "the Papists," "the Horrible Hibernians," "the Nomads," and "the Ramblers." By 1927 the epithet "Irish" was in common use, and that year President Matthew Walsh, whose father had emigrated to Chicago from County Cork, officially approved the term "Fighting Irish" as the University's athletic sobriquet.

Numerous Irishmen—Layden, Leahy, Brennan—have coached the Notre Dame Irish in stadium combat. Assuredly the most Irish-Catholic of them all was Frank William Leahy (V-16-17), heir to the Rockne legend and perpetuator of Notre Dame invincibility. In his eleven years as coach, the brooding, enigmatic Leahy recorded four national championships and coached six unbeaten teams. When he returned to Notre Dame after serving in World War II, he turned down a professional football coaching contract (supposedly with a *carte blanche* salary figure) and vowed to coach Notre Dame undefeated for the next decade. For almost five years he did not lose a contest, com-

V-15

V–16–17. "The Coach," 1941–53
Photo V–16 shows Frank W. Leahy, his "lads," and athletic director Edward "Moose" Krause along the sidelines of the stadium; V–17 shows Leahy, inheritor of Rockne's mantle, in his appropriately decorated Breen-Phillips office.

V–16

V–17

V–18–20. The Field, 1899–1928
The evolution of Cartier Field: V–18, ca. 1900, with a 500-seat covered grandstand, limited bleacher area, and wood fence from Warren Cartier's Michigan lumber mill; V–19, first football homecoming game, November 1920, Notre Dame 28–Purdue 0, seating capacity, 10,000; V–20, ca. 1928, football stands at their greatest extent, approximately 35,000 capacity.

V–20

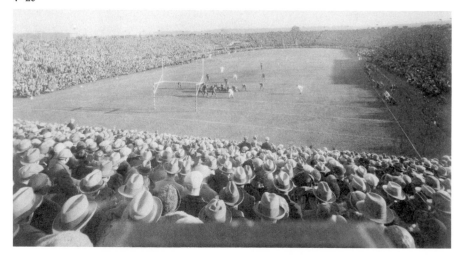

V–18

V–19

piling a winning streak that extended through thirty-nine games.

The Leahy years, roughly coincident with the 1940s, like the Rockne years two decades before, were an exciting, victorious, some would say fanatical, football era at Notre Dame. With such athletic success came the inevitable and unfortunate reputation of being a football factory. Leahy always insisted that he kept athletics subordinate to academics. He often, however, goaded his "lads" to victory by casting them as defenders of the faith, Saturday afternoon warriors doing chivalric battle for "God, Country, and Notre Dame." Winning was such a Leahy tradition that University officials, including the president, constantly had to defend Leahy's success against the criticism of many contemporary coaches, teams, and writers.

Despite his convoluted, polysyllabic Victorian phraseology and his exaggerated moralism, Leahy always commanded respect from his assistants, his players (many of whom were hardened World War II veterans personally recruited by him), and most of his opponents.

V–21

V–21–22. The Fans, ca. 1900
Gentlemen students properly attired to witness autumnal combat at preinflation prices.

V–22

He and his "lads"—Creighton Miller, Angelo Bertelli, Zygmont Czarobski, Johnny Lujack, Leon Hart, "Six-Yard" Sitko, George Ratterman, Johnny Lattner—rewrote many of Notre Dame's football records. Sportswriter Bill Furlong identified his 1947 season as the "Year South Bend Had an NFL Franchise" because forty-two of Leahy's players that year went on to play professional football. A martinet on details, organization, and fundamentals, Leahy drove himself and his teams unmercifully. By the early 1950s, although still winning, he

was a physical wreck. "Coaching burns out a man's insides," he admitted. "It's more than tensions. Ooooh, it was far worse." Forced into retirement, he was replaced by twenty-five-year-old Terry Brennan in 1953.

Leahy spent the next two decades always as "the coach," but never again on the sidelines with a Notre Dame eleven. His official biographer, Wells Twombly, aptly called him an American Don Quixote, "who genuinely believed in all the old frontier verities, now dying; who chased the American dream

with a single-minded passion, and who may have been America's last knight-errant."

G *Walk north along the back of O'Shaughnessy via the service road and stop at the north end of the building; face northeast toward the Memorial Library (72).*

As a center and left tackle, Leahy had played under Rockne on the University's original Cartier Field (V–18–20), a multipurpose athletic area that has had two locations in its seventy-five-year existence. In 1887 Notre Dame played its first

intercollegiate football match losing 8–0 to the University of Michigan in an open field (V–23) now occupied by Nieuwland Science Hall (52) and Chemistry Hall (53). In that same year on the same field, Adrian "Pop" Anson, who had attended Notre Dame in 1869 and later became a star third baseman and the first manager of the Chicago Cubs, showed the students how to play a nine-man game with a bat and ball, popularly called "rounders" but also known as baseball (V–23). By 1899 these sports, plus track and field, required more adequate space.

V–23. Brownson Campus, 1888
Site of most major collegiate intramural and varsity outdoor sports before Cartier Field was created from thirteen acres across the county road (Juniper), the Brownson campus is distinguishable here by the first tree line in the background.

V–24. Baseball Varsity, 1899
The baseball team was coached by Frank Hering (top row, third from left), who, while a law student, was also the first football coach. Hering, as a leader in the F.O.E., later originated the American Mother's Day.

V–23

V–24

Warren A. Cartier, who graduated with a bachelor of science in chemical engineering in 1877, volunteered to purchase a ten-acre plot across what was then Juniper Road (V–15 and 19), to supply the lumber for an enclosing fence, and to construct a 500-seat covered grandstand. This first Cartier Field was a large, enclosed multipurpose athletic area. A 220-yard straightaway ran almost diagonally across the main field. On the north side of this track were one of the two football gridirons and an adjoining grandstand. South of the runway was a quarter-mile track banked at the turns so as to provide thrills for the bicyclists of that day. Inside this enclosure was another football field and a baseball diamond. A one-mile cinder track encircled all these fields. With various modifications over the next six decades (President Matthew Walsh expanded the bleachers twice to accommodate increased football crowds), Cartier Field was the site of diverse activity: Notre Dame's 1905 defeat of the American College of Medicine and Surgery, 142–0; World War I and II drill practices and military maneuvers (IV–5; V–

6 and 25); Rockne's flamboyant and Leahy's interminable scrimmages; track-and-field competitions (V–26); Notre Dame's first homecoming (V–19), when football tickets were cheaper (V–21); and, of course, forty seasons of baseball, coached by Clarence "Jake" Kline since 1934. In 1962, with the groundbreaking for the development of the Memorial Library Quadrangle, Cartier Field was moved further southeast to a site behind the Athletic and Convocation Center (79).

H *Walk back to the South Quadrangle via the path along the north side of O'Shaughnessy Hall; continue west until you reach the intersecting path leading north in front of the main entrance of Chemistry Hall (53).*

Like athletics, teaching and research in science have long been traditional strengths of Notre Dame. Beginning in 1852, the chemical sciences stand out as a particular institutional forte. From its earliest days the chemistry department has engaged such talent as Fathers Thomas Vagnier, Joseph Carrier,

V–25

V–26

John Zahm, and Julius Nieuwland, and Professors Henry Froning, Kenneth Campbell, George Hennion, and Charles Price.

Chemistry was the first department of the University to have a separate building (Hoynes Hall, 1902, III–54). After that building (42) was partially destroyed by a phosphorous fire (III–56) in 1916, the present structure (V–27), designed by Edward Tilton of New York, was built, and the chemistry department occupied it the following year. An addition to this structure for the chemical engineering department was added at its east end in 1934, and a former campus post office (IV–9) was moved to its rear in 1940 to serve as a library.

I *Walk to the front of Nieuwland Science Hall (52).*

Julius Arthur Nieuwland, whose achievement is perpetuated in the University's history by the science complex named in his honor, was probably Notre Dame's most outstanding research scientist in the early twentieth century. Born in Europe in 1878 and raised in Belgian community of Mishawaka (Indi-

ana), Nieuwland was educated at Notre Dame (B.A., 1899) and at Catholic University (Ph.D., 1904). Though trained as a chemist, he first taught botany when he returned to Notre Dame in 1904. As a botanist, he founded and edited a bimonthly journal, *The American Midland Naturalist*, and also developed the University herbarium and botanical library.

Organic chemistry, however, most

intrigued Nieuwland ever since he had written his doctoral thesis, "Reactions of Acetylene." By 1918 he had become director of chemical research at Notre Dame and devoted his energy solely to the teaching of graduate students (V–29) and his own research (V–28). In a paper read before the Organic Chemical Symposium at Rochester, New York, in 1926, he disclosed his now famous catalytic polymerization of

V–25–26. Cartier Field, 1916–41
Among its many uses, Cartier Field and its surrounding terrain have been the site of military drill and calisthenics and Notre Dame outdoor track-and-field events since 1900.

V–28–29. Julius A. Nieuwland, 1878–1936
V–28, in his laboratories with an associate chemist; V–29, in front of Science Hall (III-45) with the first class of doctoral students in chemistry and the largest contingent in the newly created 1918 summer session for advanced studies.

V–27. Chemistry Hall, 1917
This structure was originally intended to be another limestone building like the Lemonnier Library (14), which was erected the same year. President Cavanaugh had to settle for a three-storey brick structure when the provincial council cut his original budget request.

V–27

V–28

V–29

acetylene which culminated in the basic patents in the manufacture of neoprene, or "synthetic rubber." E. I. du Pont de Nemours and Company immediately became interested in Nieuwland's research, subsidizing it as well as paying him handsome consulting fees which he, in turn, used to augment the chemistry library holdings. The royalty income from the Nieuwland patents was later used by the University to cover a part of the cost of constructing Nieuwland Science Hall in 1952.

J *Continue walking north in front of Nieuwland Science Hall to the center of the path between Nieuwland and the Old Fieldhouse (57).*

The new science complex was built on the recreation and athletic fields known as the Brownson, or seniors' campus (V–30) throughout the nineteenth century. Here, reports the 1865 *Guide to the University*, was "a well-constructed ball alley solidly built of brick, plus poles, hand swings, balladores, spring boards, and the various et ceteras of gymnastic exercises, very puzzling and confusing to the uninitiated, though familiar to the ath-

V–30. Brownson Campus, 1893
The Athletic fields and bleachers were directly behind the Science Hall (now La Fortune Student Center) and in front of the first main gym (III–34), pictured here at the extreme right.

V–31. Electrostatic Generator (Atom Smasher)
Built in the basement annex of old Science Hall by Professors Bernard Waldman (VI–34) and George Collins and completed in 1942, this atom smasher was the second of four built by the physics department on the campus.

letes who there develop agility and muscular strength." Subsequently, the site was also a baseball diamond (V–23), rugby, soccer, and football gridirons, and military drill fields.

In appropriate proximity to these fields were the University gymnasiums, the first (III–34) built in 1882 on a site now occupied by Cavanaugh Hall (51) and the Fieldhouse (57), erected in 1898. The Fieldhouse, now a decrepit hulk falling down about itself, was once an imposing, castellated edifice (V–33) and the pride of President Andrew Morrissey who built it. Morrissey, as his corpulence indicated, was not a practitioner of athletics, but he did believe in the classical ideal, *mens sana in corpore sano* ("a healthy mind in a healthy body"). Unfortunately, the 1898 gymnasium that he built burned down in 1899 (V–32). Undaunted, Morrissey promptly authorized the immediate reconstruction of "one of the largest college gymnasia in the United States." Despite Morrissey's claims of its modernity, he did not hesitate to reuse its old 1893 cornerstone (note the stone at the building's southwest corner).

V–30

V–31

V–32

V–33

V–32–34. University Fieldhouse
V–32, aflame, 1898; V–33, reconstructed, 1899; V–34, concessioned, 1914.

V–34

The rebuilt Fieldhouse (V–33) was fireproof (a distinction given all Notre Dame buildings when they had been reconstructed after fires), and its interior space (180′ × 100′) was used for track-and-field events as well as indoor baseball and football practice. Basketball was played on a clay court that had to be watered down and rolled daily. Resembling a great white train shed with 122 skylights of fluted glass, the inside of the building's half-domed ceiling was finished in pressed steel of classical and Renaissance designs. In 1925 a basketball annex (V–38), complete with a movable hardwood court and a gallery seating 6,000 spectators, was added to the 1899 building. This extension, whose public entrance was on old Juniper Road, enabled the basketball varsity to play its home games on campus instead of at the South Bend YMCA. Gate receipts from Notre Dame's first and only

V–35. Pep Rally, ca 1940s
Frank Leahy addresses a rare daytime and
relatively somber student rally. Favorite
speakers besides the prolix Leahy
over the years included Clarence Manion,
Father Tom Brennan, sportswriter Arch
Ward, and actor Pat O'Brien, who
reenacted his Rockne impersonation.

V–35

V–36. Pep Rally, ca. 1950s
On any given Friday evening before a
home game, 6,000 or so students, alumni,
and visitors would follow the marching
band around the campus in a torchlight
parade, concluding their revelry in
the dirt pit of the Fieldhouse with an
hour of boosterism, effigy-hanging, and
general bedlam.

V–36

Rose Bowl appearance in 1925 helped pay for the new addition.

For more than three-quarters of a century, the Fieldhouse has had a multifaceted history. Its basketball arena, first a dirt-floor anachronism and then a pressurized capsule of cacophony (V–38), was always a disarming experience for opponents. From its balcony the rituals of mass hysteria known as football pep rallies (V–35–36) were enacted on appropriate Friday evenings each autumn. In its central arena, various initiation rites took place such as the annual Bengal Boxing Bouts (V–37) and the June commencement exercises. Here Rockne and Westbrook Pegler shook hands, supposedly to end a famous feud; here occupants of Carroll Hall refectory would compete in relay races for special cherry pastry tarts; here visiting dignitaries (FDR, W. B. Yeats, G. K. Chesterton) addressed the University; here the students held their Mock Political Convention and their annual Mardi Gras; and now here the art department has many of its studios, a huge ceramics workshop and kilns, and the Isis student art gallery.

K *Walk north in front of the Fieldhouse, pass the entrance to the Isis gallery (open Monday through Friday afternoons), and proceed northeast along the diagonal path to the center of the North Quadrangle.*

During the late 1930s and throughout the 1940s and 1950s, campus expansion shifted from the southeast to the northeast. Here a North Quadrangle was eventually created on what had first been University farmland, then the minims' playing fields (III–31–32), and, by the 1920s, the location of the now demolished Freshman and Sophomore Halls (V–39–40). These two hastily erected temporary wooden structures were built by the Uni-

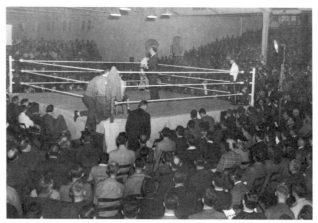

V–37

V–38

V–37–38. Fieldhouse Sports
V–37, Bengal Bout finals before 3,500 spectators in 1946; V–38, basketball in the 1940s before a capacity crowd.

V–39–40. Beginnings of Underclassmen's Quad, 1922–23
V–39, Freshman Hall, a two-storey (270' × 45'), clapboard structure accommodating 176 men; V–40, Sophomore Hall, built at right angles to Freshman Hall.

V–39

V–40

V–41. **Farley Women, 1974**

V–42. **Navy Drill Hall, 1943–62**

versity's engineering department in 1922 and 1923 to alleviate the housing shortage caused by the student influx soon after the First World War. Freshman Hall was located approximately in the center of the quadrangle just east of Zahm Hall (50). Sophomore Hall stood almost exactly on the site of the present Farley Hall (59). These two "cardboard palaces" enabled 362 men to move back on campus and were used extensively until they were torn down in 1932 (Freshman Hall) and 1936 (Sophomore Hall, which was renamed Freshman Hall in 1932).

With the removal of these temporary barracks, the University began rebuilding in its now familiar collegiate Gothic mode. Cavanaugh Hall (51), named in honor of the eighth president (III–77), began the North Quad in 1936. Zahm Hall, to perpetuate the memory of the C.S.C. scientist (III–46), opened the following year, and in 1939 the outlines of the new quad became distinguishable with the siting of Breen-Phillips Hall (58), named for two alumni and benefactors—Frank B. Phillips and William P. Breen,

both of Fort Wayne, Indiana. With the additions of the Wenninger-Kirsch Building (1936; renovated in 1974 and renamed Haggar Hall), Farley Hall (59), built in 1947, Keenan (49) and Stanford (48) Halls in 1957, and the North Dining Hall (60) in 1957, the quad was complete. The tradition of locating underclassmen on this north end of the campus (begun with Freshman and Sophomore Halls) continued until 1962 when the quadrangle's six dormitories became multiclass residences just like the other campus dormitories. Now two of them, Breen-Phillips and Farley, are dorms for undergraduate women (V–41).

In 1936, the year that the first dormitory was being constructed on the North Quad, the Wenninger-Kirsch Hall was also being erected. A tribute to the two teachers (V–43 and 44) who pioneered in expanding the natural sciences at Notre Dame and to the University's traditional expertise in biology, the structure's new classrooms, laboratories, herbarium, greenhouses, library, and scientific apparatus initially appeared adequate. It soon became necessary to expand the facility, es-

V–41

V–42

V–43–45. Three Generations of Biologists
Since 1882 when Alexander Kirsch (1855–1923) returned to Notre Dame from Louvain to teach anatomy, cytology, and bacteriology, the University's biology department has expanded its reputation. Francis Wenninger (1888–1940) (V–43) succeeded Kirsch (V–44) as department head and then became dean of the College of Science. Wenninger recruited J. Arthur Reyniers (1908–67) (V–45), whose pioneering work with germfree animals and isolation techniques led to the establishment of LOBUND.

V–43

V–44

V–45

pecially in the area allotted to the bacteriological research begun by Professor James A. Reyniers (V–45). Encouraged by Dean Wenninger and later by President O'Hara in his innovative attempts to obtain and sustain germfree laboratory animals, Reyniers's first lab specimens were nurtured in fruit jars in the old Science Hall (III–49). In 1936 his research quarters were moved into twenty-three laboratories (which he designed) in the basement of the new biology building. By 1947 three additional structures—a machine shop (66) in which to fashion tools and machinery, a storage laboratory for the animals (mostly monkeys and rats), and the Germfree Life Building (68)—were built to the north of the biology complex. Although Reyniers eventually left the research institute, his pioneer work continued under the direction of former associates and graduate students. The entire program was known by the acronym LOBUND (Laboratories of Bacteriology at the University of Notre Dame) and divided into three divisions: germfree life, biological engineering, and micrurgy. Although Wenninger-

Kirsch Hall has been converted to Haggar Hall (and now houses the psychology department), LOBUND continues its research in the ancillary structures behind the building and in the Paul V. Galvin Life Sciences Center (84).

L *Walk northeast across the North Quad to the path between Breen-Phillips Hall (58) and Farley Hall (59) and proceed east across the service road and along the path to the left of the WNDU building (70) until you reach the Vetville historical marker at the north side of Memorial Library (72).*

Completion of the North Quadrangle was one University response to the pressure of increased student enrollment in the late 1930s and 1940s; the creation of Vetville for married students was another response. With the termination of World War II, over one-and-one-half million veterans wanted to resume or to begin a college education supported by the Servicemen's Readjustment Act, more popularly known as the "G.I. Bill." Unlike many other major universities that were faced with increased postwar

V–46

V–47

V–46–47. LOBUND
Figure V–46 shows scientists in the
Reyniers Germfree Life Building (68)
transferring a monkey into apparatus
preparatory to performing a Caesarian
section to obtain germfree animals
for scientific research; V–47 shows
a technician, outfitted in a special sterile
suit, preparing equipment for rearing a
colony of germfree animals.

student enrollments, Notre Dame's problem was complicated by its traditional policy against admitting married men to its undergraduate colleges. During the war years this policy had often been waived for certain students living in South Bend, but no provisions had been made to house married students with families on the campus.

By the spring of 1946, both on- and off-campus housing were at a premium. In May of that year University officials and the Federal Housing Authority announced plans for dismantling thirty-nine prisoner-of-war barracks at a military camp in Weingarten, Missouri, and transporting and reconstructing them on a thirteen-acre site (V–48) now occupied by the Memorial Library and its surrounding structures. The University allocated $40,000 to clear the site of some of its farm buildings (V–15), to plat the village tract, to construct roads, and to install water mains and sewers. The government subsidized ($400,000) the transfer and rebuilding of the temporary structures.

Each of the barracks (V–50) was divided into three small apartments

which, in turn, were subdivided by thin partitions into a kitchen (V–49), two bedrooms, a living room, and a bath. These apartments provided cheap housing (in 1946, rent was $27 a month) for 117 families. Only families (V–52) could qualify for such housing, and their financial situation was another factor in the ultimate selection. Quarters were often furnished in the decor of "early marriage" via purchases from Goodwill stores and the St. Vincent de Paul Society.

While carrying a full undergraduate load of studies, practically all these married students worked in factories or business in South Bend or neighboring cities. Many wives also had full-time jobs outside the home. For example, Eugene Jaeger, a father of four in 1951, commuted two days a week to an East Chicago steel plant while his wife, June, worked the three-to-eleven shift for U.S. Rubber Company in Mishawaka. When his G.I. Bill benefits ran out and his wife became pregnant, Jaeger began a hectic daily schedule: 8:00 A.M. to noon he worked as an engineer at Bendix in South Bend, 1:00 P.M. to 5:00 P.M.

V–48. Vetville, ca. 1954
This airview, looking west, shows (l. to r.) Cartier Field (V–26), the Navy Drill Hall (V–42), Vetville Recreation Hall, and the thirty-nine apartment dwellings. Juniper Road was curved to force it along the perimeter of Cartier Field. Bulla Road (lower right) still penetrated the campus to the site of the present WNDU-TV station.

V–49. Vetville Interior

he attended his University classes, and 6:00 P.M. to 10:00 P.M. he continued his job at Bendix. In between, he studied.

Although not all married Notre Dame students faced as extreme financial pressures as the Jaegers, life in Vetville was a hardscrabble existence for most of the young parents. Pooling of resources (baby-sitters, laundry facilities, autos, foodstuffs, medicines, even finances) was a necessity. Named the "fertile valley" by its residents, 106 babies were born to Vetville parents in the 1946–47 school year and the birthrate climbed during the next decade. Given the generational continuity of many Notre Dame students, a number of undergraduates by the mid-1960s could list their birthplace as none other than the Notre Dame campus.

The Vetville community governed itself through a legislative council elected from the six wards into which the village was divided. Residents also elected a mayor, who was charged to negotiate with the University administration for better garbage collection, paved streets, food cooperatives, and playgrounds.

Like any other municipality, Vetville occupants badgered the appropriate civic agencies for improved bus and phone service and police protection. Eventually they convinced the Federal Housing Authority to build a recreation hall (V–48) and playgrounds (appropriately enough on land where the minims [III–31] had formerly taken their recess periods). They also persuaded the University to permit them the use of the Navy Drill Hall (V–42) for dances, potluck suppers, and other social events. Their own newspaper, *The Vetville Gazette*, trumpeted these community action successes as well as new births, jobs, and residents.

Vetville housed married students and their families until 1961, when its buildings were bulldozed and burned to make way for the Memorial Library. That same year the University secured a federal loan of $1 million to construct new married-student housing known as University Village (4), located to the north and west of the main campus along U.S. 31-33.

Federal assistance, a series of major fund-raising campaigns, and sev-

V–48

V–49

V–50–52. Vetville, ca. 1940s
The view in V–50 was taken atop the
Administration Building, looking
east to the married students' complex. In
the background, especially at the top
right, can be seen some of the remaining
farm buildings (note the circular barn)
from the relocated Notre Dame farm.
Photos V–51–52 show other aspects of
Vetville life.

V–50

V–51

V–52

V–53. Ellerbe Projection, 1967
Ellerbe Associates designed this
architectural scale model for a new
quadrangle to be created north of the
Memorial Library (top left). Only Grace
(90) and Flanner (89) Towers have
been built.

V–54. St. Joseph's Farm, 1974
All Notre Dame farm operations were
moved from the campus proper eight miles
east to Granger, Indiana, where the
brothers' community had maintained
another farm since Sorin purchased the
land in 1865. This air photograph
shows the extent of the complex in 1974.

V–54

eral generous private donors all helped transform the Vetville site into still another quadrangle. In 1962 the Stepan Center (69), one of the earliest geodesic-domed structures in the nation, was donated by Alfred C. Stepan of Chicago and erected as a general student-activity building. Then in the late 1960s, five new high-rise student residence halls were tentatively projected to form a semicircle around a proposed modern chapel (V–53). Only two of the eleven-storey skyscraper dormitories have been built: Flanner Tower (89), a gift of Mrs. John L. Kellogg in memory of her son, Thomas Flanner; and Grace Tower (90), donated by J. Peter Grace in the name of his father, Joseph P. Grace. Both dorms, which together house 1,056 students, were built in 1969.

The Memorial Library Quadrangle was not built until the late 1960s, but it is, in part, the logical outgrowth of trends already evident in the presidential administration of John J. Cavanaugh in the late 1940s. Post–World War II Notre Dame faced many of the problems (increased enrollment, need for endow-

ment and academic upgrading, football fame) that the post–World War I institution had encountered. John Cavanaugh (V–55). president from 1946 to 1952, met some of these challenges and passed others on to his designated successor, Theodore M. Hesburgh.

Cavanaugh's personality, aspirations, and achievements link early twentieth-century Notre Dame with the University of the past two decades. After working as a private secretary in the office of Henry Ford, young John came to Notre Dame and served a two-year secretarial apprenticeship (1917–19) under President John W. Cavanaugh (no relation) and briefly under President James Burns. As a lay student he was a popular campus leader, head of the early SAC, and a recipient of one of the University's first four-year bachelor degrees in commerce in 1923. After graduation he worked in the South Bend offices of Studebaker as an advertising manager. In 1926 he resigned to enter the Holy Cross novitiate. Earning a master's degree in English a year later, he studied theology in Washington, D.C., was ordained in 1931, took a

V–55

V–56

V–55. University Executives, 1922–75
Four Notre Dame presidents whose combined tenure spans over a half-century include: (l. to r.) John F. O'Hara (1934–40), Theodore Hesburgh (1952–), Matthew J. Walsh (1922–28), and John J. Cavanaugh (1946–52).

V–56. University President Cavanaugh and President Truman

V–57. Student "Extras" in 1940
This group of undergraduates acted as typical Notre Dame students in the 1940 Warner Brothers' film, **Knute Rockne, All-American.**

licentiate in philosophy at the Gregorian University in Rome, and returned to Notre Dame to succeed John O'Hara as university prefect of religion. Appointed University vice-president and chairman of the Faculty Board of Athletics that would hire Frank Leahy, he assisted President Hugh O'Donnell during the World War II years. Father Cavanaugh, although a devoted cleric, employed his business and secular experience to grapple with various problems in his own postwar administration. A gracious man with numerous non-University con-

tacts and friends (V–56), he avoided the moral calisthenics of O'Hara and the insecure pomposity of Hugh O'Donnell in articulating his vision for the future Notre Dame.

President John J. Cavanaugh's plans for the University remarkably paralleled President Burns's aspirations of a quarter of a century earlier. Quick to recognize the necessity of, and changes in, academic fund-raising as a constant of modern University existence, Cavanaugh, along with his tireless alumni association president, Harry Hogan, set up the Notre Dame

Foundation in 1947. Its goal: raise $25 million in a decade. Funds were solicited to build Nieuwland Science Hall, O'Shaughnessy Hall, the E. M. Morris Inn (21), and the Fred and Sally Fisher Hall (9). The foundation also was to be the beginning of a permanent University endowment. At the end of his first three years as president, Cavanaugh, like Burns at the beginning of his first three years, reorganized the University administration in order to meet the multiple needs of both academic and physical expansion. To a cabinet of four C.S.C. priests who

served as his vice-presidents, Cavanaugh delegated various responsibilities: Howard Kenna, academic affairs; John J. Burke, business affairs; Joseph A. Kohoe, student affairs; John Murphy, public relations. Theodore M. Hesburgh, a thirty-two-year-old theology instructor and popular chaplain of Vetville, was named executive vice-president.

During his six-year term, Cavanaugh endeavored to upgrade the academic quality of his University. He authorized the Institute of Medieval Studies, brainchild of Philip Moore (V–63); an annual nat-

V–57

V–58. Walsh Hall Dormitory Residents, ca. 1950

V–58

ural law institute; the Committee on International Relations; and LO-BUND (V–46–47). The expansion of advanced studies and research became a high priority under Cavanaugh, and the number of students in the Graduate School rose from 96 in 1946 to 450 in 1951. He created resentment among certain old-guard faculty members when he announced the need for a Distinguished Professors Program, implying that certain current faculty did not compare favorably with those he planned to recruit from other institutions. He also sought to establish lay advisory councils for each of the University's colleges. Finally, he used Notre Dame as a platform from which to raise a perennial question of twentieth-century American Catholic intellectual history: "Where are the Catholic Salks, Oppenheimers, Einsteins?"

Cavanaugh hoped, as had Sorin, Lemonnier, and Burns before him, that such Catholic intellectuals would come from Notre Dame. By the late 1940s an eager and dedicated, but still woefully underpaid, faculty (V–59–64) was endeavoring to achieve academic viability in

teaching, research, and publication. Representative scholars included John Frederick (English), Henry Bolger (physics), Leo R. Ward (philosophy), Karl Menger (mathematics), Philip Moore (medieval studies), Charles Price (chemistry), and Waldemar Gurian (politics).

Menger (V–62) and Gurian (V–64) were just two of the over forty European scholars who helped to enrich and professionalize the Notre Dame faculty during the period 1930–60. Part of a larger academic, scientific, and artistic migration that would enhance and enliven American educational, intellectual, and cultural history, some of the first Notre Dame refugee scholars (for example, Menger and Gurian; Eugene Guth, physics; Arthur Haas, physics; Ferdinand Hermens, politics) emigrated when the Anschluss and other repressive measures were begun by the Axis powers in the 1930s. Others (for example, Boleslaw Szczesniak, history; Astrik Gabriel, medieval studies; Stephen Kertesz, politics) came after the war. A third wave of scholars (for example, Gerhart Niemeyer, politics; Ernest Brandl, architecture; Eric

Voegelin, politics) joined the faculty ranks in the 1950s. Part of what historian John Nef has called "the Notre Dame Renaissance," these professors and their colleagues enlarged Notre Dame's participation in the wider American academic community via the sponsorship of symposia, their outside lecturing and publishing, and their personal contacts with refugee scholars in other havens such as Princeton's Center for Advanced Study and the Committee on Social Thought at the University of Chicago. Notre Dame's foreign-trained faculty also brought a new cultural heterogeneity to the campus, helped make research and publication an integral part of University life, and contributed greatly to the expansion of the Graduate School.

One of the chief characteristics of Notre Dame undergraduate students during the Cavanaugh era (V–57–58), many of whom were the sons of European immigrants, was their tremendous numerical increase. In fact, one of Cavanaugh's and the University's most crucial decisions was whether Notre Dame should attempt to maintain the status quo of its pre-

V–59

V–60

V–62

V–61

V–59. Ivan Mestrovic, Artist-in-Residence

V–60. John T. Frederick, Professor of American Literature

V–61. Arthur Haas, President John O'Hara, Arnold Lunn

V–62. Karl Menger, Professor of Mathematics

V–63. Philip Moore, Medievalist and Director of the Graduate School

V–63

V–64. Waldemar Gurian, Founder and Editor of The Review of Politics

V–65. Notre Dame, 1954

V–64. Waldemar Gurian, Founder and Editor of The Review of Politics

war enrollment of approximately 3,200, or whether the University could safely expand to absorb the tremendous demands for postwar college education. Cavanaugh decided to let Notre Dame grow beyond its earlier self-imposed enrollment limit to a high of 5,100 undergraduates in 1952, an increase of better than 62 percent during his six-year tenure.

This rapid increase in the student population naturally overcrowded all available housing, feeding, and teaching facilities. Dormitory singles became doubles; doubles were converted into triples. Vetville housed some returning veterans, but other students, married and single, again were forced to search South Bend for private rooms and apartments. All available classrooms were used, and temporary buildings, constructed by the navy during the war, were (and still are) utilized to accommodate the overflow classes. Student life, despite the increased size of the student body, appeared to resist, through the resident-hall system, the potential impersonality of an expanded University. New activities (for example, student coun-

cil, Young Christian Students, Notre Dame Symphony, Notre Dame Chamber of Commerce, the *Tech Review*, Aesculepians) expanded extracurricular life, and new academic departments (for example, economics, and sociology-anthropology) stimulated a more diverse intellectual life. As Professor Richard Sullivan remembers the 1940s, discipline regulations were almost as demanding as student days of the late 1920s: "a certain number of appearances have to be made at chapel, morning and evening; no student can ordinarily be out later than midnight; freshmen get that late hour only once a week, and if they otherwise conduct themselves in seemly fashion; a letter from home has to justify in advance any weekend spent away; students journeying forth check out and, returning, check in; room lights are turned off by a master switch at eleven o'clock at night in most halls; those reserved for upperclassmen sometimes, by traditional arrangement, get electricity until twelve; drunkenness and gambling are matters for instant suspension or expulsion; cars may be owned or driven only by

special and rare permission, under elaborate restrictions."

John J. Cavanaugh presided over such an institution during the crucial years of transition, 1946–52. However, he also prodded the University into a greater emphasis on secular education and primed Notre Dame for an unprecedented era of change that his successor would oversee for the next two decades. Cavanaugh, desirous by his own account of "breaking Notre Dame out of the monastic mentality," set a now familiar style for the University chief executive. He carried Notre Dame's name and needs to the committees of the American Council on Education and the Ford Foundation. He served on the Board of Visitors to the U.S. Naval Academy and on the Board of Directors of the Great Books Foundation. He hobnobbed with diplomatic, governmental, and military officials as well as wealthy alumni and men of business. When his term expired in 1952, one significant chapter of the University's history was concluded. Another chapter began when he chose Theodore M. Hesburgh as his presidential successor.

VI. The University, 1952-76

VI–1. Notre Dame, 1957
An aerial view taken looking toward the northwest and illustrating the expansion of the campus in the late 1950s along the North Quadrangle located in the middle right of the photograph.

Chapter VI does not follow the format of the previous chapters in that it does not have an accompanying campus walk. Instead, the reader is invited to walk (south) to the front of the Memorial Library reflecting pool in front of the library mural plaque (see drawing right marked *). At this location, the reader will be in the center of the Memorial Library Quadrangle and in a position to survey several important structures—Memorial Library, Radiation Research Building, Computing Center and Mathematics Building, Paul V. Galvin Life Sciences Building, and the Athletic and Convocation Center—that were erected in the 1960s. The library mall was also the location of several important communal campus activities and rallies during this decade. In the 1952–76 period, the University experienced the greatest physical growth in its history. The twenty-four new buildings, four major renovations, and two additions undertaken during this time are depicted (by cross-hatching) on this drawing. A number of the new structures were sited according to a new master campus plan (VI–10) drawn by Ellerbe Associates in 1967.

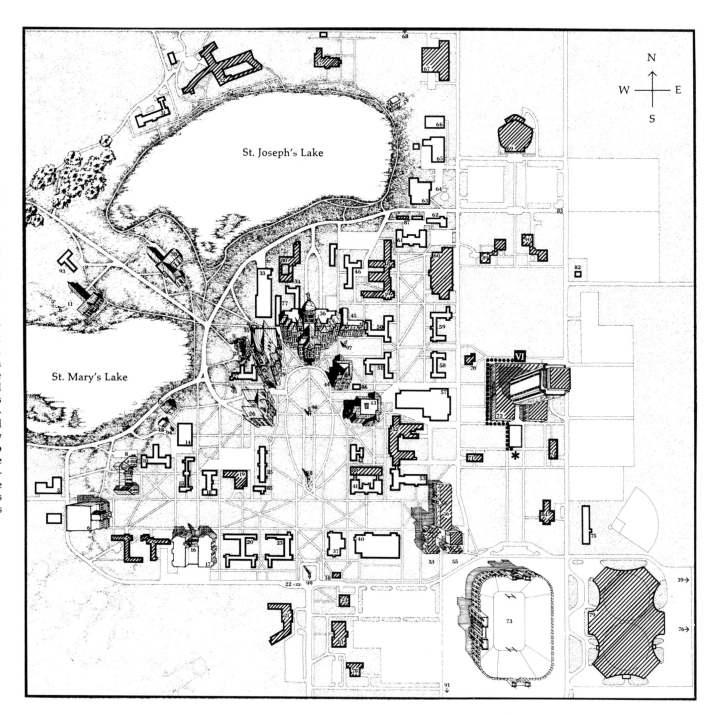

Hesburgh, Academic Growth, Coeducation

NO MAN HAS GOVERNED the University of Notre Dame longer than Theodore Martin Hesburgh (VI–2–8). Contemporary observers of the University's past two decades have depicted Hesburgh's presidency as the one constant factor in a period of unprecedented change. One author simply entitled the last third of his University history: "Hesburgh." Two other writers named their book on student life in the 1960s: *Hesburgh's Notre Dame: Triumph in Transition.* Numerous other Notre Dame observers saw that Hesburgh came to personify the University in the public mind. The *New York Times* considered him the chief reason for Notre Dame becoming "a citadel of liberalism among Catholic universities," while *The Nation* described him as not only the last of the high-powered, domineering, aggressive American college presidents, but also perhaps the "first of

Notre Dame in 1976
Acreage: 1,250   Buildings: 85
Faculty: 656   Tuition: $2,782
Students: 8,750
Room/board: $1,169

a new breed of low-profile, priest-politicians."

Born in Syracuse, New York, in 1917, Theodore Hesburgh began his undergraduate education at Notre Dame in 1934. James Burns, superior of the C.S.C. Indiana Province, recognized a young man whose special talents could be used by the community and sent him off for advanced study at the Gregorian University in Rome in 1937 before the young Hesburgh had even completed his bachelor's degree. While pursuing further graduate work in theology, Hesburgh was ordained a priest of the Congregation of Holy Cross in 1943. After receiving his doctorate in sacred theology from Catholic University in 1945, he returned to teach at Notre Dame. Thereafter he rose rapidly in the University's administration. Named theology department chairman in 1948, he became executive vice-president of the University in 1949 and president in 1952. Highlights of his public service record include participation on the U.S. Commission on Civil Rights (VI–5), the International Atomic Energy Agency (VI–7), the Carnegie Commission

on the Future of Higher Education, the Board of Directors of the Chase Manhattan Bank, and the Rockefeller Foundation. He, and indirectly the University, was honored by receiving the U.S. Medal of Freedom, the Meiklejohn Award of the American Association of University Professors, the Charles Evans Hughes Award of the National Conference of Christians and Jews, and the Reinhold Niebuhr Award. A recipient of honorary degrees from over forty colleges and universities, Hesburgh has traveled extensively (averaging over 130,000 miles a year) while performing a myriad of academic, university, civic, and ecclesiastical duties.

One way to essay Notre Dame and President Hesburgh in the post–World War II period is to divide the era into its two decades. In the 1950s young Hesburgh (he was thirty-five when he assumed the presidency) issued a challenge to his institution to become what he termed the "new Notre Dame." He set himself three tasks which he sought to accomplish simultaneously: build a first-rate undergraduate college and upgrade the

Graduate School; reorganize Notre Dame as a modern University; and create what, in his estimation, had heretofore been only an ideal—a Catholic university.

Hesburgh decided to restrict undergraduate enrollment to 5,500, demand higher Scholastic Aptitude Test scores from students for admission, and reform the curricula in the arts and letters, law, and engineering colleges. A galaxy of visiting lecturers (for example, historian Arnold Toynbee, theologian Martin D'Arcy, classicist Sir Richard Livingstone) and permanent faculty (for example, mathematician Vladimir Seidel, biochemist Charles E. Brownson, political theorist Stephen Kertesz) were recruited to promote academic excellence. The first comprehensive faculty manual in the University's history was compiled in 1954. Its subsequent revisions in 1967 and 1973 document the increasing role that the faculty has begun to play in the University's governance. By the conclusion of his first six-year presidential term in 1958, Hesburgh's Notre Dame already had several of the traits that would continue to characterize the

VI–3

VI–2

VI–2–4. Father Hesburgh at Home
Meeting with undergraduates (VI–2) in
the 1950s; officiating at the 1960
commencement exercises (VI–3) with
Cardinal Giovanni Baptista Montini
(later Pope Paul VI) and Dr. George
Shuster, Laetare medalist that year;
conferring with students (VI–4) in
the 1960s.

VI–4

VI–5

VI–6

VI–5–7. Father Hesburgh Abroad
Participating in a meeting of the U.S.
Civil Rights Commission with President
Kennedy in 1961 (VI–5); singled out for
outstanding national educational and
civic achievement in a cover story of
Time magazine (VI–6); representing the
Vatican at the International Atomic
Energy Agency in 1965 (VI–7).

VI–7

VI–8. Theodore Martin Hesburgh, C.S.C.,
Priest and President

VI–8

institution into the 1970s: academic development, increased faculty and student self-perception, and aggressive presidential leadership.

In the summer of 1958 the Congregation of Holy Cross voted to separate the superiorship of the C.S.C. religious community at Notre Dame from the University presidency, allowing Father Hesburgh to continue as the University's chief executive officer without a terminal date. (Since 1919 Notre Dame's president had also acted as the religious superior of the Holy Cross priests and brothers who lived and worked at the institution. The president-superior had thereby been limited to a term of six years under Canon Law 505. See Chapter IV.) Certain other occurrences in 1958 were indicative of the emerging modern Notre Dame: the Holy Cross sisters' convent closed, ending 115 years of service to the University; President Hesburgh began his first full year as a member of the U.S. Commission on Civil Rights; and eighteen undergraduate Notre Dame students were named to Woodrow Wilson Teaching Fellowships, the fifth largest number in the nation to merit this academic accolade.

The Ford Foundation selected Notre Dame in 1960 as one of six rapidly improving universities (others were Johns Hopkins, Vanderbilt, Denver, Brown, and Stanford) that would receive a grant of $6 million each if a matching $12 million could be raised from other sources within three years. The Ford grant, known in the University fund-raising parlance as Challenge I, was both an acknowledgment of the University's growth in the preceding decade and the beginning of the institution's constant quest for philanthropic income in the years to follow. Challenge I raised money for faculty development, increased student aid and scholarships, and funded a Freshman Year of Studies program and various area study programs (Latin America, East Europe, and Africa). This first major campaign of the 1960s also financed the construction of several facilities that symbolized new or expanded interests of the University: the Computing Center and Mathematics Building (74), erected in 1962; the Memorial Library (72), built in

VI–9–10. Memorial Library Construction, 1960–63

A view from the east, VI–9 shows the steel-frame skeleton of the library (left) and the Computing Center and Mathematics Building (right) in 1962. In the foreground is Cartier Field, and in the background the buildings of the Notre Dame farm can still be seen. Figure VI–10 illustrates the growth of the Library Quadrangle, flanked by old and new Juniper Roads, and shows (bottom to top of the aerial view): the stadium (73); then, within the quadrangle to the northwest, the Radiation Building (71); and to the northeast, the Computing Center and Mathematics Building (74); the Memorial Library (about to have its mural installed); and the Stepan Center (69), behind the library to the north.

VI–9

1961–63 (VI–9–10); and Lewis Hall for women religious (80), finished in 1965. While not a part of Challenge I, Skidmore, Owens, and Merrill's simple but extremely well-designed Radiation Research Building (71) was constructed by funds from the U.S. Atomic Energy Commission in 1963.

Subsequent financial campaigns raised an additional $80 million for the University. Challenge II (1963–66) financed the Athletic and Convocation Center (79), the renovation of the Lemonnier Library as the new residence of the School of Architecture (14), and the expansion of the power plant (63) and other service facilities. The SUMMA campaign (1967–72), the University's third major capital drive in less than ten years, secured $62 million to endow distinguished professorships, expand graduate education, provide for minority scholarships and student loans, and inaugurate special projects such as the Institute for Advanced Religious Studies. Blueprints for nine new buildings, including designs for a major high-rise dormitory complex and a new campus church (V–53), were pre-

pared as part of a new master campus plan (VI–12). Twenty-four new structures, four major renovations, and two building additions completed during the 1952–76 period drastically transformed Notre Dame. This physical expansion to the south and east (see map accompanying Chapter VI) embodied what some claimed to be the modern University's "edifice complex."

Various criticisms were leveled at Notre Dame's newest architecture: its exaggerated masses (particularly evident in the Memorial Library); its weakening of the campus's dramatic entrance (structures strung out along Notre Dame Avenue); and its confused dual-axis focal points (the visual conflict between the new library quadrangle and the old main quadrangle). In 1920 Francis Kervick had warned against building in "unharmonious scale" and producing "vertical monotony." He argued that "huge apartment-type residence halls" were incompatible with the University's traditional architectural ambience. Kervick likewise opposed stringing out unrelated buildings along the axial French boulevard (Notre Dame Avenue) first created

VI–10

VI–11. Library Mural, 1964
The 132-foot-high stone mosaic was patterned after Millard Sheets's painting, *The Word of Life*, with Christ as teacher surrounded by his apostles and an assembly of saints and scholars who have contributed to knowledge throughout the ages. A gift of Mr. and Mrs. Howard Phalin, the mural contains eighty-one different types of stone material from sixteen countries. Its fabrication was done in 171 finishes and the total composition contains 5,714 individual pieces. (A complete description of the mural's figures can be found on a plaque south of the library's reflecting pool.)

VI–11

by Sorin. "The beautiful and picturesque site of the University," insisted Kervick in his 1920 campus plan (IV–29), "will be negated and the buildings will front upon an uninteresting road with an indefinite beginning given to the campus and always with the buildings having the appearance of stragglers on the road to town."

Many architectural historians believe the Memorial Library (VI–11), designed by Ellerbe Associates in 1961–63, embodies several of Kervick's general caveats. Yet the building is a testament, if in too monumental a manner, to the academic and scholarly excellence to which Notre Dame now aspired. Various epithets given the building by students—"the largest grain elevator in the Midwest," "the brain silo," "Ted's Mahal," "Mount Excellence," or "the world's largest holy card"—attest to the structure's obvious visual incompatibility with the rest of the campus architecture (despite its being fifteen feet shorter than the Administration Building's golden dome), while at the same time acknowledging it as representative of the University's intellectual

VI–12. Master Campus Plan, 1967
Designed by Ellerbe and Associates, the new master plan was divided by the architects into three categories: A) existing buildings, particularly those nearing completion such as University Club (1), LOBUND Laboratory (2), power plant addition (3), and, Athletic and Convocation Center (4); B) SUMMA program buildings, which included life sciences (5), engineering (6), chemistry (7), North Dining Hall addition (8), undergraduate residences (9), business administration (10), advanced religious studies (11); and C) proposed future buildings such as mathematics (12), faculty offices (13), classroom buildings (14), aero engineering (15), fine arts (16), academic center (17), olympic swimming pool (18), physics (19), and Cardinal O'Hara Chapel (20) (Numbers here correspond to this blueprint of the 1967 master plan.)

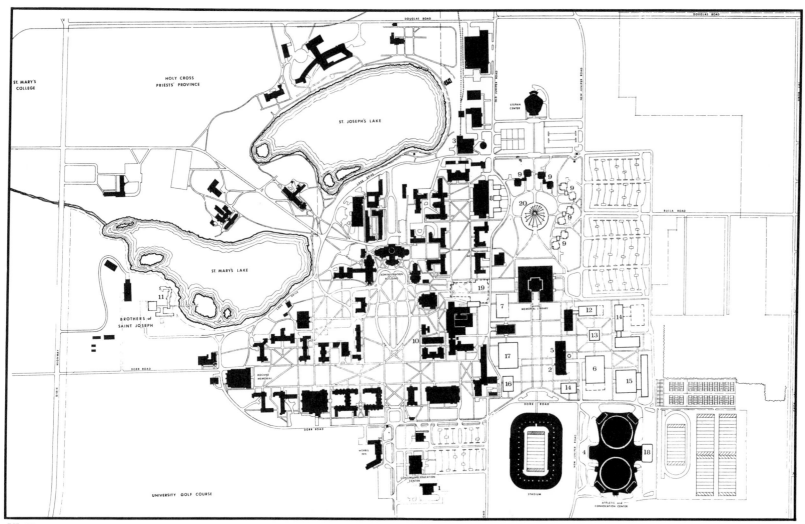

VI–13. Coach Ara Parseghian
Hoisted atop the shoulders of his team and fellow coaches, a jubilant Parseghian is carried across the field at the Cotton Bowl after Notre Dame's victory over the University of Texas in 1971.

VI–14. Sugar Bowl Postgame Victory Celebration, 1974

VI–13

VI–14

growth and aspirations since the early 1960s.

In the meantime, Notre Dame football, after a decade of disappointing seasons, returned to its winning ways under coach Ara Parseghian (VI–13), who continued the traditions of Rockne (for example, reading one of his teams an inspirational letter from a previously injured backfield star) and Leahy (for example, constantly stressing fundamentals and extensive pregame strategy). During his first season as head coach in 1964, Parseghian led Notre Dame (which had been 2–7 the previous year) to a 9–1 record and the MacArthur Bowl Award. Before resigning in 1974, he compiled a record of ninety-five wins, seventeen losses, and four games tied. In 1970 a longstanding tradition was overturned when Notre Dame played the University of Texas in its first postseason bowl competition since it had met Stanford in the 1925 Rose Bowl. The University's administration justified its change of policy by saying that it wished to use the game's proceeds to expand a minority scholarships program. Winning seasons under

VI–15. Athletic and Convocation Center, 1968
In part of the opening-week ceremonies of the new athletic and convocation facility, the Notre Dame basketball team, led by All-American Austin Carr (shooting in this photograph), defeated UCLA.

VI–15

Parseghian permitted Notre Dame to continue this arrangement, returning to bowl competition (VI–14) repeatedly in the early 1970s.

The 1960s, however, marked a time of tension as well as growth and renewed football fame. Influenced by internal issues (debates over student regulations, University governance, and coeducation) and important external events (the Peace Corps, civil rights, Vatican Council II, and the Vietnam War), Notre Dame entered a decade of turmoil in which an intense internal debate was waged over the University's future direction, identity, and purpose. A narrative of the numerous, and often interrelated, events of this time reveals that while a great deal changed, much remained the same. A longer perspective will be necessary to write an adequate historical study of the University's recent past; what is now possible is to attempt to narrate what now appear to have been the crucial events of the period, to estimate the major changes that occurred, and, where possible, to suggest something of the temper of the transition, if not its total meaning.

In the early 1960s there were portents of the contention that would erupt in the last half of that decade. There were student protests over the disciplinary regimen such as a demonstration in front of Corby Hall in 1960 when students pressed their demands for an end to excessive dormitory regulations. Arguments for increased intellectual excellence surfaced in an eighty-page report written and submitted to the administration in 1961 by student leaders and fellowship recipients known as the Committee of Nineteen. Student journalists on *The Scholastic*, attempting to print various student proposals for restructuring the University, chafed under editorial censorship.

In April 1963, President Hesburgh countered these criticisms in the first in a series of long, personal letters that he would write during the decade. These "Epistles of Hesburgh to His Constituencies," as student journalists called them, became one of the forums whereby Father Hesburgh endeavored to assess, redirect, or initiate the multiple changes that his institution underwent throughout the decade.

VI–16

VI–17

VI–16–17. Notre Dame Abroad
Professor Donald Costello (VI–16), director of the Notre Dame Innsbruck Program in Austria from 1973 to 1975, lectures on modern European drama in the baroque *Claudia Saal, Institut für Finanzwissenschaft, die Universität Innsbruck.* Photo VI–17 shows Joseph Keyerleber (left) and David Coombs (right), Notre Dame class of 1961, on assignment with the Peace Corps in 1963, offering instruction to two young Chilean students.

Debate over University governance began in 1963 and was to continue in attempts by students and some faculty members to divide the executive powers that Father Hesburgh held into separate offices of president and chancellor. In that year the reformers, concerned that Father Hesburgh was frequently absent from the University due to the press of his numerous national and international responsibilities, advocated having a layman take over the office of president, a position that would remain the chief internal office of the University and its principal academic policymaking position. George N. Shuster (VI–3), former chairman of Notre Dame's English department, former president of Hunter College, and a special assistant to President Hesburgh since 1961, was often proposed as a possible candidate in this early effort at a partial laicization of the University power structure. In 1969 students proffered Willis D. Nutting (VI–33), associate professor in the general program of liberal studies and faculty member at Notre Dame since 1936, for the presidency in a later attempt to broaden the base of University executive authority. In both instances, the chancellor (whom the reformers always anticipated would be Hesburgh) would continue to represent Notre Dame in the national Catholic community and in national and international circles.

The misgivings over President Hesburgh's authority was only one manifestation of the preoccupation with challenge and change that marked the decade. The world outside the University came under special scrutiny. Social science research was expanded with the creation of the Center for the Study of Man in Contemporary Society. Undergraduate foreign study campuses were established at Innsbruck, Austria (VI–16), and later at Angers (France), Sophia (Japan), Cali (Colombia)—changed to Anahuac, Mexico, in 1970—and Taipei (Taiwan). Notre Dame students were also eligible to participate in the St. Mary's College program in Rome, Italy. Specialized curricula were likewise begun by the Law School in London, by the School of Architecture in Rome, and by the English department in Dublin. Political and social concerns were expressed by student involvement in the Mississippi voter registration projects in 1961–63 and in the Peace Corps (VI–17). The Second Vatican Council (1962–64) prompted increased theological speculation, innovative liturgical programs, and nascent plans for an ecumenical Center for Advanced Religious Studies at the University.

By 1967 a Catholic pentecostal movement had gathered momentum among a vocal group of students as well as a few faculty and staff people. Notre Dame's administration hosted a seminar at Land O'Lakes, Wisconsin, that produced an important position paper, "On the Nature of the Contemporary Catholic University," stressing intellectual autonomy and academic freedom. The statement, signed by twenty-six prominent Catholics (virtually all top officials of Catholic institutions of higher learning in North America), was later adopted by the International Federation of Catholic Universities at Louvanium University, Kinshasa, Congo.

Through a complex mixture of internal and external factors, the University's development was being shaped both by the individuals who were directing and debating its policies and by the historical milieu in which it was maturing. This dialectic, always present in an institution's history, reached a high intensity during the final five academic years of the 1960s.

Notre Dame experienced its first major anti–Vietnam War activity when a daylong teach-in was held on October 16, 1965. Faculty, students, and two non-University speakers debated American involvemen in Southeast Asia for over twelve hours. The political spectrum represented the nation in microcosm: Students for a Democratic Society, *realpolitikers*, Young Americans for Freedom, cold-war liberals, pacifists, and radicals. Two students, Joel R. Connelly and Howard J. Dooley, who wrote about their undergraduate years at Notre Dame in the 1960s, saw the 1965 Vietnam symposium as indicative of the temper of Notre Dame student protest movement for the remainder of the decade. In their estimation, "a pattern emerged here which set its stamp on Notre Dame's anti-war activism for the duration of the war-protest phenomenon. Notre Dame students remained by and large non-ideological in their anti-Vietnam stance, thus avoiding much of the factionalism and irrational one-upmanship which made a shambles of the ideologically committed New Left. Notre Dame students also, for the most part, remained tactical moderates, preferring peaceful demonstrations to bear witness to their concern rather than more violent activism." In 1967, two hundred students, faculty, and religious protesters (VI–18), demonstrated against the job interviewing which was being conducted at the University Placement Bureau by Dow Chemical Company. Dow produced, among other things, napalm, which was being used by the U.S. military in the war in Southeast Asia.

Student unrest, which had been sputtering at Notre Dame since the first anti-Vietnam teach-in in 1965, boiled over in various directions during 1968–69. A Student General Assembly was held in the Stepan Center by students who hoped to galvanize current discontent and draw up agendas for reform. Student body presidents ran on "student power" platforms of varying militancy. Various student newspapers, such as the underground *Thursday Throwback* and the student government's *Voice*, emerged in the early 1960s only to disappear by the middle of the decade. Another student paper, *The Observer*, appeared in 1966 and survived to report, instigate, and occasionally misrepresent the student agitation. In the tempest, students expressed their personal frustrations, genuine social interests, petty grievances, and idealistic concerns. They protested against the University's lack of a totally open speakers policy, disciplinary regulations and parietal restrictions, the presence and accreditation of the ROTC, the small number of minorities on the faculty and in the student body, campus job interviewing by the Central Intelligence Agency, and the escalation of the Vietnam War. Students and faculty debated the issues and personalities in the turbulent 1968 presidential primaries: some got "clean for Gene," while others insisted "Nixon's the one" (the traditional Patriot of the Year Award of the senior class—given to Richard Nixon in 1960—was replaced in 1968 by the Senior Fellow Award, the first recipient being Eugene McCarthy). Throughout 1968–69, rallies and counterrallies, demonstrations and counterdemonstrations (VI–20), created cultural as well as academic confusion. A University-sanctioned, week-long, student-organized seminar on pornography and censorship, held in February 1969, turned into a comedy of errors, unnecessary police harrassment, and sophomoric embarrassment to everyone involved.

Later that month, President Hesburgh released another long letter to the entire University community. In his statement, popularly promulgated in the national media as Notre Dame's "Tough Fifteen-Minute Rule," Hesburgh spelled out what would occur should militants abuse the right of dissent and needlessly disrupt the Notre Dame academic community: 1) dissent would be permitted, even encouraged; 2) interference with the civil rights of others, however, would not be allowed; 3) students, faculty, or staff who violated this principle and persisted in disregarding the rights of other individuals and the University community-at-large would be given fifteen minutes to reflect on their actions; if they persisted their identity cards would be requested and confiscated; they would thereby forfeit their membership in the University community and be subject to civil arrest as intruders; 4) it would be assumed that those individuals who would not surrender their University identity cards were not members of the Notre Dame community. "I have no intention of presiding over a spectacle," wrote Hesburgh. "Too many people have given too much of themselves and their lives to this University to let this happen here. Without being melodramatic, if this conviction makes this my last will and testament to Notre Dame, so be it."

The president's eight-page letter was accompanied by endorsements from the Student Life Council (an elected board consisting of eight students, eight faculty, and eight administrators when created in 1967–68 and charged with making student affairs policy), the Faculty Senate, the University Academic Council, and the alumni officers.

Not all students, faculty, and alumni supported Hesburgh's position. Vigorous debate continued in various faculty councils and in the student press as to the legal and moral limits of the right to dissent. Confrontations still continued to occur. At a national conference on institutional racism sponsored by the National Student Association and held at Notre Dame, Hesburgh, a charter member of the U.S. Civil Rights Commission, was heckled by students who demanded greater minority enrollment; others argued for the withdrawal of academic credit from ROTC programs and urged an end to the U.S. military presence in Southeast Asia.

In October 1969, Father Hesburgh publicly joined the increasing national disenchantment with the U.S. policy in Vietnam. On the New Mobilization Committee's announced Vietnam Moratorium Day (October 15th), the president signed an open letter with certain other U.S. college and university presidents calling on the government to accelerate its withdrawal of military forces from Vietnam. The Notre Dame community participated in the national moratorium in several ways. At a peace rally at "the circle," a series of speakers explored the religious implications of the war. Students, faculty, and staff then marched (VI–21) across the South Quadrangle to Notre Dame's ROTC Building (5), where students planted wooden crosses (VI-22) commemorating each Notre Dame graduate killed in the war. Then the assembly solemnly marched back across the campus to the center of the Memorial Library Quadrangle. Here over 2,500 Notre Dame and St. Mary's students, faculty, and staff (including President Hesburgh, who had joined the procession en route) gathered to participate in a Mass for peace (VI-23), concelebrated by the seventy-seven-year-old English archbishop Thomas Roberts, several C.S.C. clergy, and a diocesan priest. Archbishop Roberts spoke of the Christian's obligation to resist immoral behavior by the state: "You may be the only university in the world where the Mass has been connected with the offering of draft cards," he told

VI–18–20. Campus Antiwar Dissent
Demonstrations took place at the
University's placement bureau (VI–18)
annually from 1967 to 1970, while other
confrontations (VI–19) and symbolic
protests (VI–20) resulted from rallies,
marches, and other forms of civil
dissent.

VI–18

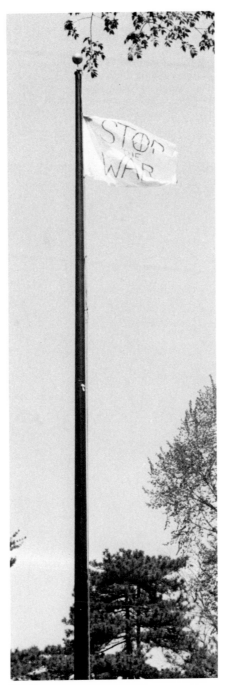

VI–19

VI–20

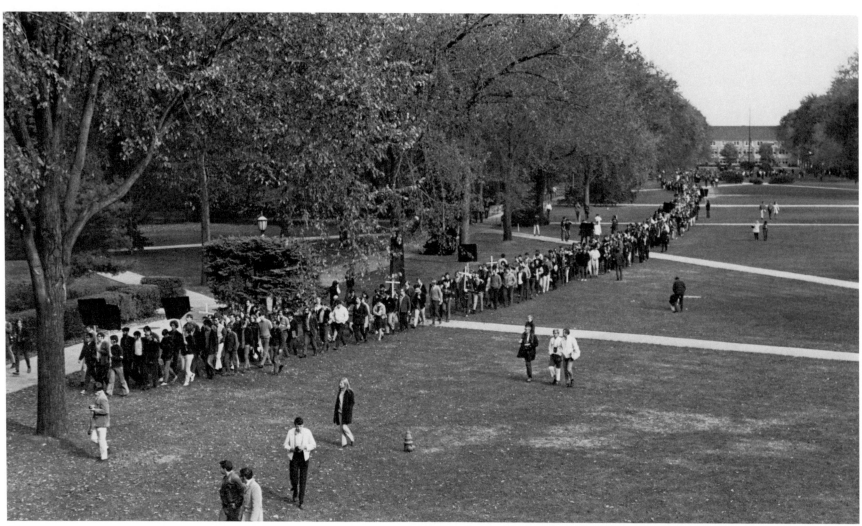

VI–21–23. Moratorium Day, 1969
Students, faculty, and staff march (VI–21)
from a peace rally held at "the circle"
across the South Quadrangle to the
ROTC Building where they planted
wooden crosses commemorating each
Notre Dame graduate killed in the
Vietnam war (VI–22). The assembly then
proceeded to the Library Quadrangle to
participate in a Mass for peace (VI–23).

VI–23

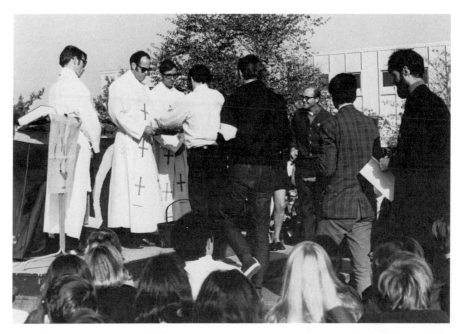

VI–22

the outdoor congregation. "But
when you and I go to daily Mass,
more often than not we celebrate
the feast of a martyr who was put
to death for some form of civil disobedience. We have learned from
them that we ought to obey God,
not man."

At the offertory of the Eucharist
service, four students, an assistant
professor in the University's non-
violence program (initiated by
Father Hesburgh in 1967 to enable
students to study alternatives for
effecting peaceful social change),
and an assistant professor of mathematics at St. Mary's College destroyed their draft cards, with the
assistance of a St. Mary's student,
as an act of civil disobedience
against the U.S. government's pros-

ecution of the Vietnam War. The
liturgy concluded with a fervent
prayer for world peace. This moratorium protest, like the majority of
Notre Dame's antiwar activities
throughout the 1960s, was nonviolent, nondestructive of campus
property, and highly religious in its
motivation, rhetoric, and execution.

Student agitation against the
Vietnam War continued when Dow
Chemical Company and the CIA
attempted to recruit on campus.
Due to the enforcement of Hesburgh's previously announced fifteen-minute rule, this 1969
confrontation resulted in the expulsion of five students and the suspension of five others, known in
the parlance of the day as the
"Notre Dame Ten." With the U.S.

VI–24   VI–25

VI–24. War Protest, May 1970
In order to demonstrate their opposition to the United States military invasion of Cambodia and the killing of students at Kent State University in Ohio and Jackson State in Mississippi, many Notre Dame students registered their outrage with petitions to Congress, a student strike, and Masses for peace such as this liturgy held on the campus at "the circle."

VI–25. War Cease-Fire, 1973
An observance of the Vietnam peace was held on January 28, 1973, in the University's Athletic and Convocation Center. The program was planned by Notre Dame faculty, students, and administrators and was open to the public. It included an hour of readings, talks, and music relating to the theme of peace, followed by a concelebrated Mass with President Hesburgh as homilist and principal celebrant. A simple meal was served in the building after the Mass.

military invasion of Cambodia and the killing of students at Kent State University and Jackson State University in 1970, horror and outrage swept the Notre Dame campus. Mass meetings were organized, memorial liturgies held, protest rallies conducted, a student strike proclaimed, and Masses for peace celebrated (VI–24). Large numbers of faculty members, many of whom had formerly supported the war effort or eschewed any involvement whatsoever in the campus demon-

strations, joined students in all-night, informal discussions over the University community's proper response to the national and international events. President Hesburgh issued an unequivocal public statement outlining his personal opposition to the war and decrying the paucity of moral leadership in America. In a nonviolent protest, about one thousand Notre Dame students followed their president's suggestion and collected over 23,000 signatures from South Bend

residents on a petition to be sent to Congress endorsing Hesburgh's antiwar position. Protest activism at Notre Dame throughout the 1960s was permeated by a distinct tone of Christian moral outrage. Significantly, when a cease-fire to the Vietnam War was officially declared in 1973, the University community gathered for a Eucharist liturgy in the Athletic and Convocation Center (VI–25) to pray for a reconcilation of differences and for the strength to strive in concert to cre-

ate a lasting peace at home and abroad.

During the 125th anniversary of the University's founding (1967), the Notre Dame community speculated about its present and future much more than it celebrated its past. The entire tenor of the 1960s lent itself more to reevaluation than to commemoration. At a special convocation ostensibly designed to signalize the institution's nineteenth-century origins, President Hesburgh spoke of his future dreams, which he hoped to see realized at Notre Dame. As he had done earlier in calling for a threefold goal for his "new Notre Dame," so too here he expressed himself with three metaphors. The University should become: "a *beacon*, shining with the great light of intelligence illuminated by faith"; "a *bridge* across the chasms of misunderstandings that divide so profoundly so much of the modern world"; and "a *crossroads*, where all the intellectual currents of our times meet in dialogue."

To assist in accomplishing these objectives, Hesburgh, strongly supported and encouraged by his provincial, Father Howard J. Kenna, and his superior-general, Father Germain M. Lalande, decided to recommend to the C.S.C. community that the University's Board of Trustees be laicized and expanded. Operating under the University's original 1844 charter of incorporation, the institution had been governed by a self-perpetuating, six-man Board of Trustees composed of members of the Congregation of Holy Cross. In 1967 the C.S.C. community considered relinquishing direct control of the institution that it had founded and fostered for 125 years as its most prestigious educational establishment.

Several factors conditioned this contemplated break with the past. A number of Catholic institutions, such as St. Louis University and the C.S.C.'s own University of Portland, had already announced the adoption of lay-dominated boards. More significant to some members of the Holy Cross congregation were the directives of the Second Vatican Council that had urged religious communities to share their ministries and monies more generously with the laity in the common Christian effort of the Church. There were also the empirical realities of Notre Dame in 1967. Among the more than seven hundred members of the teaching and research faculty, only fifty-five were C.S.C. priests or brothers. Other duties formerly handled entirely by the Congregation—fundraising, lower- and middle-level administration, maintenance—were now done by lay people. In fact, in 1966 James W. Frick, who had joined President John J. Cavanaugh's Notre Dame Foundation office after graduating from Notre Dame in 1951, was named the head of the public relations and development office, becoming the first layman to hold a University vice-presidency. Another index of increased lay involvement in University governance was the later appointment (1967) of Dr. Frederick Rossini to a newly created post of vice-president for research and sponsored programs.

Moreover, most of the University's $30-million annual operating budget was derived from secular sources. Nondenominational foundations and government agencies often looked askance at Notre Dame's clerical domination. In words reminiscent of James Burns's argument (see Chapter IV) for the creation of the Board of Associate Lay Trustees in 1922, President Hesburgh insisted that the only way the University could pursue long-range fund-raising goals and expand its endowment was to assume a lay-oriented power structure.

After four days of closed debate by forty-five priests in Sacred Heart Church, a special session of the provincial chapter of the C.S.C. community filed out of the historic structure and announced their decision to alienate their ownership of the Notre Dame campus, an investment that in 1967 had a book value of $133.5 million (a replacement value of $192.5 million), minus land value. Alumni were reassured that the essential character of the University as a Catholic institution of higher learning could not be altered except with the concurrence of at least two-thirds of the twelve Fellows of the University (an executive group of trustees designated by the new bylaws to be composed of six priests of the Congregation of Holy Cross and six lay persons, with whom the technical ownership of the University now rested). Furthermore, the president of Notre Dame would continue to be a Holy Cross priest of the Indiana Province, appointed by a board of thirty trustees.

By the autumn of 1970, coeducation became the focus of debate within the University community. Attempts had been made to entice several Midwest Catholic women's

VI–26. St. Mary's–Notre Dame Merger Agreement, May 1971
Officials from the two college communities sign and approve the first official agreements to merge their institutions into a coeducational unit. Six months later both schools decided not to merge. Left to right are President Hesburgh; Sister M. Olivette Whelan, C.S.C., superior-general of the Sisters of the Holy Cross; Edmund Stephan, chairman of the University Board of Trustees; and Sister M. Alma Peter, C.S.C., acting president of St. Mary's.

VI–26

colleges to relocate on or near the Notre Dame campus in the early 1960s. Female students had been present at the University since 1918 when women religious (V–29) first entered the summer session for advanced studies. Women religious and laywomen enrolled in the Graduate School when it began in 1932. Occasionally, a laywoman had earned her bachelor's degree on a part-time basis or by special arrangement, but until 1965, women studying at Notre Dame usually were members of religious communities or in the Graduate School.

In 1965, however, the Co-Exchange Program was instituted with St. Mary's College, whereby Notre Dame students could take classes at the neighboring women's college and St. Mary's students could do coursework in certain of the University's colleges. By the fall of 1970 a merger of St. Mary's and Notre Dame seemed probable. The faculties and administrations of both schools spent the year attempting to arrange and adjudicate the details of such a decision. In May 1971 the trustees of both institutions ratified the recommendations

of the executive committees of their respective Boards of Trustees for unification (VI–26). The proposed merger was suspended indefinitely, however, in November 1971 by a mutual decision of both schools. Notre Dame announced at that time that it would accept a limited number (365) of women undergraduates into its 1972 freshman class, thus beginning the first phase of a multi-year plan to implement coeducation.

Notre Dame's decision grew out of an aspiration to improve the quality and the totality of the education it provided. It was anticipated that a general upgrading of the academic environment and an overall improvement in the quality of student life would result. By 1975 the undergraduate student body had a ratio of four men to every woman (17:1 had been the beginning ratio in 1972). Sister Suzanne Kelly, O.S.B. (VI–27), and Dr. Josephine Massyngberde Ford (VI–28) became the first women in modern times to receive full-time, formal faculty appointments during the regular academic year (1965). In general, however, the presence of women on the University's teach-

ing and research faculty remains small.

Women at Notre Dame experienced their share of misunderstandings, inequities, frustrations, and stereotyping. As it happened, the advent of women at Notre Dame as undergraduate students (VI–29–31) coincided with a new emphasis on and concern with the nature of women's position in society. Hence, there was spoken and unspoken pressure on both the University and its women to be attentive to their public images and the need to achieve genuine equity. By 1975 most women appeared to feel that there was increasing mutual respect and understanding between men and women both in the classroom and out of it. The integration of women into an all-male institution, previously run by men for men, went remarkably smoothly. Coeducation provided wider dimensions of intellectual and social experience for both men and women students; it was also assuredly a significant turning point in the University's history.

During the preparations for a proposed merger with St. Mary's College and the decision unilaterally

VI–27–28. Women Faculty, 1965
Sister Suzanne Kelly, O.S.B. (VI–27), an instructor in the history and philosophy of science, and Dr. Josephine Massyngberde Ford (VI–28), a biblical and liturgical scholar, were the first women appointed to full-time positions on the teaching and research faculty in 1965. Dr. Ford later became the first woman to receive tenure at the University.

VI–29–31. Coeducation at Notre Dame, 1972
Beginning with the freshman class of 1972, the University began the first phase of coeducation, whereby women students were fully integrated into Notre Dame's academic (VI–29 and 31) as well as social (VI–30) life.

VI–28

VI–30

VI–27

VI–29

VI–31

VI–32. University Provost
Appointed in 1970 to the newly created office of university provost, James T. Burtchaell, C.S.C., became the University's chief academic officer and the acting president in the absence of

the president. A scholar in biblical theology, Father Burtchaell studied and engaged in research at six institutions in this country, Europe, and the Middle East before returning to teach in Notre Dame's theology department. A Fellow and trustee of the University, he also chaired the Committee on University Priorities.

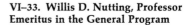

VI–33. Willis D. Nutting, Professor Emeritus in the General Program

VI–34. Bernard Waldman, Professor of Physics and Dean of the College of Science

VI–32

to implement coeducation, the University's Board of Trustees created a new and a powerful position within the Notre Dame administration. The provost's office replaced an often lethargic academic affairs vice-presidency. The provost became the second-ranking executive officer of the University and to him was delegated direct control over all academic affairs and indirect supervision of student life. James T. Burtchaell (VI–32), C.S.C. priest, foreign-trained (Jerusalem and Cambridge) biblical scholar, and chairman of the theology department from 1967–70, was named to the position in September 1970. With the creation of a provost's office, the earlier proposals by students and faculty in 1963 and 1969 for a shared University executive appeared to have been partially implemented.

With a new provost, a commitment to become a coeducational institution, and a recent decade of turmoil, expansion, and unprecedented change behind it, Notre Dame entered the 1970s. Increased attention to academic excellence was visible in the demand for the

doctorate as a necessity for most faculty appointments and in the University's expanded quest for endowed professorships. The clerical–lay person composition of the faculty (VI–33–38) in 1975 was proportionally nearly the reverse of the ratio in the University's early years. Only one out of every ten who taught full-time on the faculty of over seven hundred was a religious or a cleric. Few bachelor-dons (IV–37) lived in the undergraduate dormitories; with the 1974 death of Francis "Frank" O'Malley (VI–36), perennial guru of Notre Dame freshmen since the 1940s, a distinctive faculty type passed from the modern scene. The current University faculty has become more professionally organized (via the University Academic Council, five individual college councils, and a faculty senate) and more nationally recognized (two faculty members, Joseph M. Duffy and John S. Dunne, C.S.C., [VI–38], were awarded the prestigious Harbison Award for Excellence in Teaching in the 1960s). Alumni, after training in graduate schools at other major universities, have returned in large

VI–33

VI–34

VI–36. Francis J. "Frank" O'Malley, Professor of English, 1909–74.

VI–35. Milton Burton, Professor of Chemistry and Former Director of the University Radiation Laboratory

VI–37. Bachelor-Dons
Faculty residents of campus dormitories for over forty years, Paul Fenlon, (left), and Joseph Ryan (right), professors emeriti of English, in Fenlon's Sorin Hall room.

VI–38. John S. Dunne, C.S.C., Professor of Theology and Harbison Teaching Award Recipient

VI–39

VI–39–40. Student Body Presidents, 1968 and 1972
Contrasting leadership styles can be suggested by comparing the tenures of Richard Rossi and Robert Kersten. In a 1968 student political meeting in Washington Hall, Rossi (VI–39) argued for "student power" and greater involvement of undergraduates in University governance. In 1972 Kersten (VI–40), urged by his section mates in Walsh Hall, conducted a satirical spoof of student government activities, ran for the crown of campus "King" (instead of student body president), won the student election, and "reigned" for the academic year.

VI–41–42. Contemporary Student Life, 1975
Sorin Hall men's dormitory (VI–41); Badin Hall women's dormitory (VI–42).

VI–42   VI–41

VI–40

VI–43–44. **Contemporary Extracurricular Life, 1975**
The "An Tostal" spring festival hog wrestle (VI–43); student volunteer at the Northern Indiana Children's Hospital (VI–44).

numbers to teach (over a fourth of the faculty members in 1975 held a Notre Dame degree).

The modern Notre Dame student (VI–39–44) is difficult to categorize in other than statistical terms. A survey of the incoming freshman class of 1975–76 reveals that 24 percent of the students ranked within the top five positions of their graduating class. Over 60 percent of the 1975 freshmen were in the top 10 percent of their class and over 80 percent in the top 20 percent. The entire Notre Dame student body was made up of students from all fifty states and fifty-seven foreign countries. Over 75 percent of the undergraduate students resided on the campus. Fifty-seven percent of the undergraduates received financial aid, which in 1975 totaled $6.7 million from all sources.

By the mid-1970s certain striking characteristics of student life in the 1960s had disappeared: the trend toward assertive self-government, the demand for "student power," and high-profile student body presidents (compare VI–39 with VI–40); the flamboyant rhetoric of the po-

litical minority groups; and aggressive idealism and heady social activism.

Several trends continued, however. Social concern could still be seen in students' involvement in tutoring programs and social service work (VI–44) in the neighboring South Bend community. In postconciliar Notre Dame the attempt to define the nature of the University's catholicity continued as the University president and provost attempted to clarify their position on such a crucial issue. Debate over parietal hours and judicial codes still occupied meetings of the Student Life Council despite the fact that the student disciplinary code during the 1960s had undergone the most extensive liberalization in the University's history.

Observers came to visit and interpret the "new Notre Dame" in much the same way that foreign travelers such as Alexis de Tocqueville and James Bryce once came to probe the meaning of nineteenth-century America. Most Notre Dame interpreters have sought to analyze the University by focusing on a single event as symbolic of what

VI–43

VI–44

VI–45. Committee on University Priorities

Pictured clockwise around the conference table are: Father Ernan McMullin, professor of philosophy (secretary); Dr. Yusaku Furuhashi, professor of marketing management; Mr. Frank Palopoli, graduate student in government and international studies; Dr. James Daschbach, associate professor of aerospace and mechanical engineering;

Mr. Howard Bathon, senior in arts and letters and chemical engineering; Father James T. Burtchaell, C.S.C. (chairman); Dr. Thomas Shaffer, dean of the Law School; Dr. James Frick, vice-president for public relations and development; Father David Burrell, C.S.C., associate professor of theology and philosophy; Dr. Robert Gordon, vice-president for advanced studies; Dr. O. Timothy O'Meara, professor of mathematics; and

Dr. Marshall Smelser, professor of history. Also appointed to the committee, but not pictured here, were Sister Madonna Kolbenschlag, H.M., assistant professor of American studies, and Father James Flanigan, C.S.C., associate vice-president for student affairs.

they think typifies the changed Notre Dame. Some point to the fact that a recent student body president was not only a Protestant but also a black; others note that the 1974 valedictorian was a woman; the fact that most clergy go about in secular garb or that the theology department enjoys academic respectability attract the attention of other observers. Many feel that Notre Dame's one-time aspiration to be the "Catholic West Point" has been replaced by a vision of becoming a "Catholic Princeton."

In 1972 Notre Dame decided to study itself. The Committee on University Priorities (COUP) was appointed by President Hesburgh. Its dual charge was to identify the institution's traditional strengths that were worth maintaining and to recommend new priorities deserving the future attention of the institution. After meeting in more than thirty plenary sessions and commissioning four task-force reports from four separate subcommittees (academic discipline, research and instruction, enrollment, and physical facilities), the fourteen-member committee (VI–45) issued its findings as *The Report of the Committee on University Priorities* (Notre Dame, 1973). The committee hoped that its estimate of Notre Dame would become a useful working paper for discussion, a possible agenda for future growth, and a provocative document for continual self-evaluation. It concluded its forty-page report with a series of recommendations that were singled out for special emphasis and listed in the order of importance. In many ways, these recommendations may prove to be an important benchmark of Notre Dame's achievement and aspirations in the mid-1970s:

1. The University should continue its traditional commitment to freedom of inquiry and thought.

2. The University should have a faculty and student affairs staff among whom committed Catholics should predominate.

3. The University's endowment should have the highest priority in the allocation of unrestricted income.

4. The University and its colleges should encourage departmental initiatives in teaching, including designation of appropriate persons whose task would be to support good teachers and help others to become such.

5. The University should recognize that it must apply its resources in such a way as to increase excellence in all its disciplines, including those that now enjoy academic distinction.

6. The University's library book budget should be increased significantly, and an endowment specifically restricted to purchases of books, periodicals, and related learning materials should be set up, not as a substitute for the book budget but as a supplement to it.

7. The University's advanced programs should concentrate on improvement through greater selectivity in enrollment, and within the next five years each advanced studies unit should undertake a self-study according to a schedule set up by the vice-president for advanced studies.

8. The University should eliminate overcrowding in residence halls and study specific ways of enhancing the intellectual role of the rector, possibly through formal and informal educational programs involving hall staffs and faculty.

9. The University should establish a temporary committee of outside consultants, charged specifically with determination and assessment of needs, use, and controlled growth of an optimal computer configuration for the campus.

10. The University should institute a procedure for long-range planning, perhaps through a committee charged with rating the relative importance of its physical needs by means of a continual, regular review of the functioning and maintenance of campus buildings and grounds. This group would also receive and approve all requests for major renovation and construction and present solutions for the improvement of the campus environment, including those centering on preventive maintenance.

The Report of the Committee on University Priorities obviously does not represent all that Notre Dame is, or is not, as the University enters the last quarter of the twentieth century. It does suggest, however, that Notre Dame, altered considerably by the internal pressures and external events of the past two decades, is still engaged, as were its original founders, in discovering what it is and what it can become.

VI–46

Transept Frescoes (Epistle side, s.e.)

Upper Panel: *The Nativity of Virgin Mary*

Lower Panels: 1. *Child Mary Tending Flowers in Garden While St. Anne Sits Reading a Scroll*

              2. *St. Anne Teaches Child Mary to pray*

Transept Frescoes (Epistle side, s.w.)

Upper Panel: *Presentation of Virgin Mary in the Temple*

Lower Panel: *Child Mary and Her Parents Preparing for the Presentation*

Nave Central Wall Frescoes (Epistle Side)

Standing in the center aisle, look up to the left, below the clerestory on the upper wall; begin with the figure (St. Cecilia) closest to the transept and view the following figures on the upper wall spandrils back down the center aisle.

1. *St. Cecilia*	4. *St. Thomas Aquinas*	7. *St. Mary Magdalene*
2. *St. Lucia*	5. *St. Benedict Labre*	8. *St. Paul the Hermit*
3. *St. Bonaventure*	6. *St. Alexis*	9. *St. John the Baptist*

III. Inventory of Murals in the Administration Building

A. Luigi Gregori Wall Murals (second floor entrance hall)

This series of twelve paintings, representing incidents in the life of Christopher Columbus (1451–1506), was done between 1882 and 1884 by Luigi Gregori (1819–96) while serving as University artist-in-residence on leave from the Vatican. The paintings, varying in width from five-and-one-half to nineteen feet, are all eleven feet high; they are not true frescoes, since they were painted on dry plastered walls. View the murals by beginning at the vestibule entrance to the Administration Building and walking north toward the central rotunda.

The model for Gregori's painting, *Christopher Columbus, Discoverer* (left), as he was for all likenesses of Columbus except the deathbed scene where Father Sorin was the model, was Father Thomas E. Walsh, C.S.C., Notre Dame's seventh president. Columbus is here pictured in full court regalia. The globe by his side is turned to show the new world, and one of the explorer's fingers rests upon the North American continent.

Isabella the Catholic, Protectress of Columbus (right), represents the queen whose patronage gave her immortal fame. Shown descending her throne arrayed in royal robes, she holds in her hands the box of jewels that she pawned to aid Columbus.

The story of Columbus begins when he begs for bread for his son, Diego. *Columbus at the Gate of the Convent of La Rabida* (right) shows the travel-weary and dejected mariner, whose theories of a new route to the East Indies have been rejected by Spanish and Portuguese authorities, about to turn to France, when Father Juan Perez de Marchena hears of his story and intercedes with Queen Isabella.

Father Perez Blesses Columbus before He Embarks (left) shows the embarkation site at Palos on August 3, 1492. Father Perez, whose intercession gained Columbus his patronage and by whose kindness Columbus was fed and sheltered, is seen blessing the explorer in the early morning of that fateful day. .

Columbus's journey took seventy days across uncharted seas. It was interrupted by a mutiny (*The Mutiny at Sea* [left]) by despairing and angry sailors, who insisted that Columbus turn back before food supplies were exhausted. Columbus's calm is in strong contrast to the violence of the mutineers.

After calming his men, Columbus pushed on, finally sighting land on October 12, 1492. *Discovery of Land Friday, October 12, 1492* (right), depicts the great exhilaration of the sighting; the leaders of the mutiny kneel before Columbus. Models for this painting include Arthur J. Stace (man with beard in foreground) and Joseph Lyons (smooth-shaven man in foreground), professors of poetry and drama at Notre Dame, as well as the University's first librarian, James F. Edwards, seen here at the rail looking out to sea.

Taking Possession of the New World (right) shows the discoverer planting the cross, claiming the territory in the name of Ferdinand and Isabella. Near Columbus stand the two Pinzon brothers who commanded the *Nina* and the *Pinta*, and by himself a bit further out stands the man who would give his name to the new continent, Amerigo Vespucci.

The largest of the murals, *Return of Columbus and Reception at Court* (left), depicts Columbus's triumphant return to Granada. The U.S. Post Office chose this as a design for a commemorative stamp issued in conjunction with the Columbian Exposition in Chicago in 1893. Among the models used in this painting, the artist has included himself (the man with the mustache behind the red drape at the far upper right corner). Father Stoffell, professor of Greek, was the model for the man looking over the artist's shoulder. Farther toward the front on the same side are the likenesses of Mrs. Rhodius and her son of Indianapolis, clad in elaborate court costumes. Mrs. Rhodius was one of the early benefactors of the University.

Bobadilla Betrays Columbus (left) represents the mariner as a victim of treachery by Francisco Bobadilla, a Spanish nobleman appointed as one of the rulers of the new territories. The scene is the cottage of Columbus.

Columbus was sent back to Spain in chains, where authorities dropped all charges against him. He retired to a monastery, where he died in 1506 at the age of sixty (*Death of Columbus, Valladolid, May 20, 1506* [right]). Among the friends in attendance was a Franciscan monk at the foot of the bed leaning on a cane. Gregori used Father Louis Neyron, priest-scientist at Notre Dame and surgeon in Napoleon's army at Waterloo before his ordination, as his unwilling model for the monk. The Franciscan brother standing beside the monk bears the likeness of Brother Albeus, C.S.C.

The final paintings, *Father Diego de Deza, Protector of Columbus at Salamanca* (left) and *Luis de Santangel, Treasurer of Aragon* (right), show two men instrumental in Columbus's voyage.

B. Luigi Gregori Dome Mural (inner dome mural)

After completing the Columbian murals, Gregori turned his attention to the rotunda of the Administration Building. The eight figures, allegorical representations of Religion, Philosophy, History, Science, Fame, Music, and Poetry, are in various states of repose.

Religion, reclining on a terrestrial globe in the center of the rotunda, holds an open book and casts her eyes heavenward. Her colorful robe symbolizes the three theological virtues, faith (white), hope (green), and charity (red). The Holy Spirit, in the form of a dove hovering overhead, exemplifies divine inspiration.

Philosophy, on the south quadrant and the only figure looking virtually straight ahead, is grave and modest. Seated on a marble throne with a gold diadem on her forehead, she holds two open books, bearing the inscriptions *Naturalis* and *Moralis*. The following descriptions are of the figures as they are seen clockwise from *Philosophy*.

History, in a two-figure grouping, is represented by a noble, winged matron, robed in white, symbolic of truth. Father Time holds a book for her to write upon, and in his infirmity he seems intent upon seeking knowledge at her feet.

Science is a matron robed in the gold and purple of royalty, symbolic of power and majesty. The open book on her knees represents wide teaching, and the scepter with a radiant sun upon it symbolizes the darkness-dispelling light that she brings.

Fame, the only figure represented as flying (perhaps Gregori's commentary on fame's fleet-footedness), holds two trumpets in her hands (one gold and the other silver), representing her clarion call for both the greater and lesser accomplishments of man.

Music, playing her lute, wears a seven-diamond crown representing the seven musical tones. She appears lost in her playing, indifferent to everything around her.

Poetry is depicted with upraised quill, a thoughtful and serene expression upon her face. Her blue robe symbolizes her celestial gifts, the laurel crown upon her head signifies the glory that she seeks, and the lyre represents the correspondence between the harmony of her art and that of music. She writes the words *Numine afflor*.

IV. Inventory of Campus Sculpture

Title	Location	Artist	Title	Location	Artist
Christ and the Samaritan Woman at the Well	O'Shaughnessy Hall Sculpture Courtyard	Ivan Mestrovic	St. Patrick	Dillon Hall south facade	John J. Bednar
St. Luke the Evangelist	Sculpture Courtyard	Ivan Mestrovic	Cardinal Newman	Dillon Hall southwest entrance, door facade	John J. Bednar
St. John the Evangelist	Sculpture Courtyard	Ivan Mestrovic			
Descent from the Cross	Sacred Heart Church	Ivan Mestrovic	St. George	Sacred Heart Church Memorial Door (right)	John J. Bednar
The Return of the Prodigal Son	Sacred Heart Church	Ivan Mestrovic	St. Joan of Arc	Sacred Heart Church Memorial Door (left)	John J. Bednar
Madonna and Child	O'Shaughnessy Hall great hall	Ivan Mestrovic	St. Joseph	Lyons Hall archway facade	Eugene Kormendi
Madonna and Child	Lewis Hall Court	Ivan Mestrovic	The Good Shepherd	Student Infirmary west doorway facade	Eugene Kormendi
Bust of Basil A. Moreau	Moreau Seminary	Ivan Mestrovic	St. Raphael	Student Infirmary west facade	Eugene Kormendi
The Last Supper	North Dining Hall	Ivan Mestrovic	St. Thomas More	Law Building west doorway facade	Eugene Kormendi
Christ as a Young Boy Teaching	Stanford-Keenan Hall lobby	Ivan Mestrovic	Christ the King	Law Building south tower facade	Eugene Kormendi
The Ashbaugh Madonna	Art Gallery permanent exhibition	Ivan Mestrovic	The Madonna	Alumni Hall north facade	Eugene Kormendi
Head of Moses	Memorial Library second floor	Ivan Mestrovic	St. Christopher	Rockne Memorial east doorway facade	Eugene Kormendi
Crucifix	Stanford-Keenan Hall chapel	Ivan Mestrovic	"Joe College"	Alumni Hall north tower facade	Eugene Kormendi
Crucifix	O'Shaughnessy Hall great hall	Ivan Mestrovic	Crucifix	Sacred Heart Church	Eugene Kormendi
St. Thomas Aquinas	Alumni Hall inner court, north facade	John J. Bednar	St. Andrew	Morrissey Hall east doorway facade	James Kress
St. Bonaventure	Alumni Hall inner court, north facade	John J. Bednar	Edward F. Sorin	Main Quadrangle	Ernesto Biondi
St. Augustine	Dillon Hall southeast entrance, door facade	John J. Bednar	Our Lady of the University	Campus Entrance "the circle"	Anthony J. Lauck, C.S.C.
St. Jerome	Dillon Hall inner court, north facade	John J. Bednar	Prayer Symbol	Moreau Seminary, garden	Anthony J. Lauck, C.S.C.

Title	Location	Artist
Titus I	Front of Art Gallery	Michael Todd
Moses	Memorial Library west side	Joseph Turkalj
St. Thomas	Hoynes Hall south wall addition	Patrick J. Weishapl
Stations of the Cross	St. Joseph's Lake southwest shore	Ernest Thorne Thompson
St. Joseph	Columba Hall east side	N. Serf
Centennial Bas-Reliefs University of Notre Dame 1842–1942	Sacred Heart Church main entrance vestibule	Eugene Kormendi
St. Timothy	Howard Hall south archway	Raymond Cusick
St. Edward	St. Edward's Hall front garden	Froc-Robert
Sacred Heart	Main Quadrangle	Robert Cassiani
William J. Corby	Corby Hall	Samuel Murray
Christ the Teacher	Library front facade	Millard Sheets
Mary, Queen of Heaven	Corby Hall south facade	Unknown
Knute Rockne	Rockne Memorial memorial foyer	Nison Tregor
Our Lady of Lourdes	Grotto niche	Unknown
Our Lady of Notre Dame	Administration Building dome	Giovanni Meli
The Holy Spirit	Moreau Seminary south facade	David Hayes
Jeremiah	Grace-Flanner courtyard	Waldemar Otto
Pietà	Moreau Seminary garden	Waldemar Otto

Selected Bibliography

Armstrong, James E. *Onward to Victory: A Chronicle of the Alumni of the University of Notre Dame, 1842–1973.* Notre Dame, Ind.: University of Notre Dame, 1974.

Arthur, David J., C.S.C. "The University of Notre Dame, 1919–1933: An Administrative History." Ph.D. dissertation, University of Michigan, 1973.

Beirne, Killian, C.S.C. *From Sea to Shining Sea: A History of the Holy Cross Brothers.* Notre Dame, Ind.: Holy Cross Press, 1966.

Brosnahan, M. Eleanore, C.S.C. *On the King's Highway: A History of the Sisters of the Holy Cross of St. Mary of the Immaculate Conception, Notre Dame, Indiana.* New York: D. Appleton & Co., 1931.

Catta, Etienne, and Catta, Tony. *Basil Anthony Mary Moreau.* 2 vols. Milwaukee: The Bruce Company, 1955.

Connelly, Joel R., and Dooley, Howard R. *Hesburgh's Notre Dame: Triumph in Transition.* New York: Hawthorn Books, 1972.

Federowicz, John, C.S.C. "Forces Affecting the Development of Libraries at the University of Notre Dame, 1843–1968." Master's thesis, Kent State University, 1968.

Gillespie, Mary of St. Angela, C.S.C. *Life of Reverend Francois Cointet, Priest and Missionary of the Congregation of Holy Cross.* Cincinnati: J. P. Walsh, 1855.

Grant, Chet. *Before Rockne at Notre Dame: Impression and Reminiscence.* Notre Dame, Ind.: Dujarie Press, 1968.

Heston, Edward. *Father Dujarie: Founder of the Sisters of Providence and the Brothers of Holy Cross (1767–1838).* Milwaukee: The Bruce Press, Catholic Life Publications, 1960.

Hope, Arthur J., C.S.C. *Notre Dame: One Hundred Years.* Notre Dame, Indiana: University of Notre Dame Press, 1943.

Howard, Timothy. *A Brief History of the University of Notre Dame Du Lac, Indiana, from 1842 to 1892.* Chicago: The Werner Company, 1895.

Katz, Fred. *The Glory of Notre Dame.* Hong Kong: Bartholomew House Ltd., 1971.

Kearney, Anna Rose. "James A. Burns, C.S.C.—Educator." Ph.D. dissertation, University of Notre Dame, 1975.

Lenoue, John, C.S.C. "The Historical Development of the Curriculum of the University of Notre Dame." Master's thesis, University of Notre Dame, 1933.

Lyons, Joseph A. *Silver Jubilee of the University of Notre Dame.* Chicago: E. B. Meyers and Co., 1869.

McAllister, Anna Shannon. *Flame in the Wilderness: Life and Letters of Mother Angela Gillespie, C.S.C., 1824–1887.* Paterson, N.J.: St. Anthony Guild Press, 1941.

McAvoy, Thomas, C.S.C. *Catholic Church in Indiana 1789–1834.* New York: AMS Press, Inc., 1940.

_____. *Father O'Hara of Notre Dame: The Cardinal-Archbishop of Philadelphia.* Notre Dame, Ind.: University of Notre Dame Press, 1967.

McCandless, Kenneth William. "The Endangered Domain: A Review and Analysis of Campus Planning and Design at the University of Notre Dame." Master's thesis, University of Notre Dame, 1974.

Moore, Philip, C.S.C. "Academic Development: University of Notre Dame: Past, Present, Future." Mimeographed. Notre Dame, Ind.: University of Notre Dame, 1960.

Morin, Garnier, C.S.C. *Holy Cross Brothers: From France to Notre Dame.* Notre Dame, Ind.: Dujarie Press, 1952.

Schauinger, J. H. *Stephen Badin: Priest in the Wilderness.* Milwaukee: The Bruce Company, 1956.

Sorin, Edward, C.S.C. "Chroniques de Notre Dame du Lac." Provincial Archives of the Congregation of Holy Cross, n.d.

_____. *Circular Letters of the Very Rev. Edward Sorin.* 2 vols. Notre Dame, Ind.: privately printed, 1885, 1894.

Sullivan, Richard. *Notre Dame: Reminiscences of an Era.* Notre Dame, Indiana: University of Notre Dame Press, 1961.

Trahey, James, C.S.C. *The Brothers of Holy Cross.* Notre Dame, Ind.: The University Press, 1901.

Wack, John T. "The University of Notre Dame du Lac: Foundation, 1842–1857." Ph.D. dissertation, University of Notre Dame, 1967.

Wallace, Francis. *Notre Dame: Its People and Its Legends.* New York: David McKay, 1969.

Weber, Ralph E. *Notre Dame's John Zahm: American Catholic Apologist and Educator.* Notre Dame, Ind.: University of Notre Dame Press, 1961.

Photograph Credits

The majority of the photographs that I have used in this study can be found in four principal depositories located on the University of Notre Dame campus:

University of Notre Dame Archives
Office of Information Services
Office of Printing and Publications
University Photographer's Office

I would also like to thank several other institutions for granting me permission to reproduce photographs from their archives:

Northern Indiana Historical Society
Ellerbe Associates
Art Gallery, University of Notre Dame
Office of Sports Information, University of Notre Dame
Department of Earth Sciences, University of Notre Dame
Office of Public Information, St. Mary's College
Congregation of Holy Cross Archives, Indiana Province
Office of Campus Engineer, University of Notre Dame
Department of Special Collections, Memorial Library, University of Notre Dame

Numerous individual collectors have generously permitted me to research their private holdings of photographs of Notre Dame. I am particularly indebted to Mr. Francis P. Clark for permission to reproduce an extremely large number of photographs. Others who have consented to my reproducing photographs from their collections include:

James K. Newkirk
Grover Miller
Arthur Shea
Mrs. J. Sean Keenan
Franklin L. Long
Charles Parnell
Bernard Waldman

INDEX